365 Potluck Dessert Recipes

(365 Potluck Dessert Recipes - Volume 1)

Olive Chen

Copyright: Published in the United States by Olive Chen/ © OLIVE CHEN

Published on July, 24 2020

All rights reserved. No part of this publication may be reproduced, stored in retrieval system, copied in any form or by any means, electronic, mechanical, photocopying, recording or otherwise transmitted without written permission from the publisher. Please do not participate in or encourage piracy of this material in any way. You must not circulate this book in any format. OLIVE CHEN does not control or direct users' actions and is not responsible for the information or content shared, harm and/or actions of the book readers.

In accordance with the U.S. Copyright Act of 1976, the scanning, uploading and electronic sharing of any part of this book without the permission of the publisher constitute unlawful piracy and theft of the author's intellectual property. If you would like to use material from the book (other than just simply for reviewing the book), prior permission must be obtained by contacting the author at author@voilacookbook.com

Thank you for your support of the author's rights.

Content

365 AWESOME POTLUCK DESSERT RECIPES 8

1. 3 Layer Cheesy Strawberry Cake 8
2. 4 Ingredient Sweet And Spicy Chicken Wings 8
3. All American Jello Salad 9
4. Almost Fat Free Cheesecake 9
5. Amish Sticky Buns, Sweet Rolls Wow Wow Wow! 10
6. Angel Cake Delight 11
7. Annie Glenn's Chocolate Chip Cookies ... 11
8. Apple Cinnamon Coffee Cake 12
9. Apple Cobbler With Oatmeal 12
10. Apple Crisp For THe Microwave 13
11. Apple Milk Indian Delicacy(Seb Rabdi) 13
12. Apple Pear Compote 14
13. Apple Mango Crisp 14
14. Apricot Mashed Sweet Potatoes 15
15. Apricot And Oat Fingers 15
16. Bacardi Rum Cake 16
17. Balsamic Bleu Pears 16
18. Banana Butterfinger Cake 17
19. Banana Cream Pie(Cook's Country) 18
20. Banana Cupcakes With Cream Cheese Frosting 19
21. Banana Poi 20
22. Banana Split Cake 20
23. Banana Split Pie For A Crowd....no Raw Eggs 20
24. Banana Yogurt Bundt Cake 21
25. Base Jello Shots Recipe With Fruit Floaters 22
26. Bavarian Strawberries 22
27. Berry Pudding 23
28. Best Blueberry Cobbler 23
29. Big Boy's Strawberry Pie 24
30. Bisquick Coffee Cake 24
31. Bisquick Fruit Cobbler 25
32. Bite Sized Chocolate Meringues 25
33. Bittersweet Chocolate Pound Cake With Decadent Glaze 26
34. Blueberry Bread Pudding, Wonderful And Easy! 27
35. Blueberry Cobbler In A Bottle 27
36. Blueberry Fool 28
37. Bourbon Sweet Potatoes 28
38. Bran Apple Crisp 29
39. Breakfast Cookie 29
40. Brownies In A Jar 30
41. Buckeye Brownies 30
42. Buried Treasure Cupcakes K 31
43. Calypso Coffee Cake With Butter Rum Glaze 31
44. Candy Corn Marshmallow Crispy Treats ..32
45. Captain Krunchers 33
46. Caramel Apple Brickle Dip 33
47. Caramel Chocolate Bars 34
48. Caramel Peanut Popcorn 34
49. Carob Nut Fudge 35
50. Carrot Sheet Cake With Frosting 35
51. Cashew Peach Sweet Potatoes 36
52. Cheater's Carrot Cake 36
53. Cheeseburger In Paradise Cookies 37
54. Cheesecake Topped With Fresh Fruit 38
55. Cherry Cheesecake Cups 38
56. Cherry Crunch Coffee Cake 39
57. Cherry Nectar Cake 39
58. Cherry Time Cobbler 40
59. Chewy Chocolate Macaroons 40
60. Chewy And Fudgy Brownies 41
61. Chewy, Loaded, Oatmeal, Peanut Butter Bar "cookies" 42
62. Chex "Cookies" 43
63. Chex Candy Clusters 43
64. Chili And Cornbread Cupcakes 44
65. Chocolate Gingernut Ripple Cake 44
66. Chocolate Almond Fudge Cake 45
67. Chocolate Bonbons 45
68. Chocolate Cheese Eclairs 46
69. Chocolate Cherry Pudding Cake 47
70. Chocolate Chip Almond Cake 47
71. Chocolate Chip And Peanut Cookies 48
72. Chocolate Covered Raisins 48
73. Chocolate Dipped Almond Cookies 49
74. Chocolate Gobs With Icing 49
75. Chocolate Granola Candies 50
76. Chocolate Hazelnut Dessert Pizza 50
77. Chocolate Layer Delight 51
78. Chocolate Mascarpone And Strawberry Tart 51

79. Chocolate Nutella No Bake Cookies 52
80. Chocolate Toffee Graham Treats 52
81. Chocolate, Butterscotch, Pb Rice Krispies Treats 53
82. Chocolate Banana Trifle 53
83. Chocolate Covered Strawberries 54
84. Cholly's World Famous Gingerbread Cake 55
85. Chow Mein Noodle Cookies 55
86. Chris's Favorite Cherry Jello 56
87. Classic Buttercream Frosting 56
88. Cocoa Cream Roll 57
89. Coconut (Almond) Joys 57
90. Coffee Marshmallow Sponge 58
91. Coffee And Mascarpone Slice 58
92. Cracker Custard 59
93. Cranberry Crisp With Autumn Fruit 60
94. Cranberry Glazed Pound Cake 60
95. Cranberry, Chocolate Chip And Coconut Cookies 61
96. Cream Cheese Almond Bars 61
97. Creamy Pineapple Peach Dessert 62
98. Crock Pot Bread Pudding 63
99. Crock Pot Peach Dump Dessert 63
100. Crock Pot Rice Pudding 64
101. Crunchy Cereal Bars 64
102. Custard (Vanilla) Slice 64
103. Custard/Pudding 65
104. Daffodil Dessert 66
105. Dark Chocolate Cake 66
106. Date Raisin Squares Microwave 67
107. Delicious Healthy Truffles 67
108. Dessert Lovers Sweet Rice 68
109. Dimple Icing 69
110. Dolly Parton's Green Tomato Cake 69
111. Donut Pudding With Quick Easy Zabaglione 70
112. Double Cherry Crumble 71
113. Double Frosted Bourbon Brownies 71
114. Double Banana Pound Cake 72
115. Double Dark Mocha Drops 73
116. Dreamsicle Jello Salad 73
117. Dump Cake (Only 3 Ingredients!) 74
118. Eagle Brand Chocolate Sheet Cake 74
119. Easter Nests With Jelly Bean Eggs (Peanut Free) 75
120. Easy Ambrosia Parfait 75
121. Easy Butterscotch Chip Chocolate Cookies 76
122. Easy Chocolate Chip Oatmeal Cookies 76
123. Easy Chocolate Dipped Apricots (Apricot Chanukah Gelt) 77
124. Easy Lemon Pudding 77
125. Easy Rhubarb Upside Down Cake 78
126. Easy Rocky Road Brownies 78
127. Easy Snickers Bar Pie 79
128. Edinburgh Gingerbread 79
129. Elsie's Pineapple Oatmeal Bars 80
130. Emz Luscious Lemon Slice 80
131. English Blackberry Cobbler 81
132. FUDGY Peanut Butter Bars 82
133. Fabulous Fat Free Pineapple Cake 82
134. Fantasy Ribbon Fudge 83
135. Fast, Easy Apple Cobbler 83
136. Fat Free Gingersnaps 84
137. Five Flavor Pound Cake 84
138. Fresh Peach Crumble 85
139. Fruit Custard Pizza 86
140. Fruit Jello Delight 86
141. Fruit Salad For A Crowd 87
142. Fruity Vanilla Cupcakes 87
143. Fudge Macaroons 88
144. Fudgy Chocolate Layer Cake 88
145. Ginger Chocolate Shortbread 89
146. Ginger Lemon Cookies 89
147. Gingersnaps! 90
148. Graham Cracker Oatmeal Crust 91
149. Gramma's Old Fashioned Cinnamon Sweet Rolls 91
150. Grammy's Famous Raspberry Jello Mold . 93
151. Grandma Rampke's Easy Rhubarb Custard Pie 93
152. Grandma's Jello Salad 94
153. Grandma's Spaghetti And Cheese Pudding 94
154. Granny's Banana Cream Pie 95
155. Grape Salad With A Twist 95
156. Guiness Ginger Cupcakes 96
157. Gujiya Or Perakiya(Indian Pastry Sweet) . 96
158. Gwyn's Orange Jello Salad 97
159. Halo Halo Hawaiian Filipino Dessert 98
160. Ham Swiss Bread Pudding I 98
161. Hardee's Peach Cobbler Copycat 99
162. Hawaiian Pie 99

163. Hawaiian Sweet Rolls (Bread Machine)...100
164. Hazelnut Chocolate Pastries......................100
165. Healthy Apple Pear Cake............................101
166. Healthy Chocolate No Bake Oatmeal Cookies...102
167. Healthy Sorbet...102
168. Hg's Bananarama Wafer Puddin' Ww Points = 3   103
169. Homemade Banana Pudding.....................103
170. Honey Apple Noodle Kugel 104
171. Honey Bun Cake 1st Umc 104
172. Honey Lime Fruit Toss 105
173. Hot Sweet Potato Salad..............................105
174. Impossible Peanut Butter Cookies...........106
175. Impossibly Easy Pumpkin Pie (Bisquick...too Easy :) 106
176. Incredible Ice Cream Sandwich Sundae Dessert...107
177. Incredibly Easy Amazing Strawberry Shortcake...107
178. Irish Apple Crumble 108
179. Jack Daniels Bread Pudding 109
180. Julia Child's Cherry Clafouti 110
181. Kids' Fruit Salad 110
182. Kiwi And Cream Pie 110
183. Kumara / Sweet Potato Buns 111
184. Layered Ice Cream Candy Cake!...............111
185. Lemon Cake With Crackly Caramel Glaze 112
186. Lemon Frosted Golden Raisin Buns 113
187. Lemon Krisp Cookies 113
188. Lemon Meringue Cake With Strawberries 114
189. Lemon Pastry Shell 115
190. Lemon Raspberry Cheesecake Squares ...115
191. Lennie's Special Shortbread.......................116
192. Light Fresh Peach Cobbler 116
193. Light Pineapple Pudding............................117
194. Light And Tasty Pumpkin Cheesecake Bars 117
195. Lil's Chocolate Cookies (Wheaties)...........118
196. Limoncello Cream Cupcakes 118
197. Linda's Peanut Butter Cookies..................119
198. Louisiana Caramel Pralines 120
199. Low Fat Noodle Kugel 120
200. Low Fat Pumpkin Cake 121
201. Low Fat Triple Fruit Pizza 121
202. Lox Mousse 122
203. Loz (Almond Sweetmeats).........................122
204. M. Cunningham's Almond Butter Cake . 123
205. Maple Krispie Cookies 124
206. Maple Pecan Squares..................................124
207. Martin's Mum's Gingernuts 125
208. Mellow Yellow Jello Salad 125
209. Melting Moments..126
210. Mile High Lemon Pie..................................126
211. Mini Chocolate Chip Cheese Pie 127
212. Mirj's Easy Sweet And Spicy Fat Free Curry Flavored Pumpkin 127
213. Mocha Butter Cupcakes With Mocha Butter Frosting...128
214. Mom's Infamous Mincemeat Pie 129
215. Most Incredible No Fail Pie Crust 129
216. My Grandma's Applesauce Spice Cake .. 129
217. My Mom's Oatmeal Cake...........................130
218. My Momma's Pear Salad 131
219. My Sister's Sweet Potato Bread................131
220. Nana's Special Cookies 131
221. Nicole's Punch Bowl Cake 132
222. Nigerian Fruit Salad 133
223. Nutty Oatmeal Raisin Chews 133
224. Oat N' Toffee Cookies 134
225. Oatmeal Apple Cookies..............................134
226. Oatmeal Applesauce Cookies 135
227. Oh My D Lux Chocolate Chip Cookies . 135
228. Old Fashioned Banana Pudding 136
229. Old Fashioned GingerBread Cookies 136
230. One Bowl Chocolate Mocha Cream Cake 137
231. One Pan Fruit Brownies.............................138
232. Orange Dessert Squares 138
233. Orange Honey Cake....................................139
234. Orange Mousse Dessert 140
235. Orange Walnut Bar Cake 141
236. Orange Chocolate Ice Cream Sauce........141
237. Oreo Pudding...142
238. Our Family Fried Pies.................................142
239. Parmesan Shortbread 143
240. Peanut Butter Cut Out Cookies 143
241. Peanut Chubbies 144
242. Peanut Parfait Dessert 145
243. Pear Pudding Cake (Or Apple, Peach...) In Crock Pot 146
244. Pears Poached In Red Wine 146

245. Pecan Sandies Cake Mix Cookies 147
246. Perfect Peanut Butter Cookies 147
247. Pina Colada Cheesecake With Coco Nut Crust 148
248. Pine Bark (Homemade Toffee) 149
249. Pineapple Coconut Cream Dream Pie 150
250. Pink Fantasy Salad 150
251. Plum Streusel Kuchen 151
252. Poppy Seed Plum Cake 151
253. Poppycock 152
254. Possum's Apple Crisp 153
255. Potato Salad With Sweet Onion Dressing 153
256. Praline Brownies 154
257. Praline Pumpkin Pie 154
258. Pumpkin Cake Bars With Cream Cheese Frosting! 155
259. Pumpkin Gooey Butter Cake (Paula Deen) 156
260. Pumpkin Apple Cake(s) 156
261. Pumpkin Spice Bundt Cake 157
262. Queen Elizabeth's Own Cake 158
263. Quick Easy Fruit And Dip 158
264. Quick And Easy Chocolate Chip Cookie Dough Brownies 159
265. Quick And Easy Eggless Banana Bread .. 159
266. Quick And Easy German Chocolate Cake 160
267. Quick And Easy Ice Cream Pie 160
268. Raspberry Rave 161
269. Raspberry Sunshine 161
270. Raspberry Apple Crumble (Volumetric) . 162
271. Rawai (Parsee Sweet) 162
272. Red Raspberry Holiday Trifle 163
273. Red Velvet Chocolate Cake Icing 164
274. Red, White, And Blueberry Pudding (Raw Vegan) 164
275. Rhubarb Cake 165
276. Rhubarb Upside Down Cake 165
277. Rice Cakes With Sweet Potatoes Soy Ginger Glaze 166
278. Rice Pudding Mexican Style, Arroz Con Leche 167
279. Rich, Fudgy Vegan Brownies 167
280. Roasted Pumpkin And Sweet Potato Soup 168
281. Rocky Road Brownies 169
282. Rolled Chocolate Sugar Cookies 169
283. Rum Cream Apple Pie 170
284. Russian Teacakes 170
285. S'mores Pizza 171
286. SO EASY SO GOOD Fruit Dip 171
287. Salad With Eight Fruits 172
288. Santa's Whiskers 172
289. Scottish Fruited Gingerbread 173
290. Scottish Tablet II 173
291. Scripture Cookies 174
292. Sex In A Pan 174
293. Sheet Cake Icing 175
294. Simple Cathedral Windows 175
295. Simple Chocolate Cupcakes 176
296. Simple Jello Salad 176
297. Simply Fresh Fruit Salad 177
298. Six Spice Oatmeal Raisin Cookies 177
299. Sky High Strawberry Pie 178
300. Slow Cooker (Crock Pot) Pumpkin Apple Dessert 178
301. Slow Peaches 179
302. Smucker's Strawberry Angel Cookies 179
303. Snickers Caramel Apple Salad 180
304. Soft 'N Chewy CHOCOLATE SANDWICH COOKIES 180
305. Sour Cream Fresh Blueberry Peach Cobbler 181
306. Southern Pride Sweet Cornbread 181
307. Spiced Sweet Potato Casserole 182
308. Spicy Baked Sweet Potato "fries" 183
309. St. Paddy's Day Pound Cake 183
310. Strawberry Angel Fluff 184
311. Strawberry Cucumber Veloute 184
312. Strawberry Peach Gelatin Dessert 184
313. Strawberry Pretzel Potluck Salad 185
314. Strawberry Streusel Squares 185
315. Strawberry Trifle No Cream Cheese 186
316. Sue B's Blueberry Buckle 187
317. Sugar Dusted Banana Cake 187
318. Sugarless Apple Cookies 188
319. Sunflower Centerpiece 188
320. Super Easy Peanut Butter Fudge 189
321. Super Easy Peach Cobbler 189
322. Super Rich No Bake Chocolate Peanut Butter Pie 190
323. Swedish Rice Dessert 190
324. Sweet Fry Bread Enough For An Army! 191

325. Sweet Iced Cinnamon Tea 191
326. Sweet Pineapple Cranberry Sauce 192
327. Sweet Potato Boats 193
328. Sweet Potato With Brandy And Raisins .. 193
329. Sweet Potatoes (Yams) With Apricots ... 194
330. Sweet Potatoes With Rum 194
331. Sweet Tea Chicken 195
332. Tate's Bake Shop Chocolate Chip Cookies 195
333. That Yummy Pink Salad 196
334. The Bestest Butter Cookies (Rolled) 196
335. The Only Chocolate Cake Recipe You'll Ever Need! (Devil's Food) 197
336. The Ultimate Strawberry Shortcake 198
337. Theepless (Almost Funnel Cake) 198
338. Tikvenik Bulgarian Sweet Pumpkin Pie .. 199
339. Toffee Almond Bars 199
340. Toffee Cornflake Cookies 200
341. Torrones A Christmas Time Nougat Candy 200
342. Tres Leches (Three Milk Cake) 201
343. Triple Dark Chocolate Mousse Pie 202
344. Tropical Breakfast Ambrosia 202
345. Tropical Paradise 203
346. Ultimate Mars Bar Slice 203
347. Unemployment Cake (Poudding Chomeur) 204
348. Vanilla Cinnamon Fruit Salad 204
349. Vanilla Fruit Salad For Sixty Plus 205
350. Vegan Cranberry Cashew Biscotti 205
351. Vegetarian Sweet Potato Pie 206
352. Walnut Squares 207
353. Whipped Minted Yoghurt 207
354. White Chocolate Chunk Macadamia Cookies 208
355. White Chocolate No Bake Cheesecake Pie 208
356. White Dessert 208
357. Whole Wheat Chocolate Chip Cookies ... 209
358. Whoopie Pies (Lightened Up) 209
359. Willamette Apple And Cheddar Tart 210
360. Wonderful Lemon Fruit Salad 211
361. World's Most Amazing Simple Cobbler!! (Peach And Strawberry) 211
362. YUM YUMS (Chocolate Nut Cookies) .. 212
363. Yum Yum Yo Yo Biscuits 212
364. Yummy Caramel Frosting 213
365. Yummy Gelatin Salad 213

INDEX **215**

CONCLUSION **219**

365 Awesome Potluck Dessert Recipes

***

1. 3 Layer Cheesy Strawberry Cake

Serving: 16 serving(s) | Prep: 30mins | Ready in:

Ingredients

- Layer 1
- 1 cup flour
- 1/4 cup sugar
- 2 teaspoons finely shredded lemon zest
- 1 teaspoon baking powder
- 1/2 cup margarine, softened
- 1 beaten egg
- 1/4 cup milk
- 1/2 teaspoon vanilla
- Layer 2
- 2 (8 ounce) packages cream cheese, plus
- 1 (3 ounce) package cream cheese (low fat works fine)
- 1 1/2 cups sugar
- 1 egg
- 2 teaspoons vanilla
- 1 tablespoon lemon juice
- Layer 3
- 4 cups sliced fresh strawberries
- 1/2 cup currant jelly (at room temperature)
- 1/2 cup fresh blueberries (to garnish) or 1/2 cup toasted sliced almonds (to garnish)

Direction

- Layer 1: Make this part 4 to 24 hours ahead: Preheat oven to 350 degrees F.
- Mix dry ingredients in a bowl.
- Cut in margarine until texture feels like corn meal.
- Combine wet ingredients in a bowl and mix well. Then add all at once to the dry ingredients. Mix just enough to make a soft dough.
- Using fingers, gently pat dough into the bottom of a 9 X 13 pan.
- Layer 2: Combine all ingredients.
- Beat until creamy with mixer on high.
- Spread over dough in the pan.
- Bake at 350 for 30 minutes or until golden brown.
- Cool completely and cover.
- Refrigerate for 2 to 24 hours.
- Layer 3: 3 hours or less before serving.
- Arrange berries on top of cake.
- Stir jelly to soften, then brush jelly over berries.
- Garnish with blueberries or toasted almond slices. (Toast almond slices in a fry pan over medium heat, stirring constantly until browned a bit.).

Nutrition Information

- Calories: 337.3
- Fiber: 1.2
- Sugar: 29.6
- Total Carbohydrate: 40.1
- Cholesterol: 64
- Total Fat: 18.4
- Saturated Fat: 8.7
- Sodium: 203.2
- Protein: 4.6

2. 4 Ingredient Sweet And Spicy Chicken Wings

Serving: 4 serving(s) | Prep: 5mins | Ready in:

Ingredients

- 2 1/2-3 lbs uncooked chicken wings, cut in sections
- 1/2 cup honey
- 1/2 cup soy sauce
- 1/2 cup barbecue sauce

Direction

- Preheat oven to 350 degrees.
- Place wings in a greased 9 x 13 baking dish.
- Combine sauces and honey and pour over the wings.
- Bake for about an hour, or until juices run clear.

Nutrition Information

- Calories: 827.2
- Saturated Fat: 12.7
- Sodium: 2484.5
- Fiber: 0.6
- Sugar: 43.5
- Cholesterol: 218.5
- Total Fat: 45.4
- Protein: 55.9
- Total Carbohydrate: 48.2

3. All American Jello Salad

Serving: 6 serving(s) | Prep: 3hours | Ready in:

Ingredients

- 1 (4 ounce) package raspberry gelatin powder
- 1 (4 ounce) package berry blue gelatin mix
- 2 1/2 cups boiling water
- 1 cup crushed pineapple, packed in fruit juice, undrained
- 1/4 cup frozen unsweetened blueberries
- 1/4 cup frozen unsweetened raspberry
- 1 cup diced banana

Direction

- In a large bowl, combine dry gelatins and water.
- Mix well to dissolve gelatin.
- Stir in undrained pineapple.
- Add frozen blueberries and raspberries.
- Mix well to combine Fold in bananas.
- Pour mixture into an 8X8 dish.
- Refrigerate until firm (about 3 hours).
- Cut and serve.

Nutrition Information

- Calories: 197
- Sodium: 178.8
- Cholesterol: 0
- Protein: 3.5
- Total Fat: 0.2
- Saturated Fat: 0
- Fiber: 1.5
- Sugar: 42.3
- Total Carbohydrate: 47.8

4. Almost Fat Free Cheesecake

Serving: 12 serving(s) | Prep: 35mins | Ready in:

Ingredients

- CRUST
- 1/2 cup graham cracker crumbs
- TOPPING
- 16 ounces fat free sour cream
- 3 tablespoons sugar
- 1 teaspoon vanilla
- FILLING
- 3 (8 ounce) packages fat free cream cheese, room temperature
- 1 cup sugar
- 1 teaspoon vanilla
- 6 egg whites

Direction

- Preheat oven to 350 degrees.

- Lightly spray a 9 inch spring form pan with cooking spray and sprinkle graham cracker crumbs evenly over bottom.
- In a large bowl beat together the cream cheese, sugar, vanilla and egg whites with an electric mixer on low speed, until blended.
- Pour filling into prepared pan and bake for 45 minutes, or until centre puffs and is almost set.
- Remove from oven.
- In a medium mixing bowl combine sour cream, sugar and vanilla and mix thoroughly.
- Spread mixture over cheesecake and return to oven for 5 minutes or until topping sets.
- Chill before serving.

Nutrition Information

- Calories: 196
- Cholesterol: 10.2
- Protein: 12.7
- Total Fat: 1.4
- Saturated Fat: 0.7
- Sodium: 469.6
- Fiber: 0.1
- Sugar: 26.9
- Total Carbohydrate: 32.8

5. Amish Sticky Buns, Sweet Rolls Wow Wow Wow!

Serving: 48-52 serving(s) | Prep: 1hours30mins | Ready in:

Ingredients

- 2 tablespoons yeast
- 1 tablespoon sugar
- 1 cup water (approx. 105 degrees)
- 1 cup milk
- 6 tablespoons butter
- 1/2 cup sugar
- 1 teaspoon salt
- 7 cups flour
- 3 eggs, beaten
- Syrup
- 3 cups brown sugar
- 3/4 cup butter
- 6 tablespoons Karo syrup
- Topping
- brown sugar
- cinnamon

Direction

- Dissolve yeast and 1 tbsp. sugar in warm water.
- Scald milk, then add butter, sugar and salt.
- Cool to lukewarm.
- Add two cups flour.
- Add yeast and eggs.
- Stir in the remainder of the flour and knead lightly.
- Let rise until double.
- While dough is rising, boil all syrup ingredients for two minutes.
- Divide syrup into six 8-inch square pans (or I sometimes use 3- 9x13 pans).
- When dough is doubled, punch down and divide into two parts.
- Roll each part (one at a time) into a 12x18-inch rectangle on a well-floured board or table.
- Sprinkle with brown sugar and cinnamon.
- Roll up tightly, beginning at the wide side.
- Cut into 1 inch slices, and lay slices on top of the syrup in the pans.
- Repeat with all dough.
- Bake at 375°F for 15 minutes.

Nutrition Information

- Calories: 181.9
- Total Carbohydrate: 32
- Cholesterol: 23.8
- Total Fat: 5
- Sodium: 98.1
- Fiber: 0.6
- Sugar: 16.4
- Saturated Fat: 3
- Protein: 2.7

6. Angel Cake Delight

Serving: 1 13x9 dish, 10 serving(s) | Prep: 10mins | Ready in:

Ingredients

- 1 large angel food cake
- 2 cans Eagle Brand Condensed Milk
- 4 lemons, juiced
- 1 orange, juiced
- 1 (20 ounce) can crushed pineapple, drained

Direction

- Break angel food cake into pieces and place in 13 x 9 dish.
- Pour Eagle Brand milk in a mixing bowl.
- Add the juices separately.
- Add juice of lemons; beat well.
- Add juice of orange; beat well.
- Add drained pineapple; beat well.
- Pour over crumbled cake.
- Stir well.
- Refrigerate overnight.
- Cut in squares.
- Top with whipping cream and a cherry on each square.

Nutrition Information

- Calories: 545.3
- Sodium: 441.1
- Total Fat: 9.7
- Saturated Fat: 5.9
- Fiber: 2.9
- Sugar: 85.8
- Total Carbohydrate: 108.2
- Cholesterol: 36.4
- Protein: 13

7. Annie Glenn's Chocolate Chip Cookies

Serving: 48 cookies | Prep: 15mins | Ready in:

Ingredients

- 2 1/4 cups flour
- 1 teaspoon baking soda
- 1 teaspoon salt
- 1/2 cup butter, at room temperature (or hard stick margarine, softened)
- 1/2 cup shortening
- 3/4 cup white sugar
- 3/4 cup lightly packed brown sugar
- 1 teaspoon vanilla
- 2 eggs
- 1 (12 ounce) package semi-sweet chocolate chips

Direction

- Preheat oven to 350F degrees.
- In a mixing bowl, combine flour, baking soda and salt; set aside.
- In a large mixing bowl, with an electric mixer, cream together butter, shortening, sugars and vanilla.
- Add eggs, one at a time, mixing well after each addition.
- Mix in the flour mixture.
- Fold in the chocolate chips.
- Drop spoonfuls onto greased cookie sheets and bake in preheated oven for 10 to 12 minutes, or until golden brown.
- Note from Lennie: I would use parchment paper on the baking sheets instead of greasing them.

Nutrition Information

- Calories: 119.5
- Protein: 1.2
- Saturated Fat: 3.1
- Fiber: 0.6
- Cholesterol: 13.9
- Sugar: 10.3

- Total Carbohydrate: 15.4
- Total Fat: 6.4
- Sodium: 93.5

8. Apple Cinnamon Coffee Cake

Serving: 12-16 serving(s) | Prep: 5mins | Ready in:

Ingredients

- 1 (18 1/4 ounce) box yellow cake mix
- 3 eggs
- 1 cup plain yogurt
- 1 (21 ounce) can apple pie filling
- 3 tablespoons sugar
- 1 tablespoon cinnamon
- 2 teaspoons flour

Direction

- In large mixing bowl, combine cake mix, eggs and yogurt.
- Beat for 3 minutes.
- Spread into greased and floured 13x9 pan.
- Arrange pie filling over the batter.
- Combine cinnamon, sugar and flour.
- Sprinkle on top of cake.
- Bake at 350 for 40-45 minutes.
- Serve warm.

Nutrition Information

- Calories: 282.8
- Sodium: 332.3
- Fiber: 1.3
- Sugar: 29.8
- Protein: 4.3
- Total Fat: 7
- Saturated Fat: 1.6
- Total Carbohydrate: 51.8
- Cholesterol: 56.4

9. Apple Cobbler With Oatmeal

Serving: 6 serving(s) | Prep: 10mins | Ready in:

Ingredients

- 6 -8 baking apples (I prefer Cortland)
- 1/2 cup white sugar
- 1/2 cup margarine
- 1 tablespoon ground cinnamon
- 3/4 cup quick-cooking oatmeal or 3/4 cup rolled oats
- 3/4 cup brown sugar
- 3/4 cup white flour

Direction

- For best results with this recipe, use apples that hold their shape when baking and aren't too tart.
- Do not use Macintosh apples (too soft) or Red Delicious (too bland).
- I prefer Cortland's or Empires.
- Preheat the oven to 350 degrees- if you have a convection oven, do NOT use the convection feature- the dessert will be dry and overcooked on top.
- Use the regular baking feature.
- This recipe isn't good for microwave use.
- Peel and core the apples, then cut them into eighths or into large cubes.
- Distribute the apples evenly into a medium-sized ungreased baking dish (I like the white Corning/Pyrex oval dishes) and sprinkle the white sugar and cinnamon over top.
- Distribute 1 tbsp. of the margarine in dollops throughout the top of the apples (no need to try to stir it in).
- In a separate medium mixing bowl, combine the remaining margarine, the oats, brown sugar and flour using your hands or a pastry whisk until it forms a crumbly, dry-ish mixture.
- (Note: if you like lots of crumble topping, feel free to double the ingredient quantities for the topping).

- Pour the mixture over top of the apples and spread it out evenly so that all the apples are covered and the edges and corners hidden.
- Pat the mixture down lightly so that it looks sort of like a crust.
- Bake for 30-35 minutes, until the crumb top has darkened to a golden brown colour.
- Remove from the oven and let cool for at least 10 minutes before serving.
- Spoon out portions into large bowls and serve with ice cream, thick sweetened yoghurt or milk.

Nutrition Information

- Calories: 497.3
- Saturated Fat: 3.3
- Sodium: 188
- Cholesterol: 0
- Protein: 3.7
- Total Fat: 16.3
- Fiber: 6.5
- Sugar: 62.4
- Total Carbohydrate: 88.8

10. Apple Crisp For THe Microwave

Serving: 4 serving(s) | Prep: 15mins | Ready in:

Ingredients

- 5 medium apples, peeled and thinly sliced
- 1/2 cup packed brown sugar
- 1/2 cup quick oats
- 4 tablespoons flour
- 1 teaspoon cinnamon
- 5 tablespoons cold butter

Direction

- Put apple slices in glass dish.
- Mix the remaining ingredients to a small crumb.
- Sprinkle over fruit.
- Microwave, uncovered on hi 5 minutes.
- Let set for 5 minutes.
- Microwave again on hi for 5 minutes, or until apples are tender.

Nutrition Information

- Calories: 389.4
- Total Fat: 15.4
- Saturated Fat: 9.3
- Sugar: 44.6
- Protein: 3
- Sodium: 115.4
- Fiber: 5.7
- Total Carbohydrate: 63.8
- Cholesterol: 38.2

11. Apple Milk Indian Delicacy(Seb Rabdi)

Serving: 4 serving(s) | Prep: 30mins | Ready in:

Ingredients

- 1 1/2 liters milk
- 1/2 teaspoon green cardamom powder
- 2 teaspoons chopped cashews
- 2 teaspoons chopped plain pistachios
- 2 teaspoons saffron threads, soaked in 2 tbsps. warm milk or 2 teaspoons warm water
- 150 g sugar
- 4 apples, washed

Direction

- Bring milk to a boil in a pot.
- Remove from heat and allow it to cool down to room temperature and thicken on its own.
- Add nuts, green cardamom powder, saffron and sugar.
- Mix well and keep aside.
- Cut off the tops of the 4 apples and scoop out the centre portion with the seed.

- The centre portion will now be empty.
- In this portion, fill in the above prepared milk-sugar combo (known as "rabdi" in Hindi), very carefully.
- Make a dough of wheat flour with water and roll out a thin strip and firmly fix this onto the top of the apple so as to seal it.
- Cover the apple with aluminum foil.
- Likewise, repeat for all the apples.
- Freeze for a few hours.
- After about 4 hours, remove the apples, slice them and garnish them with rose syrup and serve.

Nutrition Information

- Calories: 481.6
- Total Carbohydrate: 75.6
- Cholesterol: 54.3
- Fiber: 3.5
- Sugar: 52
- Protein: 13.6
- Total Fat: 15.7
- Saturated Fat: 9.1
- Sodium: 201.2

12. Apple Pear Compote

Serving: 6 serving(s) | Prep: 10mins | Ready in:

Ingredients

- 4 ounces dry white wine
- 1 teaspoon honey
- 1/2 teaspoon vanilla extract
- 1/4 teaspoon ground cinnamon
- 1/8 teaspoon ground nutmeg
- 1/8 teaspoon ground ginger
- 1 granny smith apple, peeled, pared and chopped
- 1 mcintosh apple, peeled, pared and chopped
- 10 ounces pears, pared and chopped
- frozen non-dairy whipped topping, , thawed

Direction

- In large saucepan, combine wine, honey, vanilla and spices.
- Cook over high heat until mixture boils.
- Add Granny Smith apple.
- Reduce heat and cook until liquid is reduced by half, about ten minutes.
- Add McIntosh apples and pears.
- Cook until fruit is tender and liquid is mostly evaporated and syrupy.
- Top with whipped topping and serve.
- Truly delicious.

Nutrition Information

- Calories: 72.2
- Total Fat: 0.2
- Saturated Fat: 0
- Sodium: 2
- Fiber: 2.6
- Sugar: 10.6
- Total Carbohydrate: 15.3
- Cholesterol: 0
- Protein: 0.3

13. Apple Mango Crisp

Serving: 1 13x9 pan, 16 serving(s) | Prep: 15mins | Ready in:

Ingredients

- 3/4 cup rolled oats
- 1/2 cup flour
- 1/2 cup toasted wheat germ
- 1/2 cup brown sugar, packed
- 1 1/2 teaspoons cinnamon
- 1/4 cup butter, melted
- 3 green apples, cored chopped coarsely (see note)
- 3 red apples, cored chopped coarsely (see note)
- 3 tablespoons lime juice

- 1/4 cup flour
- 4 cups frozen mangoes, chopped coarsely
- 1/3 cup chopped pecans

Direction

- Preheat oven to 375. Grease a 13x9 cake pan.
- In a medium bowl, stir together first five ingredients; stir in butter--distributing evenly. Set aside.
- Place apples in large bowl, sprinkle with lime juice, then remaining flour; stir to mix, then fold in mango chunks.
- Pour apple-mango mixture into prepared pan; top with oat-sugar mixture.
- Bake (uncovered) for 30 minutes; sprinkle with pecans, bake another 10-15 minutes (apples should be tender throughout).
- Cool slightly, serve warm with whipped cream or vanilla ice cream.
- NOTE: My hubby noted that he would prefer the apples to be peeled next time.

Nutrition Information

- Calories: 170.9
- Sodium: 25.3
- Total Carbohydrate: 30.5
- Protein: 2.6
- Total Fat: 5.4
- Saturated Fat: 2.1
- Fiber: 3.3
- Sugar: 18.3
- Cholesterol: 7.6

14. Apricot Mashed Sweet Potatoes

Serving: 8 serving(s) | Prep: 5mins | Ready in:

Ingredients

- 2 1/2 lbs sweet potatoes, peeled and cut in 1/2 inch dice
- 1/4 cup apricot preserves
- 2 tablespoons butter or 2 tablespoons margarine, softened
- 3/4 teaspoon grated orange rind
- 1/8 teaspoon ground nutmeg
- 1/3 cup milk or 1/3 cup cream
- salt and pepper, to taste

Direction

- Place the sweet potatoes in a large pot; add cold water to cover by about 1 inch.
- Cover and bring to a boil; reduce the heat and boil gently until the potatoes are tender, about 15 minutes.
- Drain and return the potatoes to the pot.
- Add the remaining ingredients, except preserves, and mash with a potato masher until smooth.
- Add apricot preserves, and stir potatoes well.
- Taste and adjust seasonings.
- If the potatoes seem dry, add a little more milk.

Nutrition Information

- Calories: 178.5
- Protein: 2.7
- Sodium: 107.5
- Sugar: 9.6
- Total Carbohydrate: 35.5
- Cholesterol: 9.1
- Total Fat: 3.4
- Saturated Fat: 2.1
- Fiber: 4.3

15. Apricot And Oat Fingers

Serving: 2 serving(s) | Prep: 15mins | Ready in:

Ingredients

- 7 dried apricots
- 40 g rolled oats
- 150 ml mint tea

- 30 g chopped mixed nuts

Direction

- Soak the apricots in enough boiling mint tea to cover them for 3 hours. If you are short on time simmer the fruit in the tea for 30 minutes.
- Heat oven to 180C'350°F.
- Drain apricots and puree reserving the tea. Place in a pan with the oats, nuts and 50ml of the mint tea. Cook over a low heat for 5 minutes.
- Oil a baking sheet and press the mixture into it. Bake for 20 minutes.

Nutrition Information

- Calories: 447.8
- Sugar: 15.8
- Cholesterol: 0
- Protein: 13.1
- Total Fat: 28.4
- Saturated Fat: 3.9
- Sodium: 354.8
- Fiber: 8.5
- Total Carbohydrate: 42.1

16. Bacardi Rum Cake

Serving: 10-12 serving(s) | Prep: 20mins | Ready in:

Ingredients

- 1 cup chopped pecans or 1 cup chopped walnuts
- 1 (520 g) package yellow cake mix (You just use the cake mix as is, do not add other ingredients listed on cake box.)
- 1 (92 g) package vanilla instant pudding mix
- 4 eggs
- 1/2 cup cold water
- 1/2 cup cooking oil
- 1/2 cup dark rum or rum
- Glaze
- 1/2 cup butter
- 1/4 cup water
- 1 cup sugar
- 1/2 cup dark rum or rum

Direction

- Sprinkle nuts over bottom of greased 10 inch tube pan or 12 cup Bundt pan.
- Stir together cake mix, pudding mix, eggs, water, oil and rum.
- Pour batter over nuts.
- Bake at 325 in oven for 1 hour.
- Cool 10 minutes in pan.
- Invert onto serving plate and prick top.
- Glaze-----------------.
- Melt butter in saucepan.
- Stir in water and sugar.
- Boil 5 minutes, stirring constantly.
- Remove from heat.
- Stir in rum.
- Brush glaze evenly over top and sides of cake.
- Allow cake to absorb glaze.
- Repeat until glaze is used up.

Nutrition Information

- Calories: 669.4
- Protein: 5.9
- Total Fat: 35.9
- Saturated Fat: 9.5
- Sodium: 583.2
- Fiber: 1.6
- Cholesterol: 99.8
- Sugar: 51.5
- Total Carbohydrate: 70.7

17. Balsamic Bleu Pears

Serving: 4 serving(s) | Prep: 15mins | Ready in:

Ingredients

- 2 teaspoons balsamic vinegar

- 2 teaspoons extra virgin olive oil
- 1 lb pear, drained and sliced or julienne (canned or fresh)
- 1/4 cup chopped walnuts, toasted
- 1 -2 teaspoon crumbled blue cheese

Direction

- In a medium-size serving bowl, blend vinegar and olive oil.
- Add pears and toss gently to coat.
- Sprinkle with walnuts and cheese.

Nutrition Information

- Calories: 138.3
- Total Fat: 7.4
- Sugar: 11.7
- Fiber: 4
- Total Carbohydrate: 19
- Cholesterol: 0.5
- Protein: 1.7
- Saturated Fat: 0.9
- Sodium: 11.7

18. Banana Butterfinger Cake

Serving: 2 9 inch pans | Prep: 20mins | Ready in:

Ingredients

- FOR THE CAKE
- 2 1/4 cups cake flour
- 1 teaspoon baking powder
- 1/2 teaspoon salt
- 1/2 cup unsalted butter, room temperature
- 1 1/2 cups sugar
- 3 large eggs
- 1 tablespoon dark rum
- 1 teaspoon vanilla extract
- 3/4 cup sour cream
- 1 teaspoon baking soda
- 2 cups bananas, mashed ripe
- 1 1/2 cups butterfinger candy bars, chopped
- FOR THE GLAZE
- 2/3 cup whipping cream
- 7 tablespoons unsalted butter, cut into large pieces
- 1 tablespoon light corn syrup
- 14 ounces semisweet chocolate, chopped
- 2 teaspoons dark rum
- 1 teaspoon vanilla extract
- 1 3/4 cups butterfinger candy bars, chopped

Direction

- To make cake, position rack in top third of oven; preheat to 350 degrees.
- Butter two 9-inch-diameter cake pans with 1 1/2-inch-high sides. Line bottoms with waxed paper rounds. Butter and flour paper. Sift flour, baking powder and salt into medium bowl. Using electric mixer, beat butter in large bowl until fluffy. Gradually add sugar and beat 2 minutes. Add eggs, 1 at a time, beating well after each addition.
- Beat in dark rum and vanilla extract. Combine sour cream and baking soda in medium bowl. Add mashed bananas to sour cream mixture and stir until well blended. Add dry ingredients to butter mixture alternately with banana mixture, beginning and ending with dry ingredients. Stir in chopped Butterfinger bars. Divide batter between prepared pans. Bake until center of cake feels firm and tester inserted into center comes out clean, about 30 minutes. Cool in pans on rack 10 minutes. Run small knife around sides of cakes to loosen.
- Turn out cakes onto racks and cook. Peel off waxed paper. (Can be prepared 1 day ahead. Wrap cakes tightly and store at room temperature.)
- To make glaze, combine cream, butter and corn syrup in heavy medium saucepan. Bring to simmer over medium heat, stirring until butter melts. Remove from heat; add chocolate and stir until melted and smooth. Stir in rum and vanilla. Pour glaze into small bowl. Cover and refrigerate just until cool and thick, stirring occasionally, about 40 minutes. Transfer 1 cake layer to platter. Slide waxed

paper strips under edges of cake. Stir glaze until smooth. Spread 1°C glaze evenly over top of cake layer. Top with second cake layer. Spread remaining glaze over top and sides of cake. Cover top and sides of cake with chopped Butterfinger bars. Remove paper strips. (Can be made 2 days ahead. Cover cake and store at room temperature.).

Nutrition Information

- Calories: 5015.1
- Total Carbohydrate: 584.8
- Cholesterol: 692.8
- Protein: 71
- Fiber: 44.3
- Saturated Fat: 179
- Sodium: 2249.4
- Sugar: 323
- Total Fat: 300.6

19. Banana Cream Pie(Cook's Country)

Serving: 1 pie, 8 serving(s) | Prep: 8mins | Ready in:

Ingredients

- 5 ripe bananas
- 4 tablespoons unsalted butter
- 2 1/2 cups half-and-half
- 1/2 cup plus 2 tablespoons granulated sugar (3 1/2 ounces)
- 6 large egg yolks
- 1/4 teaspoon salt
- 2 tablespoons cornstarch
- 1 1/2 teaspoons vanilla extract
- 1 pie crust, Pillsbury Just Unroll
- 2 tablespoons orange juice
- 1 cup heavy cream
- 2 tablespoons confectioners' sugar

Direction

- 1. Peel 2 bananas and slice into 1/2-inch-thick pieces. Melt 1 tablespoon butter in medium saucepan over medium-high heat. Add sliced bananas and cook until they begin to soften, about 2 minutes. Add half-and-half, bring to boil, and boil for 30 seconds. Remove from heat, cover, and let sit for 40 minutes.
- 2. Whisk granulated sugar, egg yolks, and salt together in large bowl until smooth. Whisk in cornstarch. Strain cooled half-and-half mixture through fine-mesh strainer into yolk mixture—do not press on bananas—and whisk until incorporated; discard cooked bananas.
- 3. Transfer mixture to clean medium saucepan. Cook over medium heat, whisking constantly, until thickened to consistency of warm pudding (180 degrees), 4 to 6 minutes. Remove pan from heat; whisk in remaining 3 tablespoons butter and 1 teaspoon vanilla. Transfer pastry cream to bowl, press greased parchment paper directly against surface, and let cool for about 1 hour.
- 4. Meanwhile, roll pie dough into 12-inch round on lightly floured counter. Transfer to 9-inch pie plate, fold edge of dough under itself so edge of fold is flush with outer rim of plate, and flute edges. Refrigerate for 40 minutes, then freeze for 20 minutes. Adjust oven rack to lower-middle position and heat oven to 375 degrees.
- 5. Line chilled pie shell with 12-inch square of aluminum foil, folding foil over edges of dough. Fill with pie weights and bake for 20 minutes. Carefully remove foil and weights, rotate plate, and continue baking until crust is golden brown, 7 to 11 minutes. Let cool to room temperature.
- 6. Peel and slice remaining 3 bananas 1/4 inch thick and toss with orange juice. Whisk pastry cream briefly, then spread half over bottom of pie shell. Arrange sliced bananas on pastry cream. Top with remaining pastry cream.
- 7. Using stand mixer fitted with whisk, heavy cream, confectioners' sugar, and remaining 1/2 teaspoon vanilla on medium-low speed until foamy, about 1 minute. Increase speed to

high and whip until stiff peaks form, 1 to 3 minutes. Spread whipped cream evenly over top of pie. Refrigerate until set, at least 5 hours and up to 24 hours. Serve.

Nutrition Information

- Calories: 540
- Total Fat: 36.6
- Fiber: 2.8
- Sugar: 24.1
- Cholesterol: 222.3
- Saturated Fat: 19.1
- Sodium: 240
- Total Carbohydrate: 48.5
- Protein: 7.2

20. Banana Cupcakes With Cream Cheese Frosting

Serving: 24 mini cupcakes | Prep: 45mins | Ready in:

Ingredients

- CUPCAKES
- 3/4 cup sugar, divided
- 1/2 cup banana, ripe and mashed well
- 1/4 cup unsalted butter, softened
- 1 teaspoon vanilla extract
- 2 eggs
- 1 cup all-purpose flour (1 cup weighs 4.5 oz)
- 1/2 teaspoon baking soda
- 1/4 teaspoon salt
- 1/4 teaspoon ground nutmeg
- 1/4 cup buttermilk (I use Saco brand powdered buttermilk, reconstituted.) or 1/4 cup plain fat-free yogurt (I use Saco brand powdered buttermilk, reconstituted.)
- FROSTING
- 1 3/4 cups powdered sugar
- 1/2 cup reduced-fat cream cheese, 1/3-less-fat, chilled (0.5 cup weighs 4 oz. I use Philadelphia regular.)
- 1/2 teaspoon vanilla extract

Direction

- Preheat oven to 350 degrees F., and spray a 12-cup standard or 24-cup mini muffin tin with non-stick spray. IMPORTANT: If you use paper liners, be sure to spray the insides of the liners or the cupcakes will stick!
- CUPCAKES: Mix the mashed banana and 1/4 cup sugar and set aside.
- Beat 1/2 cup sugar, butter and 1 tsp. vanilla extract at medium speed of a mixer until well blended. Add eggs one at a time, beating well after each addition. Now add banana mixture and beat well.
- In separate bowl, whisk together flour, baking soda, salt and nutmeg. Add flour mixture to wet mixture alternately with buttermilk, mixing after each addition.
- Bake at 350 deg. for about 25 minutes (mini cupcakes, 12 to 15 minutes) or until a cake tester inserted in centre comes out clean. Cool completely on a wire rack.
- FROSTING: Beat powdered sugar, chilled cream cheese and 1/2 tsp. vanilla extract at medium speed just until blended (do not overbeat). Use the back of a spoon to spread over cupcakes.
- Store frosted cupcakes and any leftover frosting in the refrigerator, although these cupcakes don't last long enough to worry about that!

Nutrition Information

- Calories: 114.8
- Total Fat: 3.2
- Saturated Fat: 1.8
- Fiber: 0.2
- Cholesterol: 23.4
- Sodium: 83.2
- Sugar: 15.7
- Total Carbohydrate: 20.3
- Protein: 1.6

21. Banana Poi

Serving: 1 serving(s) | Prep: 5mins | Ready in:

Ingredients

- 2 cups very ripe bananas, mashed
- 2 tablespoons lemon juice
- 1 cup coconut cream

Direction

- Mash bananas until a smooth paste is formed.
- Add the lemon juice.
- Gradually add the coconut cream, stirring constantly.
- Chill and serve in glasses.

Nutrition Information

- Calories: 1330.4
- Total Carbohydrate: 228.1
- Cholesterol: 0
- Total Fat: 49.3
- Saturated Fat: 46.1
- Sodium: 109.9
- Protein: 6.8
- Fiber: 8.5
- Sugar: 189.9

22. Banana Split Cake

Serving: 12 serving(s) | Prep: 30mins | Ready in:

Ingredients

- 2 cups graham crackers (crushed)
- 1 -2 cup oleo
- 2 eggs
- 2 cups powdered sugar
- 5 bananas
- 1 (16 ounce) can crushed pineapple, drained
- 1 (8 ounce) container Cool Whip
- 1 cup crushed nuts (your choice)

Direction

- Put these ingredients in layers:
- 1st Layer: Crush crackers and mix with 1 stick melted oleo; spread in 9x13-inch pan.
- 2nd layer: Cook to a custard, 1 stick oleo, 2 eggs and 2 cups powdered sugar.
- 3rd layer: 5 bananas sliced lengthwise.
- 4th layer: Drained pineapple.
- 5th layer: Cool Whip.
- 6th layer: Crushed nuts.
- Put in refrigerator and cool.
- NOTE: You may also use other fruits such as a can of cherry pie filling, sliced sweetened strawberries, hot fudge or chocolate--but end with Cool Whip and then nuts.

Nutrition Information

- Calories: 478.8
- Sugar: 40.4
- Cholesterol: 35.2
- Protein: 5.1
- Total Fat: 28.2
- Saturated Fat: 8.3
- Sodium: 355.8
- Fiber: 3
- Total Carbohydrate: 55.3

23. Banana Split Pie For A Crowd....no Raw Eggs

Serving: 1 9 x 13 | Prep: 15mins | Ready in:

Ingredients

- 2 cups vanilla wafer crumbs or 2 cups graham cracker crumbs
- 1/2 cup melted butter or 1/2 cup margarine
- 1 (8 ounce) package fat free cream cheese (softened)
- 2 (16 ounce) containers Cool Whip

- 1 (4 ounce) package instant vanilla pudding
- 1 (20 ounce) can crushed pineapple
- 4 bananas
- Garnish
- maraschino cherry
- chocolate syrup

Direction

- Mix crumbs with butter and firmly pat the crumbs down on the bottom of a 9 x 13 pan.
- Place pan in a 350 degree oven for about 5-10 minutes or until a light golden brown.
- Set aside and let cool thoroughly.
- Meanwhile in a medium bowl, combine cream cheese, pudding, 3/4 tub of whip cream and a dash of milk and mix well.
- Then fold in the remaining 1/4 of whip cream left. The other tub of whip cream will be used for the topping.
- Spread the mixture over the crust.
- Drain pineapple and reserved the juice for later use.
- Add pineapple over topping evenly.
- Slice bananas and dip them in the pineapple juice so that they don't discolour.
- Place bananas over the pineapple.
- Spread whip cream over bananas.
- Drizzle chocolate syrup over whip cream.
- Top with cherries.
- Keep refrigerated until ready to serve.
- Enjoy!

Nutrition Information

- Calories: 7249.4
- Total Fat: 415.5
- Saturated Fat: 281.4
- Sodium: 5147.1
- Sugar: 455
- Total Carbohydrate: 846.9
- Cholesterol: 262.2
- Protein: 72
- Fiber: 25.9

24. Banana Yogurt Bundt Cake

Serving: 1 bundt cake, 16 serving(s) | Prep: 10mins | Ready in:

Ingredients

- 1/3 cup solid shortening
- 1 1/4 cups granulated sugar
- 2 eggs
- 1 teaspoon vanilla extract
- 3 medium ripe bananas, mashed
- 2 cups all-purpose flour
- 1 1/4 teaspoons baking powder
- 1 teaspoon baking soda
- 1/2 teaspoon salt
- 1 cup yogurt
- 1/3 cup chopped pecans
- 1/3 cup raisins

Direction

- In a mixing bowl, cream together shortening and sugar. Add eggs, one at a time, until well blended; stir in vanilla extract and bananas.
- In a separate bowl, combine flour, baking powder, baking soda and salt. Add to banana mixture alternately with sour cream. Stir in walnuts.
- Pour into a greased and floured 10-inch Bundt pan. Bake at 350 degrees F for 50 minutes or until done. Cool, then dust with confectioners' sugar before serving.

Nutrition Information

- Calories: 218.9
- Fiber: 1.3
- Cholesterol: 28.4
- Saturated Fat: 1.8
- Sodium: 196.4
- Protein: 3.5
- Total Fat: 7.3
- Sugar: 21
- Total Carbohydrate: 36.2

25. Base Jello Shots Recipe With Fruit Floaters

Serving: 32 shots, 10 serving(s) | Prep: 15mins | Ready in:

Ingredients

- 1 (6 ounce) boxfruit flavored Jello gelatin (large box) or 1 (5/8 ounce) boxfruit flavored sugar-free jello (large box)
- 2 cups boiling water
- 1 1/4-1 1/2 cups cold water or 1 1/4-1 1/2 cups ice water
- 1/2 cup vodka (or any liquor) or 1/2 cup light rum (or any liquor)
- 36 small paper cups
- 1/4 cup fruit juice (optional)
- 6 ounces berries (optional) or 6 ounces fruit slices, for floaters (optional)

Direction

- To make this easier, you may want to have a two quart pitcher with a handle and a pour spout to mix it with and then to pour it into the shot cups.
- First boil the water and then put it in the pitcher. Then add the package of gelatin. Stir, or shake, if your container has a tight fitting lid, to dissolve.
- Add cold water or equivalent amount of ice, fruit juice, and then liquor. Definitely use ice instead of the cold water if you are having the party in less than 4 hours because it will solidify faster. Taste to ensure there is enough liquor and consider adding more. If you use a citrus juice then you can add more liquor. Do NOT use pineapple juice, it will interfere with the gelatin setting.
- Pour the mixture into 3 oz. Dixie cups, filling 2/3 full (after all, you want enough of these to go around). I normally lay down a sheet of wax paper, and then pour the cups and place them on a cookie sheet. If you do two batches you can place the cookie sheets on top of each other in the fridge.
- Drop small fruit slices or an individual berry into each shot cup for a classy touch. Then chill for at least 3 hours.
- To bring them to your friend's party, find a cardboard box. Fill the bottom layer with shots. Lay another piece of cardboard on top of that layer and fill that layer with shots, and so on. They should make the journey with no problems.

Nutrition Information

- Calories: 90.5
- Saturated Fat: 0
- Sodium: 80.9
- Total Carbohydrate: 15.4
- Cholesterol: 0
- Protein: 1.3
- Total Fat: 0
- Fiber: 0
- Sugar: 14.6

26. Bavarian Strawberries

Serving: 6 serving(s) | Prep: 2hours15mins | Ready in:

Ingredients

- 1 quart fresh strawberries
- 1 tablespoon unflavored gelatin
- 2 teaspoons freshly squeezed lemon juice
- 3/4 cup sugar
- 4 fluid ounces cold water
- 8 fluid ounces heavy cream, whipped

Direction

- Slice the strawberries and mix with the sugar.
- Let stand until the sugar dissolves.
- Sprinkle the gelatin over cold water.

- Let stand 5 minutes, then heat gently until the gelatin dissolves completely.
- Add the gelatin and lemon juice to the sliced berries.
- Fold in the whipped cream.
- Pour into a 1-quart mold or serving dish.
- Chill until set.
- Carefully unmold and serve.

Nutrition Information

- Calories: 268.9
- Total Fat: 15
- Sodium: 18.8
- Fiber: 1.9
- Protein: 2.5
- Saturated Fat: 9.2
- Sugar: 29.5
- Total Carbohydrate: 33.6
- Cholesterol: 54.4

27. Berry Pudding

Serving: 6-8 serving(s) | Prep: 30mins | Ready in:

Ingredients

- 1 cup blueberries
- 1 cup raspberries
- 1 cup blackberry
- 3/4 cup sugar, plus more to taste
- 1/2 lemon, juice of, plus more to taste
- 1/4 ounce unflavored gelatin
- 1 1/2 cups heavy cream
- 3/4 cup sour cream

Direction

- Combine fruit and sugar with 1 cup water in a medium sauce pan over medium-low heat.
- Bring to a gentle boil and simmer for 10, until the mixture is mostly liquid and the berries are soft.
- Put through a strainer, getting as much juice as possible. Add water, if necessary to make juice mixture equal 1 quart.
- Cool. Add lemon juice. Taste and add more sugar or lemon juice if you like.
- Put 1/4 cup water in a small sauce pan and sprinkle the gelatin onto it.
- Cook over low heat until dissolved.
- Stir gelatin into the fruit juice and pour into individual bowls.
- Chill until firm.
- Whip the heavy cream until it holds soft peaks.
- Beat in 1/4 cup sugar.
- Stir in sour cream.
- Serve with berry pudding.

Nutrition Information

- Calories: 403.2
- Cholesterol: 94.2
- Saturated Fat: 17.5
- Fiber: 3.2
- Sodium: 40.9
- Sugar: 29.7
- Total Carbohydrate: 36.5
- Protein: 3.9
- Total Fat: 28.4

28. Best Blueberry Cobbler

Serving: 6-8 serving(s) | Prep: 15mins | Ready in:

Ingredients

- 2 1/2 cups fresh blueberries or 2 1/2 cups frozen blueberries
- 1 teaspoon vanilla extract
- 1/2 lemon, juiced
- 1/2 cup white sugar (to taste)
- 1/2 teaspoon all-purpose flour
- 1 tablespoon butter, melted
- 1 3/4 cups all-purpose flour
- 4 teaspoons baking powder

- 6 tablespoons white sugar
- 5 tablespoons butter
- 1 cup milk
- 2 teaspoons sugar
- 1 pinch ground cinnamon

Direction

- Lightly grease an 8 inch square baking dish. Place the blueberries into the baking dish, and mix with vanilla and lemon juice. Sprinkle with 1 cup of sugar and 1/2 teaspoon of flour, then stir in the tablespoon of melted butter. Set aside. In a medium bowl, stir together 1 3/4 cups of flour, baking powder, and 6 tablespoons sugar. Rub in the 5 tablespoons butter using your fingers, or cut in with a pastry blender until it is in small pieces. Make a well in the center, and quickly stir in the milk. Mix just until moistened. You should have a very thick batter, or very wet dough. You may need to add a splash more milk. Cover, and let batter rest for 10 minutes.
- Preheat the oven to 375 degrees F (190 degrees C). Spoon the batter over the blueberries, leaving only a few small holes for the berries to peek through. Mix together the cinnamon and 2 teaspoons sugar; sprinkle over the top. Bake for 20 to 25 minutes in the preheated oven, or until the top is golden brown. A knife inserted into the topping should come out clean - of course there will be blueberry syrup on the knife. Let cool until just warm before serving. This can store in the refrigerator for 2 days.

Nutrition Information

- Calories: 419.9
- Protein: 5.8
- Total Fat: 13.6
- Sodium: 345.4
- Fiber: 2.9
- Sugar: 36.9
- Cholesterol: 36.2
- Saturated Fat: 8.3
- Total Carbohydrate: 71.1

29. Big Boy's Strawberry Pie

Serving: 6-8 serving(s) | Prep: 30mins | Ready in:

Ingredients

- 1 pie shell, 9inch, baked
- 4 cups strawberries, fresh and sliced
- 1 1/2 cups water
- 3/4 cup granulated sugar
- 2 tablespoons cornstarch
- 3 ounces strawberry gelatin

Direction

- In baked pie crust add sliced strawberries.
- In small saucepan, mix water, sugar, and cornstarch and bring to boil. Boil until mixture is clear and thick, approximately 2 minutes.
- Remove saucepan from heat and add the strawberry gelatin, stirring until dissolved. Pour this over the strawberries in pie shell. Chill and serve.

Nutrition Information

- Calories: 343.2
- Sugar: 41.9
- Cholesterol: 0
- Saturated Fat: 2.5
- Sodium: 225.1
- Protein: 3.6
- Total Fat: 10.2
- Fiber: 3
- Total Carbohydrate: 61.3

30. Bisquick Coffee Cake

Serving: 6 serving(s) | Prep: 10mins | Ready in:

Ingredients

- Dough
- 2 cups Bisquick
- 2/3 cup water or 2/3 cup milk
- 1 egg
- 2 tablespoons sugar
- Topping
- 1/3 cup Bisquick
- 1/3 cup brown sugar
- 1/4 teaspoon ground cinnamon
- 2 tablespoons butter

Direction

- Preheat oven to 400 degrees.
- Grease a deep pie plate, 8"x8" square pan, or 9"x9" square pan.
- Mix dough ingredients and put in baking dish.
- Mix topping ingredients with a fork or pastry mixer until crumbly.
- Spread topping mix over dough and drag a butter knife across like you were making a tic-tac-toe board several times.
- Bake for 25 minutes.

Nutrition Information

- Calories: 321.8
- Sugar: 21.9
- Cholesterol: 42.2
- Total Fat: 12.3
- Saturated Fat: 4.7
- Sodium: 553.6
- Fiber: 1.1
- Total Carbohydrate: 47.8
- Protein: 5.1

31. Bisquick Fruit Cobbler

Serving: 4-6 serving(s) | Prep: 10mins | Ready in:

Ingredients

- 29 ounces fruit, undrained
- 1 tablespoon cornstarch
- 2 tablespoons cold water
- 2 cups Bisquick
- 1/2 cup milk
- 1/4 cup butter or 1/4 cup margarine, melted
- 2 tablespoons sugar, if desired

Direction

- Preheat oven to 400 degrees F. In a large saucepan add can of undrained fruit and heat through. Blend together cornstarch and water in a small bowl, mix until blended. Add mixture to fruit and boil for 1 minute. Pour thickened fruit mixture into a 2 quart baking dish and dot with butter. Set aside.
- Add Bisquick, milk, melted butter, and sugar if using, into a bowl. Stir with fork until mixture is well combined. Drop by spoonfuls over fruit. Bake for approximately 20 minutes or until shortcake is golden brown.
- Serve hot or cold.

Nutrition Information

- Calories: 427.2
- Total Carbohydrate: 50.1
- Protein: 6.2
- Total Fat: 22.5
- Sodium: 764.4
- Fiber: 1.4
- Saturated Fat: 10.5
- Sugar: 13.8
- Cholesterol: 36

32. Bite Sized Chocolate Meringues

Serving: 68-70 cookies | Prep: 20mins | Ready in:

Ingredients

- 1 cup semi-sweet chocolate chips
- 2 large egg whites
- 1/2 cup sugar
- 1/2 teaspoon vanilla

- 1/2 teaspoon apple cider vinegar

Direction

- Preheat oven to 350.
- Prepare two large cookie sheets with parchment paper. (I love this stuff because you don't need any additional grease or vegetable spray -- plus you can wash and reuse them.).
- Melt chocolate chips in the microwave. Start with 1 minute. Stir and cook another minute. Stir again and let them cool while you're making the meringue.
- Beat egg whites until foamy. Add sugar a bit at a time and continue beating until stiff.
- Beat in the vanilla and vinegar.
- Pour the melted chocolate over the top of the meringue distributing it in a stream around the top rather than all in one spot.
- Gently fold chocolate into meringue. (Option to add chopped walnuts here also.).
- Use 1/2 teaspoon rounded to drop batter onto sheets leaving about 1-1/2 inches between cookies.
- Bake for 8 minutes or until firm to touch.
- Slide parchment off cookie sheet onto cooling rack. Let stand about 10 minutes to cool before moving them and they're less likely to break.

Nutrition Information

- Calories: 18.1
- Sodium: 1.9
- Protein: 0.2
- Total Fat: 0.7
- Saturated Fat: 0.4
- Fiber: 0.1
- Sugar: 2.8
- Total Carbohydrate: 3
- Cholesterol: 0

33. Bittersweet Chocolate Pound Cake With Decadent Glaze

Serving: 12 serving(s) | Prep: 20mins | Ready in:

Ingredients

- Cake
- 6 ounces unsweetened baking chocolate, melted
- 2 cups flour
- 1 teaspoon baking soda
- 1 teaspoon baking powder
- 2 tablespoons instant coffee
- 2 tablespoons hot water
- cold water
- 2 cups sugar
- 1 cup butter, softened
- 1 teaspoon vanilla
- 3 eggs
- Dark Chocolate Glaze
- 2 ounces unsweetened baking chocolate
- 3 tablespoons butter
- 1 1/2 cups confectioners' sugar
- 3 -4 tablespoons water
- 1 teaspoon vanilla

Direction

- CAKE: Preheat oven to 325 degrees.
- Grease and flour a Bundt or tube pan.
- In a small bowl, combine flour, soda and powder.
- In a 2 cup measuring cup, dissolve coffee in hot water and add enough cold water to measure 1 1/2 cups.
- In a large mixer bowl, beat granulated sugar, butter and vanilla until creamy.
- Beat in eggs, one at a time.
- Stir in melted chocolate.
- Add flour mixture alternately with coffee mixture.
- Pour into prepared pan.
- Bake 1 hour or until center tests done.
- Cool 30 minutes and remove from pan onto a wire rack.
- Cool completely and transfer to serving dish.

- Drizzle with glaze and sprinkle with confectioner's sugar, if desired.
- GLAZE: Melt chocolate and butter, stirring until smooth.
- Remove from heat and stir in confectioner's sugar, alternately with water, until desired consistency is reached.
- Stir in vanilla extract.

Nutrition Information

- Calories: 543.9
- Saturated Fat: 18.2
- Sodium: 287.8
- Fiber: 3.8
- Total Fat: 29.8
- Sugar: 48.4
- Total Carbohydrate: 70.6
- Cholesterol: 101.2
- Protein: 6.5

34. Blueberry Bread Pudding, Wonderful And Easy!

Serving: 6 serving(s) | Prep: 20mins | Ready in:

Ingredients

- 2 cups blueberries, rinsed and picked over, remove any stems
- 2 1/2 tablespoons unsalted butter
- 3 cups bread cubes (remove crusts)
- 1/2 cup orange juice
- 1 teaspoon cinnamon
- 1/4 teaspoon nutmeg
- 1/2 cup sugar
- 2 eggs, beaten
- 1/2 cup brown sugar
- 1 teaspoon lemon juice
- 1 teaspoon Cointreau liqueur
- For garnish
- whipped cream

Direction

- Preheat oven to 400°F
- Melt the butter in a saucepan.
- Place the bread cubes in a large mixing bowl. Pour the orange juice and melted butter over the bread.
- Sprinkle on the sugar, cinnamon and nutmeg and using your hands, toss to coat the bread.
- Pour the eggs over the mixture and mix all together with a wooden spoon.
- Scrape the bread into a pie dish coated with baking spray and flatten the top with the back of a spoon. Place the blueberries on top in an even layer.
- Sprinkle with brown sugar, lemon juice and the Cointreau. Place in the oven and bake for 30-40 minutes.
- To serve:
- Cut into pie shaped wedges and serve warm or cool. Garnish with the whipped cream and any additional fresh blueberries.

Nutrition Information

- Calories: 285.6
- Total Fat: 7.3
- Sodium: 151.1
- Fiber: 1.9
- Total Carbohydrate: 53.1
- Protein: 4
- Saturated Fat: 3.7
- Sugar: 41.8
- Cholesterol: 83.2

35. Blueberry Cobbler In A Bottle

Serving: 32 oz | Prep: 5mins | Ready in:

Ingredients

- 16 ounces blueberry juice (available in the organic section of many grocery stores)
- 8 ounces absolut red label vodka (100 proof)
- 4 ounces vanilla Schnapps
- 8 ounces butterscotch schnapps

- 1/2 teaspoon lemon juice
- 1/4 teaspoon apple pie spice
- 2 cinnamon sticks

Direction

- Mix together liquid ingredients; stir in apple pie spice.
- Pour into a 32 oz. bottle, add the cinnamon sticks, and refrigerate for at least a week before serving. (We often just store it in our cool garage, which works fine.).
- Blueberry Cobbler is a group drink, often shared straight out of the bottle with folks all sitting around the campfire.
- Note: Absolut Red Label has gotten more difficult to find these days. Try to use higher proof vodka if you can, but if the Red Label is too expensive or unavailable, you can substitute another equal quality high proof vodka. Potato vodka can also be used, but check the taste before using to make sure it's something you like the taste of and that it's not too sweet for you. Higher proof is generally drier in taste.

Nutrition Information

- Calories: 17.4
- Saturated Fat: 0
- Sodium: 0.1
- Sugar: 0
- Cholesterol: 0
- Total Fat: 0
- Fiber: 0
- Total Carbohydrate: 0
- Protein: 0

36. Blueberry Fool

Serving: 6-8 serving(s) | Prep: 10mins | Ready in:

Ingredients

- 1 pint fresh blueberries
- 2 tablespoons water
- 1/2 cup sugar
- 1 pint whipping cream
- 1/2 tablespoon vanilla extract

Direction

- First, wash the blueberries and remove any over ripe or under ripe ones.
- Place the berries in a medium saucepan and stir in water and sugar.
- Cook the mixture over medium heat, stirring occasionally, for 10 minutes or until the berries are soft and have released their juices.
- Remove the pan from heat and set aside to cool.
- Pour whipping cream into a bowl and beat with an electric mixer until soft peaks form.
- Mix in vanilla extract.
- Pour cooled berries over the whipped cream and mix in carefully.
- Put into the fridge for at least 2 hours, then spoon into serving dishes.

Nutrition Information

- Calories: 368.6
- Protein: 2
- Saturated Fat: 18.3
- Sodium: 30.8
- Fiber: 1.1
- Cholesterol: 108.7
- Total Fat: 29.5
- Sugar: 21.6
- Total Carbohydrate: 26

37. Bourbon Sweet Potatoes

Serving: 10 serving(s) | Prep: 20mins | Ready in:

Ingredients

- 3 (18 ounce) cans sweet potatoes

- 1 cup sugar
- 1/3 cup Bourbon (I usually splash in a little more)
- 1/2 cup butter
- 1/2 teaspoon vanilla extract
- 2 cups miniature marshmallows

Direction

- Put sweet potatoes in a large sauce pan.
- Cook over medium heat, stirring frequently until heated through.
- Preheat oven to 350F.
- Mash sweet potatoes
- Add sugar, butter, bourbon, vanilla and beat until well blended and smooth.
- Turn into a 2 quart shallow baking dish
- Sprinkle marshmallows on top
- Bake uncovered for 30 minutes or until marshmallows are golden brown.

Nutrition Information

- Calories: 344.7
- Sodium: 157.7
- Sugar: 32.2
- Cholesterol: 24.4
- Protein: 2.7
- Total Fat: 9.3
- Saturated Fat: 5.9
- Fiber: 4.6
- Total Carbohydrate: 59

- 1/2 teaspoon cinnamon
- 1/4 cup granulated sugar

Direction

- Preheat oven to 325°F.
- In a medium bowl, combine the cereal, flour and brown sugar.
- With a pastry blender, cut in the butter until the mixture is crumbly; set aside.
- In a separate bowl, combine the apples, cinnamon and granulated sugar.
- Dump the apple mixture into a 2 quart baking dish.
- Sprinkle the cereal/flour mixture evenly over the apple mixture.
- Bake in the preheated 325°F oven for about 45 min.
- Serve warm with a scoop of vanilla ice cream on top of each serving.

Nutrition Information

- Calories: 195
- Sodium: 63
- Cholesterol: 15.2
- Total Fat: 6.4
- Saturated Fat: 3.7
- Fiber: 5.4
- Sugar: 23.8
- Total Carbohydrate: 37
- Protein: 2.3

38. Bran Apple Crisp

Serving: 1 batch, 8 serving(s) | Prep: 15mins | Ready in:

Ingredients

- 1 cup all-bran cereal
- 1/2 cup whole wheat flour
- 1/4 cup brown sugar, firmly packed
- 1/4 cup butter or 1/4 cup margarine
- 6 cups baking apples, unpeeled sliced

39. Breakfast Cookie

Serving: 1 serving(s) | Prep: 10mins | Ready in:

Ingredients

- 1/3 cup oats
- 1 tablespoon raisins
- 1 tablespoon flour
- 1/3 cup non-fat powdered milk

- 1/4 cup unsweetened applesauce (no-sugar-added)
- 1/4 teaspoon cinnamon
- 1/4 teaspoon baking powder
- 1 tablespoon no-calorie artificial sweetener

Direction

- Preheat oven to 350 degrees.
- Spray a LARGE cookie sheet with Pam or use two smaller cookie sheets.
- Mix all ingredients together and spoon on sheet.
- Bake for 15-20 minute.

Nutrition Information

- Calories: 433.1
- Sodium: 308.2
- Sugar: 26.7
- Cholesterol: 8
- Protein: 24.5
- Saturated Fat: 0.9
- Fiber: 7.1
- Total Carbohydrate: 76.6
- Total Fat: 4.1

40. Brownies In A Jar

Serving: 16 brownies, 16 serving(s) | Prep: 10mins | Ready in:

Ingredients

- 1 cup all-purpose flour
- 1/2 teaspoon baking powder
- 1/4 teaspoon salt
- 1 1/2 cups sugar
- 1/3 cup special dark cocoa, HERSHEY'S SPECIAL DARK
- 1 cup peanut butter chips, REESE'S (or HERSHEY'S Premier White Chips)
- 1/2 cup semisweet mini chocolate chips, Hershey's

Direction

- Stir together flour, baking powder and salt in a small bowl.
- Layer the ingredients in a clean 1-quart glass canister or jar in the following order (from bottom to top): sugar, cocoa, flour mixture, peanut butter chips and small chocolate chips. Tap jar gently on the counter to settle each layer before adding the next one.
- Cover jar and attach baking directions (see below). Makes 1 gift jar.
- Baking Directions: Heat oven to 350°F Grease and flour an 8x8x2-inch baking pan. Combine 1/2 cup (1 stick) melted and cooled butter and 2 slightly beaten eggs in a large bowl. Gently stir in jar contents. Spread in prepared pan. Bake for 35 minutes. Cool in pan. Cut into bars. Makes 16 bars.

Nutrition Information

- Calories: 189.3
- Total Fat: 5
- Total Carbohydrate: 34.1
- Saturated Fat: 2.4
- Sodium: 74.7
- Fiber: 1.4
- Sugar: 25.9
- Cholesterol: 0
- Protein: 3.3

41. Buckeye Brownies

Serving: 2-3 dozen brownies, 36 serving(s) | Prep: 10mins | Ready in:

Ingredients

- 19 1/2 ounces brownie mix (whatever brand that you want)
- 1/2 cup water (refer to your brownie package)
- 1 tablespoon vegetable oil (refer to your brownie package)

- 1 egg (refer to your brownie package)
- 2 cups powdered sugar
- 1/2 cup butter, softened
- 6 tablespoons butter, softened
- 1 (8 ounce) jar creamy peanut butter
- 1 (6 ounce) package semi-sweet chocolate chips

Direction

- Prepare and bake brownie mix in a greased 13"x9" baking pan according to package directions. Let cool.
- Mix powdered sugar, 1/2 cup butter and peanut butter. Mix well and spread over cooled brownies. Chill for one hour.
- Melt together chocolate chips and remaining butter in a saucepan over low heat, stirring occasionally until melted. Spread over brownies. Let cool; cut into squares.

Nutrition Information

- Calories: 204.8
- Sugar: 9.7
- Total Carbohydrate: 23.5
- Cholesterol: 17
- Protein: 2.8
- Total Fat: 12.3
- Saturated Fat: 4.9
- Sodium: 123.1
- Fiber: 0.7

42. Buried Treasure Cupcakes K

Serving: 24 cupcakes | Prep: 15mins | Ready in:

Ingredients

- 1 (18 ounce) package chocolate cake mix
- 1 (8 ounce) package cream cheese, softened
- 1 egg
- 2 tablespoons sugar
- 48 miniature Oreo cookies (chocolate sandwich style cookies)
- 1 1/2 cups thawed whipped topping

Direction

- PREHEAT oven to 350°F.
- Prepare cake batter in large mixing bowl as directed on package; set aside.
- WHISK cream cheese, egg and sugar in small mixing bowl until well blended.
- SCOOP cake batter, using 1/4-cup dry measuring cup, into each of 24 paper or foil-lined medium muffin cups, filling each cup about half full.
- SPOON 1/2 tablespoons of cream cheese mixture over batter in each muffin cup. Top with 1 cookie.
- Cover evenly with remaining cake batter.
- BAKE 19 to 22 minutes or until toothpick inserted in center comes out clean.
- Cool 5 minutes; remove from pans to wire racks. Cool completely.
- TOP cupcakes with whipped topping and remaining cookies just before serving. .

Nutrition Information

- Calories: 159.4
- Saturated Fat: 3.5
- Protein: 2.6
- Total Fat: 8.4
- Sodium: 230.5
- Fiber: 0.6
- Sugar: 11.2
- Total Carbohydrate: 20.2
- Cholesterol: 22.1

43. Calypso Coffee Cake With Butter Rum Glaze

Serving: 12 serving(s) | Prep: 30mins | Ready in:

Ingredients

- Streusel
- 1/2 cup sweetened flaked coconut
- 1/4 cup brown sugar, packed
- 1/2 teaspoon ground cinnamon
- 1 tablespoon flour
- Cake
- 3/4 cup butter, softened
- 1/4 cup brown sugar, packed
- 1/2 cup white sugar
- 3 eggs
- 1 cup sour cream
- 1 1/2 cups plantains, cooked and mashed
- 2 cups all-purpose flour
- 1 1/2 teaspoons baking powder
- 1 1/2 teaspoons baking soda
- 1/2 teaspoon salt
- 1 teaspoon ground ginger
- Glaze
- 1 tablespoon butter
- 1/4 cup brown sugar
- 1 tablespoon lime juice
- 1 tablespoon rum
- Topping
- confectioners' sugar

Direction

- Grease and flour a Bundt pan; preheat oven to 350°F.
- Peel the plantain(s) and slice (about 1/2 inch slices should be fine). Bring a pot of water to a boil, drop the plantain slices into the boiling water and boil for about 20 minutes until tender. Drain plantains and mash with a fork.
- While plantains are cooking, mix the streusel ingredients together in a small bowl and set aside.
- In a large mixing bowl, cream the butter, brown sugar and white sugar together.
- Add eggs, one at a time; then mix in sour cream and mashed plantains.
- In a separate bowl, mix together the flour, baking soda, baking powder, salt and ginger.
- Slowly add the dry ingredients to the wet ingredients, mixing until combined.
- Pour about 1/2 the batter in to the prepared Bundt pan. Sprinkle the streusel over the cake; finally, pour remaining batter over the streusel.
- Bake at 350°F for 55 minutes or until cake tests done with toothpick test.
- Let cake cool in pan for 30 minutes.
- While cake is cooling, prepare glaze by mixing butter, brown sugar, and lime juice in a small sauce pan and bring to a boil.
- Reduce heat and simmer for 3-5 minutes.
- Allow to cool slightly before adding rum.
- Carefully invert cake onto plate.
- While cake is still warm, slowly drizzle the glaze over the cake, allowing it to soak in to the cake.
- When cake is completely cool, dust with confectioners' sugar.

Nutrition Information

- Calories: 373.8
- Total Fat: 19.1
- Sodium: 457.8
- Sugar: 26.9
- Total Carbohydrate: 47
- Saturated Fat: 11.8
- Fiber: 1.3
- Cholesterol: 89.5
- Protein: 4.7

44. Candy Corn Marshmallow Crispy Treats

Serving: 24 Candy Corn-Marshmallow Crispy Treats, 24 serving(s) | Prep: 10mins | Ready in:

Ingredients

- 1/4 cup butter
- 6 cups jet-puffed miniature marshmallows
- 12 drops yellow food coloring
- 4 drops red food coloring
- 6 cups crisp rice cereal
- 2 cups candy corn

Direction

- Microwave butter in large microwaveable bowl on HIGH 45 seconds, or until melted. Add marshmallows; toss to coat. Microwave 1-1/2 minutes or until marshmallows are completely melted and mixture is well blended, stirring in food coloring after 45 seconds.
- Add cereal and candy corn; mix well. Press onto bottom of 13x9-inch pan sprayed with cooking spray.
- Cool completely before cutting into bars. Cut each bar diagonally in half.
- KRAFT KITCHENS TIPS:
- USE YOUR STOVE:
- Melt butter in a large saucepan on low heat. Add marshmallows; cook until marshmallows are completely melted and mixture is well blended, stirring constantly. Remove from heat. Add remaining ingredients; continue as directed.
- HOW TO PRESS CEREAL MIXTURE INTO PAN:
- Use waxed paper to press marshmallow mixture into prepared pan.
- HOW TO STORE:
- Store in airtight container at room temperature.

Nutrition Information

- Calories: 82.2
- Fiber: 0.1
- Total Carbohydrate: 16.2
- Cholesterol: 5.1
- Protein: 0.7
- Total Fat: 2
- Saturated Fat: 1.2
- Sodium: 80.3
- Sugar: 7.7

45. Captain Krunchers

Serving: 60-70 serving(s) | Prep: 15mins | Ready in:

Ingredients

- 1 (24 ounce) package white almond bark
- 1 cup peanut butter
- 8 cups Cap'n Crunch cereal
- 1 cup salted peanuts

Direction

- Melt bark according to package directions on stovetop.
- Add peanut butter and mix.
- Remove from heat and stir in cereal and nuts.
- Drop by spoonfuls onto wax paper.
- Cool.

Nutrition Information

- Calories: 66.6
- Total Fat: 4.3
- Saturated Fat: 0.8
- Sodium: 86.4
- Total Carbohydrate: 5.7
- Fiber: 0.7
- Sugar: 2.6
- Cholesterol: 0
- Protein: 2.2

46. Caramel Apple Brickle Dip

Serving: 20 serving(s) | Prep: 5mins | Ready in:

Ingredients

- 1 (8 ounce) container whipped cream cheese (tub, not the block type)
- 1 (18 ounce) container caramel apple dip
- 1 (10 ounce) bag English toffee bits

Direction

- Spread cream cheese into a pie plate.
- Spread caramel dip on top of cream cheese (you may not want all of the caramel - use your own judgment! :)).
- Sprinkle with all of the toffee bits and serve with sliced apples of your choice!

Nutrition Information

- Calories: 113.9
- Cholesterol: 15.2
- Saturated Fat: 4.4
- Sugar: 8.9
- Sodium: 71.1
- Fiber: 0.3
- Total Carbohydrate: 9.4
- Protein: 1.2
- Total Fat: 8.2

- Sprinkle chocolate chips over crust.
- Mix caramel topping with the reserved flour.
- Drizzle this over the chips.
- Sprinkle the top with the remaining crumb mixture.
- Bake for an additional 15 minutes.

Nutrition Information

- Calories: 384.4
- Saturated Fat: 6.5
- Fiber: 2.6
- Cholesterol: 0.1
- Total Fat: 18.8
- Sodium: 363
- Sugar: 28.5
- Total Carbohydrate: 54.8
- Protein: 3.8

47. Caramel Chocolate Bars

Serving: 1 9x13 pan, 20 serving(s) | Prep: 5mins | Ready in:

Ingredients

- 1 1/2 cups brown sugar, firmly packed
- 2 cups quick oatmeal
- 1 (16 ounce) bag chocolate chips
- 3/4 cup caramel ice cream topping
- 1 1/4 cups margarine
- 2 cups flour, plus
- 3 tablespoons flour
- 1 teaspoon baking soda
- 1 teaspoon salt

Direction

- Preheat oven to 350°.
- Cream brown sugar and margarine.
- Add dry ingredients reserving 3 Tbsp. of flour and stir in the oatmeal.
- Press 1/2 of the mixture in the bottom of a greased 9 x 13 pan and bake for 10 minutes.

48. Caramel Peanut Popcorn

Serving: 1 batch | Prep: 10mins | Ready in:

Ingredients

- 1/3-1/2 cup popcorn
- 3/4 cup unsalted peanuts
- 250 g butter
- 1 1/2 cups sugar
- 1/3 cup honey

Direction

- Lightly oil a 26cm x 32cm Swiss roll pan.
- Pop the popping corn, either in a pot or in a popcorn popper.
- Discard any unpopped kernels.
- Transfer popcorn to prepared Swiss roll pan.
- Sprinkle peanuts evenly over popcorn.
- Combine butter, sugar and honey in medium pan and stir over a low heat until sugar is dissolved.

- Bring to the boil and boil uncovered about 4 minutes or until syrup is a rich golden brown colour.
- Pour all over popcorn.
- Stand about 15 minutes and cut into pieces.

Nutrition Information

- Calories: 3950.1
- Sodium: 1447.8
- Sugar: 392.6
- Cholesterol: 534.3
- Protein: 19.2
- Total Fat: 262.2
- Saturated Fat: 137.5
- Fiber: 6.2
- Total Carbohydrate: 417.2

49. Carob Nut Fudge

Serving: 6-8 serving(s) | Prep: 15mins | Ready in:

Ingredients

- 1/2 cup peanut butter
- 1/2 cup honey
- 1 teaspoon vanilla
- 1 cup walnuts, chopped (you can substitute and use other nuts or a combination of nuts)
- 1 cup soy powder (you can use regular milk powder either)
- 4 tablespoons carob powder

Direction

- Cream together the peanut butter and the honey.
- Add the vanilla, nuts, soy powder, and carob powder and mix together.
- Press in a pan and put it in the fridge until chilled. Enjoy!

Nutrition Information

- Calories: 341.9
- Total Fat: 23.6
- Saturated Fat: 3.5
- Sodium: 100.3
- Sugar: 25.8
- Protein: 8.4
- Fiber: 2.6
- Total Carbohydrate: 30.2
- Cholesterol: 0

50. Carrot Sheet Cake With Frosting

Serving: 24-30 serving(s) | Prep: 25mins | Ready in:

Ingredients

- 4 eggs
- 1 cup vegetable oil
- 2 cups sugar
- 2 cups all-purpose flour
- 2 teaspoons baking soda
- 1/4 teaspoon baking powder
- 2 teaspoons ground cinnamon
- 1/2 teaspoon salt
- 3 cups carrots, shredded
- 2/3 cup walnuts, chopped
- FROSTING
- 1 (8 ounce) package cream cheese, softened
- 1/2 cup butter or 1/2 cup margarine, softened
- 1 teaspoon vanilla extract
- 4 cups icing sugar
- 2/3 cup walnuts, chopped, for garnish

Direction

- Preheat oven to 350 degrees Fahrenheit.
- Grease a 15" x 10" x 1" baking pan (I use Pan Release Recipe #78579).
- In a mixing bowl, beat eggs, oil and sugar until smooth.
- Combine flour, baking soda, baking powder, cinnamon and salt; add to egg mixture and beat well.
- Stir in carrots and walnuts.

- Pour into prepared baking pan.
- Bake in preheated 350 degree Fahrenheit oven for 35 minutes or until a toothpick inserted near the center comes out clean.
- Cool on a wire rack.
- FROSTING:
- Beat cream cheese, butter and vanilla in a mixing bowl until smooth.
- Beat in icing sugar.
- Spread over cake.
- Sprinkle with chopped nuts.

Nutrition Information

- Calories: 388.9
- Saturated Fat: 6.1
- Sugar: 37.5
- Total Carbohydrate: 47.6
- Protein: 3.9
- Total Fat: 21.3
- Sodium: 245.1
- Fiber: 1.3
- Cholesterol: 51.6

51. Cashew Peach Sweet Potatoes

Serving: 6-8 serving(s) | Prep: 7mins | Ready in:

Ingredients

- 6 medium sweet potatoes, boiled until tender, drained, peeled and cubed
- 1/2 cup brown sugar, packed
- 1/3 cup cashews, coarsely chopped
- 1/2 teaspoon salt
- 1/4 teaspoon ginger
- 1 (15 1/4 ounce) cansliced peaches, drained
- 3 tablespoons butter

Direction

- Preheat oven to 350°F.
- Combine brown sugar, cashews, salt and ginger in small bowl.
- Spoon half the sweet potatoes into 11-inch x 7-inch baking dish.
- Top sweet potatoes with half the peaches and ½ brown sugar mixture.
- Repeat layers.
- Dot the top of casserole with butter.
- Cover with foil and bake 30 minutes.
- Remove foil and bake additional 10 minutes.

Nutrition Information

- Calories: 303.8
- Cholesterol: 15.3
- Total Fat: 9.5
- Saturated Fat: 4.4
- Sugar: 29.5
- Total Carbohydrate: 53.4
- Sodium: 362
- Fiber: 5.2
- Protein: 3.9

52. Cheater's Carrot Cake

Serving: 12 serving(s) | Prep: 5mins | Ready in:

Ingredients

- 1 2-layer yellow cake mix
- 1 1/4 cups Miracle Whip
- 4 eggs
- 1/4 cup cold water
- 2 teaspoons cinnamon
- 2 cups finely grated carrots
- 1/2 cup chopped walnuts, , toasted
- cream cheese frosting, either your favourite or from a can

Direction

- Preheat oven to 350F; spray a 13x9 cake pan with Pam (non-stick cooking spray) and set aside.
- In a large bowl, combine dry cake mix, Miracle Whip salad dressing, eggs, water and

cinnamon at medium speed until well blended.
- With a wooden spoon, stir in carrots and walnuts.
- Note that putting the nuts in the cake is optional; you also use them as a garnish after the cake is iced.
- Pour the batter into prepared pan and bake for 35 to 40 minutes, until a toothpick or cake tester comes out clean.
- Cool completely and then frost.

Nutrition Information

- Calories: 315.8
- Fiber: 1.7
- Sugar: 22.8
- Total Carbohydrate: 41.1
- Total Fat: 14.8
- Saturated Fat: 2.4
- Sodium: 544.5
- Cholesterol: 69.8
- Protein: 5.1

53. Cheeseburger In Paradise Cookies

Serving: 20 cookies | Prep: 30mins | Ready in:

Ingredients

- 2 (12 ounce) boxes vanilla wafers
- 1 egg white
- ¼ cup sesame seeds
- 4 cups sifted powdered sugar
- 4-5 teaspoons milk
- ½ teaspoon almond extract
- green food coloring
- yellow food coloring
- red food coloring
- 1 cup shredded sweetened coconut
- 2 (10 ounce) packages peppermint patties (anything resembling the girl scouts' "thin mints")

Direction

- Place whole, perfect vanilla wafers on 2 trays; one with wafers facing up, the other with wafers facing down.
- Each tray should have the same number of wafers (35-40).
- Brush wafers (rounded side up) with egg white and sprinkle with sesame seeds.
- Set aside.
- To colour coconut, place in small container with several drops of green food colouring.
- Shake well and let sit.
- To make "cheese" frosting, whip powdered sugar and milk together till smooth.
- Add yellow and red food colouring till desired orange tint is achieved.
- To assemble "cheeseburgers", use dab of frosting to glue peppermint cookies into place on to wafer (flat side up).
- This is your "burger".
- Now spread frosting "cheese" on and sprinkle with green coconut "lettuce".
- Dab with frosting again and top with sesame wafer.
- Repeat until all "burgers" are made.

Nutrition Information

- Calories: 286.1
- Total Fat: 8.7
- Fiber: 1.3
- Sugar: 25.1
- Protein: 2.1
- Saturated Fat: 3
- Sodium: 120.3
- Total Carbohydrate: 50.9
- Cholesterol: 0.1

54. Cheesecake Topped With Fresh Fruit

Serving: 4-6 serving(s) | Prep: 15mins | Ready in:

Ingredients

- Crust
- 1 package Duncan Hines blueberry muffin mix (reserve the blueberries)
- 1/2 cup butter
- Filling
- 8 ounces cream cheese
- 16 ounces frozen Cool Whip
- 1/4 cup sugar
- 1 teaspoon vanilla extract
- 1 kiwi (sliced)
- 1 star fruit (sliced)
- 1/2 cup strawberry (sliced)

Direction

- Prepare the crust.
- Pour muffin mix into a bowl, cut in the butter.
- Sprinkle into a cake pan or cookie sheet.
- Bake in a 400 degree preheated oven for 10-12 minutes.
- Stir mixture, and then press into a pie pan sprayed with non-stick spray.
- Let cool.
- Blend the cream cheese, Cool Whip, sugar and Vanilla extract.
- Drop by spoonful into crust.
- Garnish with the fresh fruit and reserved blueberries arranged on top.
- Chill for at least 2 hours.

Nutrition Information

- Calories: 837.8
- Saturated Fat: 51.8
- Sodium: 360.9
- Sugar: 42.3
- Cholesterol: 123.4
- Protein: 6.5
- Total Fat: 71.7
- Fiber: 1.6
- Total Carbohydrate: 46

55. Cherry Cheesecake Cups

Serving: 24 serving(s) | Prep: 25mins | Ready in:

Ingredients

- Crust
- 1 (18 1/4 ounce) packageduncan hines moist deluxe devil's food cake mix (or the Classic Yellow Cake Mix)
- 1/4 cup margarine or 1/4 cup butter, melted
- Cheese Filling
- 2 (8 ounce) packages cream cheese, softened
- 3 eggs
- 3/4 cup sugar
- 1 teaspoon vanilla extract
- Topping
- 1 1/2 cups sour cream
- 1/4 cup sugar
- 1 (21 ounce) can cherry pie filling (or whatever is your fave flavor)

Direction

- Preheat oven to 350 degrees, and place foil or paper liners in 24 (2 1/2 inch) muffin cups.
- For Crust:
- Combine cake mix and melted margarine in a large bowl.
- Beat at low speed with electric mixer for 1 minute. Mixture will be crumbly.
- Divide mixture evenly among the muffins cups; level them, but do not press down.
- For Cheese Filling:
- Combine cream cheese, eggs, 3/4 cup sugar, and vanilla extract in medium bowl.
- Beat at medium speed with electric mixer, until smooth.
- Spoon evenly into muffin cups, and bake for 20 minutes, or until set.
- For Topping:

- Combine sour cream and 1/4 cup sugar in a small bowl.
- Spoon evenly over cheesecakes and return to oven for 5 minutes.
- Cool completely then garnish each cheesecake with cherry pie filling.
- Refrigerate until ready to serve.

Nutrition Information

- Calories: 276.4
- Total Carbohydrate: 32.2
- Fiber: 0.7
- Saturated Fat: 7.3
- Sodium: 276.8
- Sugar: 16.7
- Cholesterol: 53.5
- Protein: 4
- Total Fat: 15.5

56. Cherry Crunch Coffee Cake

Serving: 9 serving(s) | Prep: 15mins | Ready in:

Ingredients

- 1/2 cup brown sugar
- 2 tablespoons flour
- 1 tablespoon butter
- 1/3 cup chopped walnuts or 1/3 cup pecans
- 1 1/2 cups flour
- 1 1/2 teaspoons baking powder
- 1/4 teaspoon salt
- 2 eggs
- 1 cup sugar
- 1/4 cup butter, melted and cooled
- 1/2 cup milk
- 1 can cherry pie filling

Direction

- Mix first 4 ingredients for topping; set aside.
- Sift flour, baking powder and salt together.
- Beat eggs until fluffy, slowly add sugar, beating well.
- Stir in melted butter.
- Add flour mixture alternately with milk.
- Beat until smooth.
- Spread half in greased 9x9 baking pan.
- Top with pie filling.
- Add remaining batter.
- Sprinkle with topping.
- Bake at 350* for 45-50 minutes.

Nutrition Information

- Calories: 400.5
- Total Fat: 11.1
- Sodium: 209.9
- Sugar: 34.2
- Cholesterol: 65.8
- Protein: 5.2
- Saturated Fat: 5
- Fiber: 1.3
- Total Carbohydrate: 71.3

57. Cherry Nectar Cake

Serving: 8-10 serving(s) | Prep: 5mins | Ready in:

Ingredients

- Cake
- 1 box yellow cake mix
- 3/4 cup Wesson Oil
- 1/2 cup apricot nectar
- 4 eggs
- 1/4 cup cherry juice
- 1 (3 1/2 ounce) box cherry Jell-O
- Glaze
- 1/4 cup cherry juice
- 1 cup powdered sugar

Direction

- Combine ingredients for cake.
- Mix well.

- Pour into prepared Bundt pan.
- Bake in preheated 300 degree oven 1 hour or until done.
- Mix glaze ingredients.
- Poke holes in cake.
- Pour glaze over cake while warm.

Nutrition Information

- Calories: 613.9
- Protein: 10.4
- Sodium: 486
- Fiber: 0.8
- Total Carbohydrate: 75.9
- Cholesterol: 107.1
- Total Fat: 30.7
- Saturated Fat: 4.6
- Sugar: 45.4

58. Cherry Time Cobbler

Serving: 4-6 serving(s) | Prep: 15mins | Ready in:

Ingredients

- 2 cups cherries
- 1 cup flour
- 1 teaspoon baking powder
- 1 teaspoon salt
- 1 egg
- 2/3 cup sugar
- 1/2 cup milk
- 1/4 cup butter or 1/4 cup margarine
- 1/2 teaspoon vanilla

Direction

- Place cherries in a greased, 8 inch square baking dish.
- Mix flour, baking powder, and salt in a large bowl.
- Mix the egg, sugar, milk, butter or margarine and vanilla in a blender for 60 to 90 seconds.
- Pour the blender mixture into the flour mixture and stir lightly.
- Pour this batter over the cherries in the baking dish, spreading batter to edges of dish.
- Bake for 30 to 35 minutes at 350f degrees.
- Cobbler is done when batter is lightly browned and tooth pick inserted in centre of batter comes out clean.

Nutrition Information

- Calories: 433.1
- Sugar: 43.5
- Protein: 6.7
- Saturated Fat: 8.4
- Fiber: 2.5
- Total Carbohydrate: 71.5
- Cholesterol: 81.3
- Total Fat: 14.3
- Sodium: 807.1

59. Chewy Chocolate Macaroons

Serving: 8 dozen, 96 serving(s) | Prep: 5mins | Ready in:

Ingredients

- 1 (14 ounce) package angel flake coconut
- 1 (14 ounce) can sweetened condensed milk
- 2 teaspoons vanilla
- 4 baker's unsweetened chocolate squares, melted (4 ounces)

Direction

- Preheat oven to 350 degrees F.
- Combine all ingredients and mix well.
- Drop from teaspoon, 1 inch apart, onto well-greased baking sheets.
- Bake at 350 degrees F, for 10 to 12 minutes.
- Remove immediately from baking sheets.
- Makes 8 dozen.
- Note: the vanilla can be substituted with almond extract.

- Source: Moyn, at Gail's Recipe Swap.

Nutrition Information

- Calories: 39.3
- Total Fat: 2.3
- Fiber: 0.4
- Total Carbohydrate: 4.6
- Protein: 0.6
- Saturated Fat: 1.8
- Sodium: 16.2
- Sugar: 4.1
- Cholesterol: 1.4

60. Chewy And Fudgy Brownies

Serving: 1 batch, 16 serving(s) | Prep: 20mins | Ready in:

Ingredients

- 6 ounces quality semisweet chocolate (any good dark eating chocolate will do)
- 10 tablespoons unsalted butter, cut into chunks
- 3 large eggs
- 2 teaspoons pure vanilla extract
- 1 1/4 cups all-purpose flour
- 1 1/2 cups sugar
- 1/2 teaspoon salt
- 1 pinch baking powder
- 1 cup toasted walnut pieces, finely chopped (or any other kind of nut that you like) (optional)

Direction

- Preheat oven to 350°F.
- Toast nuts on a foil lined sheet pan until fragrant, about 7 minutes.
- While nuts are toasting break chocolate up into small pieces and place in a medium microwave safe bowl with the butter. Melt Butter with chocolate in the microwave, about 2 minutes at 50% power. Stir and continue to microwave at 50% power as required, stirring every 60 seconds. This can also be done over a double boiler.
- Let allow chocolate mixture and roasted nuts to cool.
- Meanwhile lightly beat eggs and vanilla in a small bowl and prepare a pan, 8 x 8 for thick brownies and 13 x 9 for thin ones. Line pan with foil or parchment and grease. Leave enough lining overhanging to lift the brownies out of the pan when complete.
- In a heavy duty plastic bag smash nuts with a rolling pin until well crushed, add remaining dry optional ingredients - shake to combine.
- Slowly pour egg mixture into chocolate while stirring, mixture will thicken slightly.
- Add dry ingredients in three batches, stir with a wooden spoon and ensure that each batch is fully incorporated before adding the next. Spread mixture into prepared pan with an angled spatula or a large spoon.
- Bake the 13 x 9 pan for 30-35 minutes, the 8 x 8 for 45-70 minutes or until a toothpick inserted in the centre of the pan comes out just slightly moist. Cooking time varies all over the place depending on type of pan and your oven. I use natural aluminum pans, have a calibrated thermometer and keep a pizza stone in the oven for consistency. Whatever you do to insure that that you don't overcook, simply start checking when they start to smell like brownies! You can rotate the pan halfway through the cooking process to even things out if desired.
- Cool in the pan on a rack. Remove from pan by lifting foil liner, place on a cutting board and cut into squares.

Nutrition Information

- Calories: 240.3
- Saturated Fat: 8.3
- Sugar: 19
- Protein: 3.6
- Total Fat: 13.8
- Sodium: 90.3

- Fiber: 2
- Total Carbohydrate: 29.5
- Cholesterol: 58.7

61. Chewy, Loaded, Oatmeal, Peanut Butter Bar "cookies"

Serving: 24 2x2 squares, 24 serving(s) | Prep: 10mins | Ready in:

Ingredients

- 2 cups oats (I think my were rolled, but I'm sure quick will work too)
- 1 1/2 cups raisins (any kind you prefer)
- 1 cup flour
- 1 cup flaked coconut
- 1/2 cup sugar
- 1/2 cup brown sugar
- 1/2 cup vanilla yogurt
- 1/4 cup butter
- 1 egg
- 3 -4 tablespoons peanut butter (I used 1/2 crunchy, 1/2 smooth, use what you prefer, you could use more, if you want more of the p)
- 2 tablespoons molasses (I used sorghum)
- 1 teaspoon vanilla extract
- 1/2 teaspoon baking soda
- 1/2 teaspoon salt
- 1/2 teaspoon cinnamon
- 1/4 teaspoon clove
- 1/4 teaspoon freshly ground nutmeg

Direction

- Preheat oven to 350.
- Grease a 12x12 pan that has at least 1" sides (obviously if you use a smaller pan, make this thicker, you will have to adjust your cooking time).
- Combine- flour, sugars, baking soda, salt and spices in a large mixing bowl.
- In the meantime, melt butter and peanut butter together over low heat, until melted combined (probably about 4 minutes, or so).
- Make a well in the center of your flour mixture, add vanilla egg, mix, then add yogurt molasses mix, (this will get the egg incorporated before you add the warmer butter mixture), make sure butter/peanut butter is slightly cooled, then add, mix well.
- Add oats, raisins, coconut, this should be fairly easy to combine.
- Transfer mixture to your pan, it's sticky and really easiest to spread using your fingers, make an even layer.
- Bake at 350 for 20-28 minutes.
- Keep checking it, remove from oven when golden, when you can tell the center is set (depending on your oven, the size of your pan thus the thickness of your mixture) it may even take 30 minutes or so, but don't overcook it if you want them to be chewy! Remember it will continue to cook set after you take it out!
- Remove from oven, and let pan stand (I cooled mine while we ate dinner before I cut them).
- Cut into squares, whatever size you desire, I used a pastry cutter (view this image to get an idea of what I'm talking about).
- http://www.atmosenergycooks.com/graphics/utensils/pastry_scraper.gif.
- I just pressed down to cut, then lifted, and moved on down the line, this method is really easiest as it is still pretty sticky.
- If you don't have a pastry cutter, seeing one should give you an idea of what else you can use for this.
- I then put the cut squares into sealed, plastic bags for storage.
- This made about 24, 2x2 squares.
- **It should also be noted that if you take this to a potluck or something, or have company, that since peanut allergies can be so deadly, you should make a little sign to put by it to let people know this has peanut butter in it, since it is not obvious that it does.

Nutrition Information

- Calories: 185.2
- Total Fat: 5.3
- Total Carbohydrate: 31.8
- Protein: 4.1
- Saturated Fat: 2.6
- Sodium: 114.5
- Fiber: 2.1
- Sugar: 16.7
- Cholesterol: 14.6

62. Chex "Cookies"

Serving: 30 cookies | Prep: 5mins | Ready in:

Ingredients

- 5 cups Rice Chex
- 1 package white almond bark
- 1/2 cup peanut butter
- 1 cup peanuts, salted
- 1 cup colored miniature marshmallows

Direction

- Melt the peanut butter and almond bark in a large saucepan.
- When melted, remove from heat and add Chex and peanuts, stir until coated.
- Add marshmallows, gently stir until coated.
- Spoon onto wax paper to make clusters.
- The trick is to get the cookies onto the paper before the marshmallows start to melt.
- Let sit for 3-4 hours to set.

Nutrition Information

- Calories: 73.8
- Saturated Fat: 0.8
- Sodium: 60.8
- Fiber: 0.7
- Sugar: 1.9
- Total Carbohydrate: 6.5
- Cholesterol: 0
- Protein: 2.6
- Total Fat: 4.6

63. Chex Candy Clusters

Serving: 24 clusters of candy, 24 serving(s) | Prep: 10mins | Ready in:

Ingredients

- 4 cups Rice Chex
- 2 cups pretzel sticks, coarsely broken
- 1 cup cashews, coarsely chopped
- 0.5 (16 ounce) package vanilla candy coating (almond bark)
- 1/2 cup semi-sweet chocolate chips

Direction

- Spray with cooking spray or grease 13x9-inch pan. In large bowl, mix cereal, pretzels and cashews.
- In 2-quart saucepan, melt candy coating over low heat, stirring constantly. Pour over cereal mixture, stirring until evenly coated. Press in pan; cool slightly.
- In microwavable bowl, microwave chocolate chips uncovered on High about 1 minute or until chocolate can be stirred smooth (bowl will be hot). Drizzle chocolate over snack. Let stand about 30 minutes or until chocolate is set. Break into clusters. Store in airtight container.

Nutrition Information

- Calories: 116
- Sugar: 8.1
- Saturated Fat: 3
- Fiber: 0.4
- Total Carbohydrate: 13.2
- Cholesterol: 1.3
- Protein: 1.8
- Total Fat: 6.8
- Sodium: 84.3

64. Chili And Cornbread Cupcakes

Serving: 18 serving(s) | Prep: 20mins | Ready in:

Ingredients

- 1 (6 1/2 ounce) envelopebetty crocker cornbread mix
- 3 tablespoons milk
- 2 tablespoons butter, melted
- 1/4 teaspoon chili powder
- 1 egg
- 1/3 cup green giant valley fresh steamers niblets frozen corn, thawed (from 12-oz bag)
- 2 (15 ounce) cans chili with beans
- 3/4 cup shredded cheddar cheese (3 oz)
- 6 tablespoons sour cream
- 1/4 cup corn chips
- 1/4 cup sliced green onion (4 medium)

Direction

- Heat oven to 400°F Place foil baking cup in each of 18 regular-size muffin cups.
- In medium bowl, stir cornbread mix, milk, melted butter, chili powder and egg just until moistened. Fold in corn. Spoon about 1 tablespoon cornbread mixture into each muffin cup. Top each with about 3 tablespoons chili.
- Bake 18 minutes; sprinkle each with 2 teaspoons cheese; bake 1 to 2 minutes or until cheese is melted. Let stand 5 minutes; remove from pan and top each with dollop of sour cream. Sprinkle with corn chips and green onions. Serve immediately.

Nutrition Information

- Calories: 142.6
- Cholesterol: 29.3
- Protein: 5.2
- Saturated Fat: 3.8
- Sodium: 380.3
- Fiber: 2.9
- Sugar: 2.9
- Total Fat: 7.9
- Total Carbohydrate: 13.8

65. Chocolate Gingernut Ripple Cake

Serving: 1 cake log | Prep: 30mins | Ready in:

Ingredients

- 1/3 cup milo
- 1/2 cup liqueur (optional) or 1/2 cup milk (optional)
- 300 ml thickened cream
- 250 g gingernut biscuits
- dark chocolate, grated, to serve

Direction

- Beat Milo and cream together until stiff peaks form.
- Spread 1 side of a biscuit with Milo mixture and sandwich together to another biscuit. Place on a tray. Spread another biscuit with mixture and sandwich to the first 2, and continue with remaining biscuits to create a log shape.
- Optional: Dip each biscuit briefly in liqueur or milk before spreading with milo mixture.
- Using a flat knife, spread remaining milo mixture over log to cover.
- Loosely cover with cling wrap and refrigerate overnight to allow biscuits to soften.
- Sprinkle log with grated chocolate. To serve, slice on an angle instead of straight across so you can see the layers of biscuit and cream.

Nutrition Information

- Calories: 1049.7
- Total Fat: 112.6

- Saturated Fat: 70.1
- Sodium: 115.6
- Cholesterol: 416.8
- Fiber: 0
- Sugar: 0.3
- Total Carbohydrate: 8.5
- Protein: 6.2

66. Chocolate Almond Fudge Cake

Serving: 16 serving(s) | Prep: 30mins | Ready in:

Ingredients

- 3 cups all-purpose flour
- 2 cups sugar
- 3/4 cup cocoa
- 1 1/2 teaspoons baking soda
- 1 1/2 teaspoons baking powder
- 1 teaspoon salt
- 3/4 cup butter or 3/4 cup margarine, softened
- 1 cup water
- 1/2 cup sour cream
- 4 eggs
- 2 teaspoons vanilla
- Frosting
- 1 cup whipping cream
- 1/4 cup cocoa
- 1/4 cup icing sugar
- 1 (100 g) package sliced almonds, toasted

Direction

- Measure all cake ingredients into large mixer bowl.
- Beat until blended, then beat on high 3 minutes.
- Pour into three parchment paper lined or greased 9 inch round layer cake pans.
- Bake at 350°F for 25 to 30 minutes or until cake tester inserted in centre comes out clean.
- Cool in pans 10 minutes, then invert onto cooling rack.
- Cool completely.
- Beat cream, cocoa and icing sugar until stiff peaks form.
- Place one cake layer on serving plate and spread with 1/3 cream mixture, sprinkle with 1/3 nuts.
- Add remaining layers with cream and nuts.
- Refrigerate until serving time.
- To toast almonds, place on baking sheet in oven for 3 to 5 minutes after cakes have baked.

Nutrition Information

- Calories: 399.8
- Sugar: 27.5
- Total Carbohydrate: 49.9
- Cholesterol: 99.3
- Protein: 7
- Total Fat: 20.9
- Sodium: 387.6
- Fiber: 3.1
- Saturated Fat: 10.9

67. Chocolate Bonbons

Serving: 30 bonbons, 15 serving(s) | Prep: 20mins | Ready in:

Ingredients

- 2 brown rice cakes, very finely crushed
- 1/4 cup brown rice syrup
- 1/4 cup natural-style peanut butter
- 1 1/2 tablespoons unsweetened cocoa
- 1 tablespoon canola oil (organic)
- 1/2 teaspoon vanilla extract

Direction

- Add syrup, peanut butter, cocoa, and oil to a medium saucepan.
- Heat over low heat until melted and well combined then remove from heat.
- Stir in vanilla.
- Stir in crushed rice cakes until mixed well.

- Cool mixture until it's not too hot to handle.
- Roll into large marble-size balls.
- Store in an airtight container at room temperature.

Nutrition Information

- Calories: 39.8
- Total Carbohydrate: 2.1
- Protein: 1.3
- Saturated Fat: 0.6
- Sodium: 4.8
- Sugar: 0.4
- Total Fat: 3.2
- Fiber: 0.5
- Cholesterol: 0

68. Chocolate Cheese Eclairs

Serving: 8 serving(s) | Prep: 45mins | Ready in:

Ingredients

- 3/4 cup all-purpose flour, plus
- 2 tablespoons all-purpose flour
- 2 tablespoons cocoa
- 1 tablespoon sugar
- 1 cup water
- 1/2 cup margarine or 1/2 cup butter
- 4 eggs
- CHOCOLATE CHEESE FILLING
- 1/4 cup semi-sweet chocolate chips
- 1 (3 ounce) package cream cheese, softened
- 1/3 cup packed brown sugar
- 1/4 cup milk
- 1/2 teaspoon vanilla
- 1 cup chilled whipping cream (heavy)
- COCOA GLAZE
- 1 cup powdered sugar
- 2 tablespoons cocoa
- 2 tablespoons milk

Direction

- Heat oven to 400°F.
- Mix flour, cocoa and sugar.
- Heat water and margarine in 3-quart saucepan to a rolling boil.
- Stir in flour mixture.
- Stir vigorously over low heat until mixture forms a ball, about 1 minute.
- Remove from heat.
- Beat in eggs; continue beating until smooth.
- Drop dough by about 1/4 cupfuls 3 inches apart onto ungreased cookie sheet.
- With spatula, shape each into finger 4 1/2 inches long and 1 1/2 inches wide.
- Bake until puffed and darker brown on top, 35 to 40 minutes; cool.
- Cut off tops; pull out any filaments of soft dough.
- Fill éclairs with Chocolate Cheese Filling; replace tops.
- Spread with Cocoa Glaze just before serving.
- Refrigerate any remaining éclairs.
- CHOCOLATE CHEESE FILLING: Heat chocolate chips in small heavy saucepan over low heat, stirring occasionally, until melted; cool.
- Beat cream cheese, sugar, milk and vanilla until smooth and creamy.
- Stir in chocolate.
- Beat whipping cream in chilled bowl until soft peaks form.
- Fold in chocolate mixture.
- COCOA GLAZE: Mix powdered sugar and cocoa.
- Stir in milk until smooth.
- If necessary, stir in additional milk, 1/2 teaspoon at a time, until of desired consistency.

Nutrition Information

- Calories: 469.5
- Total Fat: 30.9
- Total Carbohydrate: 42.6
- Cholesterol: 159.8
- Protein: 7.2
- Saturated Fat: 13.2

- Sodium: 221.5
- Fiber: 1.2
- Sugar: 28.2

69. Chocolate Cherry Pudding Cake

Serving: 14 serving(s) | Prep: 15mins | Ready in:

Ingredients

- 1 3/4 cups all-purpose flour
- 1 1/4 cups sugar
- 1/3 cup unsweetened cocoa
- 3 tablespoons baking powder
- 3/4 cup skim milk
- 1/2 cup unsweetened applesauce
- 1 cup sweet cherries (fresh or frozen)
- 1/4 cup chopped pecans
- 1 1/4 cups brown sugar
- 3 cups hot water
- 1/4 cup unsweetened cocoa

Direction

- Combine flour, sugar, 1/3 cup cocoa and baking powder in a large bowl; stir in milk and applesauce until dry ingredients are moistened.
- Fold in cherries and pecans.
- Spoon batter into a greased and floured 13 by 9 inch pan.
- Combine brown sugar, hot water and 1/4 cup cocoa in medium bowl until smooth.
- Pour over batter.
- Bake at 350 for 35-40 minutes or until set (cake will have a pudding-like texture).
- Serve warm or at room temperature.

Nutrition Information

- Calories: 239.7
- Total Carbohydrate: 55.6
- Protein: 3.2
- Total Fat: 2.1

- Saturated Fat: 0.5
- Sodium: 249.6
- Fiber: 2.1
- Sugar: 39.3
- Cholesterol: 0.3

70. Chocolate Chip Almond Cake

Serving: 16-20 serving(s) | Prep: 20mins | Ready in:

Ingredients

- 7 ounces almond paste, grated
- 3/4 cup sugar
- 1/2 cup unsalted butter, room temperature
- 5 large eggs, room temperature divided
- 1 teaspoon baking powder
- 1/2 teaspoon salt
- 1 cup all-purpose flour
- 3/4 cup mini chocolate chips or 5 ounces finely chopped baking chocolate
- 1/2 cup milk
- 1/2 cup sliced almonds
- 1/4 cup light brown sugar, firmly packed
- confectioners' sugar, garnish

Direction

- Preheat oven to 350°F
- Grease and flour a 9x9 inch baking pan.
- Add almond paste, sugar and butter to a bowl.
- Mix until combined.
- Beat on high for 3 minutes.
- Add 4 of the eggs (one at a time), beating well between each addition.
- Sift flour with baking powder and salt.
- Add chips or chopped chocolate, to flour and toss.
- Add flour mixture to egg mixture, alternately with milk.
- Gently fold together until combined.
- Pour batter into prepared pan and wipe out mixing bowl.
- In same bowl beat almonds, brown sugar and remaining egg until egg is frothy.

- Spread on top of cake.
- Bake for 40-45 minutes or until cake springs back when gently pressed with finger.
- Cool cake on rack.
- Dust with confectionary sugar if desired.

Nutrition Information

- Calories: 272.2
- Total Carbohydrate: 31.2
- Cholesterol: 82.4
- Protein: 5.2
- Total Fat: 15.2
- Sodium: 125.4
- Fiber: 1.7
- Saturated Fat: 6.2
- Sugar: 22.1

71. Chocolate Chip And Peanut Cookies

Serving: 3 dozen cookies, 36 serving(s) | Prep: 10mins | Ready in:

Ingredients

- 1/2 cup butter, softened
- 1/2 cup granulated sugar
- 1/4 cup brown sugar, packed
- 1 egg
- 1 teaspoon vanilla
- 1 cup all-purpose flour
- 1/2 teaspoon salt
- 1/2 teaspoon baking soda
- 1 cup semisweet chocolate piece (6 oz pkg.)
- 1 cup peanuts

Direction

- Preheat oven to 375°F.
- Cream butter and sugars; add egg, vanilla, and beat until light and fluffy.
- Sift together flour, salt and baking soda; stir into creamed mixture; blend well.
- Add chocolate pieces and peanuts and stir by hand.
- Drop from teaspoon about 2 inches apart on a greased cookie sheet.
- Bake in 375°F oven for 12 minutes.
- Remove from sheet immediately.

Nutrition Information

- Calories: 109.4
- Total Carbohydrate: 11.7
- Protein: 1.9
- Total Fat: 6.4
- Saturated Fat: 2.9
- Fiber: 0.9
- Sugar: 7.8
- Cholesterol: 12.8
- Sodium: 71.5

72. Chocolate Covered Raisins

Serving: 1 cups, 2 serving(s) | Prep: 1mins | Ready in:

Ingredients

- 1 cup raisins or 1 cup nuts
- chocolate, discs

Direction

- Melt chocolate discs in a double boiler.
- Dump in raisins
- Stir for a while.
- When raisins are fully covered in chocolate pour into strainer until all access chocolate is gone
- Pour the raisins onto pan and let sit until dry
- Eat.

Nutrition Information

- Calories: 216.8
- Total Fat: 0.3
- Total Carbohydrate: 57.4

- Cholesterol: 0
- Saturated Fat: 0
- Sodium: 8
- Fiber: 2.7
- Sugar: 42.9
- Protein: 2.2

- Calories: 178.3
- Total Fat: 9.5
- Saturated Fat: 3.1
- Sodium: 107.8
- Cholesterol: 6.9
- Protein: 2.2
- Fiber: 1.3
- Sugar: 11.1
- Total Carbohydrate: 21.5

73. Chocolate Dipped Almond Cookies

Serving: 20 cookies | Prep: 7mins | Ready in:

Ingredients

- 16 ounces refrigerated sugar cookie dough, mini bars, softened
- 1/2 cup almonds, chopped
- 1 cup semisweet chocolate morsel

Direction

- Preheat oven to 325 degrees.
- In a medium bowl combine the cookie dough and almonds.
- Refrigerate dough for 15 minutes to make handling easier.
- Roll cookie dough into balls and place on ungreased baking sheet.
- Bake for 15 to 17 minutes or until cookies are light golden brown around the edges.
- Let set on cookie sheets for 2 minutes before removing to wire racks to cool completely.
- Line cooled cookie sheets with wax paper.
- In a small bowl add morsels and microwave for 1 minute.
- Stir, microwave an additional 10-15 seconds intervals until morsels are just smooth.
- Dip cookies halfway into the melted chocolate and tap or shake off excess.
- Place on wax paper lined cookie sheets and refrigerate for 15 minutes or until chocolate is set.

Nutrition Information

74. Chocolate Gobs With Icing

Serving: 24 gobs | Prep: 30mins | Ready in:

Ingredients

- GOBS
- 4 cups flour
- 2 teaspoons baking soda
- 1/2 teaspoon baking powder
- 1/2 teaspoon salt
- 2 cups sugar
- 1/2 cup shortening
- 2 eggs
- 1 cup buttermilk
- 1 cup boiling water
- 1 teaspoon vanilla
- 1/2 cup cocoa
- ICING
- 1/2 cup milk
- 2 tablespoons flour
- 1 dash salt
- 1/2 cup shortening
- 1/2 cup sugar
- 1 teaspoon vanilla
- 3 - 3 1/2 cups powdered sugar

Direction

- For gobs, mix all ingredients together in large bowl with electric mixer.
- Drop on ungreased baking sheets by Tbsp.
- Bake at 350 degrees for 10-12 minutes.
- Remove to waxed paper to cool.

- For icing, in small saucepan cook the milk, flour and salt until smooth and thick, stirring constantly.
- Let cool.
- In med.
- Bowl, beat together 1/2 cup shortening and 1/2 cup sugar until creamy.
- Add cooled flour and milk mixture.
- Add powdered sugar and beat well.
- Spread about 1-2 Tbsp. of icing onto flat side of one gob and top with another gob (to make a "sandwich").
- Wrap individually in waxed paper or saran until eaten.
- Store in refrigerator.

Nutrition Information

- Calories: 311.2
- Fiber: 1.2
- Sugar: 36.2
- Protein: 3.6
- Total Fat: 9.7
- Saturated Fat: 2.6
- Sodium: 187.6
- Total Carbohydrate: 54
- Cholesterol: 18.8

75. Chocolate Granola Candies

Serving: 36-48 serving(s) | Prep: 5mins | Ready in:

Ingredients

- 2 1/2 cups granola cereal, with fruit and nuts
- 1/2 cup chopped nuts, of your choice
- 1/4 cup raisins (optional)
- 12 ounces chocolate-flavored baking chocolate (I use Wilton brand)

Direction

- In a medium bowl, combine cereal and chopped nut and (optional) raisins.
- In a heavy saucepan, melt candy coating over low heat, be careful not to overheat.
- Remove from heat.
- Drop teaspoonfuls of mixture into foil candy cups.
- Place candies in refrigerator to harden.
- Store in an airtight container in a cool dry place.

Nutrition Information

- Calories: 100.2
- Cholesterol: 0
- Protein: 2.8
- Saturated Fat: 3.6
- Sodium: 16.9
- Sugar: 1.9
- Total Carbohydrate: 7.8
- Total Fat: 8
- Fiber: 2.5

76. Chocolate Hazelnut Dessert Pizza

Serving: 1 pizza, 6-8 serving(s) | Prep: 15mins | Ready in:

Ingredients

- 6 ounces sugar cookie dough
- 1 cup cookie ready pecan pieces
- 8 ounces cream cheese
- 1/2 cup powdered sugar
- 1/4 cup rice milk
- 1 cup chocolate hazelnut spread
- 1 cup cookie crumbs, your choice
- 1 cup m candy
- 1 cup diced toasted hazelnuts
- 1 cup sweetened dried cherries
- 1/2 cup chocolate fudge topping

Direction

- Mix pecan bits into cookie dough, roll out into a circle about 8 inches wide.
- Bake on 350 for about 20 minutes.
- With an electric mixer, mix cream cheese, powdered sugar, rice milk and Chocolate spread.
- Spread over cooled "crust".
- Add other ingredients on top except fudge.
- Warm fudge in microwave about 30 seconds and drizzle over top of "pizza".

Nutrition Information

- Calories: 798.2
- Sodium: 223.4
- Sugar: 47.1
- Total Carbohydrate: 64.9
- Protein: 11.7
- Total Fat: 56.9
- Saturated Fat: 14.1
- Fiber: 7.3
- Cholesterol: 42.1

77. Chocolate Layer Delight

Serving: 6-8 serving(s) | Prep: 15mins | Ready in:

Ingredients

- 8 ounces cream cheese, room temp
- 16 ounces sugar Cool Whip Free (2 - 8oz containers) or 16 ounces Cool Whip Free (2 - 8oz containers)
- 12 ounces sugar free Oreo cookies, crushed (1 package, reserve 2 tsp for garnish)
- 3 ounces sugar-free instant chocolate pudding mix

Direction

- Beat cream cheese until creamy with mixer. Mix in 1 container Cool Whip with mixer until well mixed. Fold in crushed cookies. Place this layer in bottom of bowl. Next top with pudding, then top with remaining Cool Whip and garnish with reserved cookie crumbs.
- Place in refrigerator 1 hour prior to serving.

Nutrition Information

- Calories: 442.1
- Total Fat: 24.4
- Sodium: 797.1
- Protein: 6.6
- Saturated Fat: 10.6
- Fiber: 2.8
- Sugar: 23.4
- Total Carbohydrate: 52.5
- Cholesterol: 41.6

78. Chocolate Mascarpone And Strawberry Tart

Serving: 1 11, 12 serving(s) | Prep: 1hours30mins | Ready in:

Ingredients

- 1 (12 ounce) box vanilla wafers
- 1/2 cup butter, melted
- 20 ounces mascarpone
- 10 ounces cream cheese, room temperature
- 1/2 cup sour cream
- 1/2 cup sugar
- 8 ounces semisweet chocolate
- 1 lb strawberry

Direction

- Prepare Crust:
- Preheat oven to 350 degrees F.
- Crush Nilla Wafers into crumbs (this can be done in a food processor).
- Combine with melted butter.
- Press mixture into tart pan.
- Bake for 10 minutes.
- Cool completely! This is very important.
- Prepare Filling:

- Beat mascarpone, cream cheese, sour cream, sugar, and 6 oz. melted chocolate until creamy and whipped.
- If not serving within a few hours, stop here.
- Assemble the Tart:
- Fill cooled crust with the filling.
- Top with washed and sliced strawberries.
- Drizzle with 2 oz. melted chocolate.
- Store in refrigerator until serving.
- Enjoy!

Nutrition Information

- Calories: 443.9
- Total Fat: 33.4
- Saturated Fat: 18.8
- Sodium: 221.2
- Fiber: 4.5
- Total Carbohydrate: 38.1
- Protein: 6.1
- Sugar: 10.3
- Cholesterol: 50.5

79. Chocolate Nutella No Bake Cookies

Serving: 24 serving(s) | Prep: 10mins | Ready in:

Ingredients

- 2 cups sugar
- 1/4 cup cocoa powder
- 1/2 cup milk
- 1/2 cup margarine
- 1 teaspoon vanilla
- 1/8 teaspoon salt
- 1/4 cup peanut butter
- 1/4 cup nutella
- 2 3/4 cups quick oats
- 1/4-1/2 cup shredded coconut

Direction

- Over medium heat, cook sugar, cocoa, milk and margarine. Boil one minute.
- Remove from heat.
- Stir in vanilla, salt, peanut butter, Nutella, oats, and coconut (start with the 1/4 cup coconut and add more up to 1/2 cup to desired consistency. (I end up using around 1/3 cup).
- Stir until well-combined.
- Drop by teaspoon on wax paper and refrigerate to cool completely.
- Eat!

Nutrition Information

- Calories: 159.7
- Sugar: 19.1
- Total Carbohydrate: 26.6
- Protein: 2.5
- Total Fat: 5.4
- Saturated Fat: 2.1
- Sodium: 53.9
- Fiber: 1.6
- Cholesterol: 0.7

80. Chocolate Toffee Graham Treats

Serving: 22 treats | Prep: 10mins | Ready in:

Ingredients

- 11 whole honey graham crackers, broken into squares
- 1 cup butter
- 1 cup sugar
- 1/2 cup finely chopped pecans
- 1 -2 cup semi-sweet chocolate chips

Direction

- Preheat oven to 350*.
- Arrange graham crackers in a single layer in a 15 x 10 baking sheet.

- Combine butter and sugar in saucepan and bring to a boil over medium heat, stirring constantly until butter melts; then boil 2 minutes.
- Remove from heat and stir in pecans.
- Pour mixture evenly over crackers and spread carefully to edge of pan, covering crackers completely.
- Bake for 10 minutes.
- Remove from oven and sprinkle evenly with chocolate chips; when chips melt, smooth evenly to cover top.
- Cool in pan for 5 minutes; carefully separate and transfer squares to a wax paper lined cookie sheet.
- Refrigerate until chocolate hardens.

Nutrition Information

- Calories: 177.7
- Protein: 0.9
- Total Fat: 12.8
- Fiber: 0.8
- Sugar: 14.4
- Total Carbohydrate: 17
- Cholesterol: 22.2
- Saturated Fat: 6.9
- Sodium: 91.3

81. Chocolate, Butterscotch, Pb Rice Krispies Treats

Serving: 100-120 1x1squares | Prep: 10mins | Ready in:

Ingredients

- 1 cup peanut butter
- 1 cup light Karo syrup or 1 cup other corn syrup
- 1 cup sugar
- 6 cups Rice Krispies
- 1 (6 ounce) package semi-sweet chocolate chips
- 1 (6 ounce) package butterscotch chips

Direction

- Mix peanut butter, Karo syrup, and sugar in a pot, and bring to a slight boil. Stir until creamy.
- Take mixture off the burner, and mix with Rice Krispies cereal.
- Spread mixture in 13 x 9 inch pan.
- Melt chocolate and butterscotch chips together in microwave (start with 1-2 minutes, then, stirring intermittently, 30-second intervals until melted).
- Spread melted chips over Rice Krispies mixture.
- Refrigerate until chocolate-butterscotch mixture hardens (very quick, about 30 minutes).
- Cut into 2x2-inch squares. Enjoy!

Nutrition Information

- Calories: 56.4
- Total Fat: 2.3
- Saturated Fat: 1
- Sodium: 25.1
- Fiber: 0.3
- Sugar: 5.4
- Total Carbohydrate: 8.8
- Cholesterol: 0
- Protein: 0.9

82. Chocolate Banana Trifle

Serving: 16 serving(s) | Prep: 30mins | Ready in:

Ingredients

- 2/3 cup sugar
- 2/3 cup evaporated skim milk
- 3 tablespoons unsweetened cocoa
- 1 tablespoon cornstarch
- 1/4 cup coffee-flavored liqueur (such as Kahlua)

- 1 (16 ounce) angel food cake, cut into 1 inch cubes
- 2 (1 1/2 ounce) english toffee-flavored candy bars, crushed
- 3 cups skim milk
- 3 (3 1/2 ounce) packages vanilla instant pudding mix (not sugar-free)
- 2 cups sliced bananas
- 1 (12 ounce) container Cool Whip (reduced calorie or fat-free OK)
- 1 (1 1/2 ounce) english toffee-flavored candy bars, crushed

Direction

- Combine sugar, evaporated milk, cocoa and cornstarch in a medium saucepan and bring to a boil.
- Cook until sugar dissolves and mixture is thick (about 3 minutes), stirring frequently.
- Remove from heat and stir in coffee liqueur.
- Set aside to cool.
- When chocolate mixture is cool, combine with cake cubes in a large bowl.
- Mix 2 crushed candy bars in with cake mixture.
- Beat milk and pudding mix at medium speed of a mixer until well-blended.
- Stir into cake mixture.
- Cover and chill for 15 minutes in refrigerator.
- Spoon half of cake mixture into a trifle dish or large bowl (about 4 quart).
- Arrange half of bananas evenly over cake mixture and top with half of cool whip.
- Repeat layers, ending with cool whip.
- Sprinkle with remaining toffee bar.
- Chill for 1 hour before serving.

Nutrition Information

- Calories: 342.2
- Saturated Fat: 6.3
- Sodium: 473.6
- Fiber: 1
- Sugar: 48
- Cholesterol: 5.3
- Total Fat: 8.3
- Protein: 5.3
- Total Carbohydrate: 61.7

83. Chocolate Covered Strawberries

Serving: 28 strawberries | Prep: 20mins | Ready in:

Ingredients

- 2 pints strawberries, with stems if possible
- 1 1/2 cups semi-sweet chocolate chips (or milk chocolate chips)
- 2 tablespoons corn syrup
- 6 tablespoons butter

Direction

- Wash strawberries and pat dry.
- Place on paper towels until they reach room temperature.
- Melt chocolate chips, corn syrup and butter in a double boiler, stirring occasionally.
- Remove from heat and dip each strawberry into chocolate, coating 2/3 of strawberry.
- Allow excess chocolate to drip off into pan.
- Place stem side down on waxed paper covered baking pan or cookie sheet.
- Refrigerate until set, about 15-20 minutes.

Nutrition Information

- Calories: 77
- Sodium: 23
- Fiber: 1
- Sugar: 6.5
- Total Carbohydrate: 8.7
- Cholesterol: 6.5
- Total Fat: 5.2
- Saturated Fat: 3.2
- Protein: 0.6

84. Cholly's World Famous Gingerbread Cake

Serving: 8-10 serving(s) | Prep: 25mins | Ready in:

Ingredients

- 1 cup dark molasses
- 1 teaspoon baking soda
- 2 1/2 cups all-purpose flour
- 1 tablespoon baking powder
- 1 1/2 teaspoons ground cinnamon
- 1 teaspoon ground ginger
- 1/2 teaspoon salt
- 1/8 teaspoon ground cloves
- 1/2 cup butter, at room temperature
- 1 cup firmly packed brown sugar
- 2 large eggs

Direction

- In a 2-quart pan over high heat, bring 1 cup water to a boil.
- Remove from heat and stir in molasses and baking soda.
- After mixture stops foaming, stir in 1/2 cup cold water; let cool to room temperature, stirring often (about 10 minutes).
- (This can also be done easily in microwave).
- In a small bowl, whisk together dry ingredients.
- Preheat oven to 325 degrees F.
- In mixing bowl, with an electric mixer on high speed, beat butter and brown sugar until well blended.
- Beat in eggs until blended.
- Reduce speed and add flour and molasses mixtures alternately until incorporated, then beat on high speed until well blended.
- Pour into a buttered and floured 9-inch square pan.
- Bake in a 325 oven until a toothpick inserted in center of thickest part comes out clean, 45 to 50 minutes.
- Let cool on pan on a rack for at least an hour.
- Serving suggestion: Pour about 1/4 cup creme anglaise onto each plate.
- Cut cake into pieces and set them in sauce on plates.
- If desired, lightly sift unsweetened cocoa and/or powdered sugar over each plate and garnish with a mint sprig.
- Offer additional creme anglaise at table.

Nutrition Information

- Calories: 491.4
- Cholesterol: 77
- Sodium: 582.1
- Fiber: 1.4
- Sugar: 50.2
- Total Carbohydrate: 89.3
- Total Fat: 13.1
- Saturated Fat: 7.8
- Protein: 5.8

85. Chow Mein Noodle Cookies

Serving: 24-48 cookies, 40 serving(s) | Prep: 5mins | Ready in:

Ingredients

- 1 (5 1/2 ounce) package chow mein noodles
- 1 (6 ounce) package butterscotch chips
- 1 (6 ounce) package semi-sweet chocolate chips
- 1/2 cup chopped pecans

Direction

- In a large pot melt butterscotch chips and chocolate chips together.
- When all is melted and smooth add chow mein noodles and pecans.
- Drop onto wax paper using two teaspoons and let set.
- Then put into air tight container.
- Freezes good as well.

Nutrition Information

- Calories: 73.5
- Total Fat: 4.7
- Saturated Fat: 2
- Fiber: 0.5
- Sugar: 5.2
- Total Carbohydrate: 8
- Protein: 0.7
- Sodium: 21.6
- Cholesterol: 0

86. Chris's Favorite Cherry Jello

Serving: 9 serving(s) | Prep: 5mins | Ready in:

Ingredients

- 1 (3 ounce) package cherry Jell-O
- 1 cup boiling water
- 1 (2 ounce) package Dream Whip
- 1 (21 ounce) can cherry pie filling

Direction

- Mix Jello and water.
- Blend in pie filling and chill until slightly thickened (about 1.5-2 hours). Otherwise cherries will all sink to bottom.
- Make Dream Whip according to package and then blend in Dream Whip.
- Place in 9x9-inch pan and refrigerate.
- Can be easily doubled in a 9x13-inch pan.

Nutrition Information

- Calories: 148.8
- Cholesterol: 0
- Protein: 3.9
- Total Fat: 2.7
- Saturated Fat: 2.3
- Sodium: 35.8
- Fiber: 0.4
- Sugar: 3.3
- Total Carbohydrate: 27.6

87. Classic Buttercream Frosting

Serving: 8-12 serving(s) | Prep: 10mins | Ready in:

Ingredients

- 3⁄4 cup unsalted butter
- 1⁄4 cup shortening
- 1⁄2 cup milk
- 1⁄4 teaspoon salt
- 1 1⁄2 teaspoons vanilla
- 2 lbs confectioners' sugar (powdered sugar)

Direction

- Place butter, shortening, milk, vanilla, salt and one pound of sugar in large bowl.
- Beat at low speed until combined.
- Gradually add the other pound of sugar.
- Stop and scrape sides.
- Beat on high until mixture is light and fluffy.
- Keep covered with plastic wrap to prevent crusting.
- Chocolate Buttercream: For each pound of sugar used in the butter cream, allow 2/3 cup unsweetened cocoa, 3 tablespoons butter and 0.125 teaspoon salt.

Nutrition Information

- Calories: 662.4
- Saturated Fat: 12.9
- Sodium: 84.8
- Fiber: 0
- Sugar: 111
- Total Carbohydrate: 114
- Cholesterol: 47.9
- Protein: 0.7
- Total Fat: 24.2

88. Cocoa Cream Roll

Serving: 8-10 serving(s) | Prep: 45mins | Ready in:

Ingredients

- 1 cup sifted cake flour
- 1 teaspoon baking powder
- 1/4 teaspoon salt
- 1/4 cup unsweetened cocoa
- 3 eggs
- 1 cup sugar
- 1/3 cup water
- 1 teaspoon vanilla
- 1 pint heavy cream
- 1/4 cup dark rum
- 1/4 cup confectioners' sugar
- 2 teaspoons vanilla
- 1/4 cup ground nuts

Direction

- Grease a 15x10x1 inch pan lightly and line with aluminum foil; grease foil.
- Sift flour, powder, salt and cocoa together.
- Beat eggs in large bowl until very thick and lemon colored.
- Beat in granulated sugar gradually.
- Blend in water and 1 tsp vanilla at low speed.
- Mix in sifted dry ingredients slowly.
- Pour into prepared pan and bake at 375* for 15 minutes or until cake springs back when touched lightly.
- Sprinkle a clean dish towel with confectioners' sugar.
- Carefully turn out cake onto towel; gently peel off foil.
- Starting at narrow end, roll up cake and towel together.
- Place on rack to cool.
- Combine cream, rum, 1/4 cup confectioners' sugar and 2 tsp vanilla.
- Whip until stiff.
- Unroll cooled cake roll and spread evenly with about 2/3 of cream mixture.
- Carefully roll up cake and cream and place on a serving plate.
- Frost with remaining cream mixture.
- Sprinkle with ground nuts.
- Chill until serving.

Nutrition Information

- Calories: 433.2
- Saturated Fat: 14.5
- Sugar: 29.2
- Cholesterol: 160.8
- Protein: 5.5
- Total Fat: 24.4
- Sodium: 168.3
- Fiber: 1.2
- Total Carbohydrate: 45.7

89. Coconut (Almond) Joys

Serving: 36 candies | Prep: 30mins | Ready in:

Ingredients

- 1/2 cup butter, melted
- 2 cups confectioners' sugar
- 3 cups sweetened flaked coconut
- 2 ounces semi-sweet chocolate chips or 2 ounces milk chocolate chips, melted
- almond halves or slivered almonds (optional)

Direction

- Combine melted butter, sugar and coconut and mix well.
- Shape rounded teaspoonfuls into balls and place on cookie or baking sheet lined with waxed paper.
- Flatten each ball slightly by making an indentation in the center with thumb or finger.
- Fill centers with melted chocolate.
- Place an almond half or sliver on top, if desired.
- Chill until firm and store in refrigerator.

Nutrition Information

- Calories: 94.9
- Total Fat: 5.8
- Cholesterol: 6.8
- Protein: 0.3
- Saturated Fat: 4.3
- Sodium: 38.7
- Fiber: 0.4
- Sugar: 10.7
- Total Carbohydrate: 11.3

90. Coffee Marshmallow Sponge

Serving: 6-8 serving(s) | Prep: 15mins | Ready in:

Ingredients

- 1 (16 ounce) bag marshmallows
- 1/2 cup strong coffee
- 1 1/2 pints whipping cream (3 cups)
- 3 tablespoons sugar
- 24 ladyfingers, split in halves (use the soft type not Savoiardi)

Direction

- In the top of a double boiler set over simmering water, melt the marshmallows. Add coffee, stir until smooth. Remove from heat.
- Chill until cold.
- Beat the cream with the sugar until soft peaks form.
- Fold 2 cups of the whipped cream into the cold coffee mixture.
- Line the bottom and sides of a 9 or 10-inch springform pan with lady finger halves.
- Spread a layer of the coffee cream over the ladyfingers.
- Continue alternating layers, ending with the cream.
- Cover refrigerate for 2 hours.
- To serve, release sponge from pan dollop with remaining whipped cream.

Nutrition Information

- Calories: 838
- Total Fat: 48.2
- Sodium: 171.2
- Sugar: 61.5
- Protein: 8.5
- Saturated Fat: 29
- Fiber: 0.5
- Total Carbohydrate: 97.8
- Cholesterol: 323.6

91. Coffee And Mascarpone Slice

Serving: 16 serving(s) | Prep: 0S | Ready in:

Ingredients

- 1 sheet ready rolled shortcrust pastry
- 2/3 cup water
- 2 tablespoons caster sugar
- 2 teaspoons instant coffee
- 1/3 cup liqueur, of choice
- 4 egg yolks
- 1/3 cup caster sugar
- 250 g mascarpone cheese, softened
- 300 ml cream
- 1 (250 g) packet ladyfingers (sponge fingers)
- cocoa, for dusting

Direction

- Place the pastry sheet on a greased baking tray and prick over with a fork.
- Bake at 180 degrees C for about 10 minutes until it's golden brown.
- Cool and trim to fit a 23cm square cake tin.
- Place the water, 2 tablespoons sugar and coffee in a small saucepan and stir over a gentle heat until sugar is dissolved.
- Remove from the heat and add the liqueur.
- Cool.

- To prepare the mascarpone cream place the egg yolks and sugar in a heat-proof bowl over a saucepan of simmering water.
- Beat for 5 minutes until mixture is thick.
- Remove from the heat and continue beating for a few minutes until it cools down.
- Blend in the mascarpone.
- In another bowl whisk the cream until its stiff and fold into the mascarpone mix.
- Line the base and sides of a 23cm square cake tin with plastic wrap.
- Spread 1/3 of the cream mixture into the tin.
- Dip half the sponge fingers completely into the coffee syrup mixture and press them gently onto the cream mixture.
- Spread with half the remaining cream mix and top with the rest of the dipped sponge fingers.
- You only want to dip the sponge fingers, not soak them, they should still be firm.
- Spread with the rest of the cream mixture and put the pastry sheet on top.
- Cover with plastic wrap and refrigerate overnight.
- To serve, invert the slice onto a board so that the pastry is the base.
- Remove the plastic wrap.
- Cut into squares and serve dusted with cocoa powder and with mixed fresh berries.

Nutrition Information

- Calories: 253.9
- Saturated Fat: 5.5
- Sugar: 9.8
- Cholesterol: 125.5
- Protein: 3.4
- Total Fat: 12.1
- Sodium: 90.2
- Fiber: 0.6
- Total Carbohydrate: 21

92. Cracker Custard

Serving: 8-10 serving(s) | Prep: 10mins | Ready in:

Ingredients

- 1/2 cup sugar
- 2 eggs
- 1 1/2 cans evaporated milk
- 1 1/2 cups water
- 2 teaspoons cornstarch
- 1 teaspoon vanilla extract
- 1 box of premium saltine crackers

Direction

- Put 1/2 cup sugar and 2 eggs in pot and beat.
- Mix in water and milk with egg mixture and cook on medium heat until it steams.
- In a little bowl, add 1/3 cup water with 2 teaspoon corn starch and mix well.
- Add the 1/2 the corn starch mixture to the stove mixture; keep adding slowly to a slightly creamy consistency.
- Bring to a boil and add vanilla extract.
- Take off heat then add one package row of crackers at a time (using about 2 1/2 to 3 package rows depending on thickness).
- Be careful when adding crackers, leave some liquid since the crackers will soak the liquid up.
- Mix well and eat warm.

Nutrition Information

- Calories: 70.8
- Sugar: 12.7
- Total Carbohydrate: 13.3
- Protein: 1.6
- Total Fat: 1.2
- Sodium: 18.5
- Saturated Fat: 0.4
- Fiber: 0
- Cholesterol: 52.9

93. Cranberry Crisp With Autumn Fruit

Serving: 10 serving(s) | Prep: 10mins | Ready in:

Ingredients

- 3 cups sliced peeled tart apples
- 2 cups peeled firm pears
- 1 1/2 cups chopped frozen, chopped fresh cranberries or 1 1/2 cups chopped frozen, chopped cranberries
- 1 cup sugar
- 2 tablespoons flour
- 1/3 cup flour
- 1 teaspoon cinnamon
- 1 cup quick-cooking rolled oats
- 1/2 cup firmly packed brown sugar
- 1/4 cup butter or 1/4 cup margarine
- 1/2 cup chopped nuts
- whipped cream (for serving)

Direction

- Preheat the oven to 375°F.
- Grease a 2-quart shallow baking dish.
- In a large bowl, combine the apples, pears, cranberries, sugar, 2 tablespoons of the flour and cinnamon.
- Spread mixture evenly into the baking dish, in small bowl, combine rolled oats, brown sugar and the remaining 1/3 cup flour.
- Using pastry blender or fork, cut in butter until crumbly.
- Stir in nuts.
- Sprinkle crumb mixture evenly over fruit.
- Bate for 30 to 40 minutes or until golden brown and apples are tender.
- Serve with whipped cream.

Nutrition Information

- Calories: 298
- Total Fat: 8.8
- Sodium: 84.3
- Fiber: 4.3
- Saturated Fat: 3.5
- Sugar: 38.7
- Total Carbohydrate: 54.4
- Cholesterol: 12.2
- Protein: 3.4

94. Cranberry Glazed Pound Cake

Serving: 16 serving(s) | Prep: 20mins | Ready in:

Ingredients

- Cake
- 2 cups butter, softened
- 3 cups sugar
- 12 egg yolks, well beaten
- 12 egg whites, beaten to stiff peaks
- 4 cups flour
- Cranberry Glaze
- 2 cups water
- 2 cups sugar
- 1 lb cranberries (4 cups)

Direction

- Cake: Cream butter and sugar.
- Alternately add egg yolks, egg whites and flour to butter mixture.
- Beat until light and smooth.
- Pour into greased and floured 10" tube pan.
- Bake in preheated 325* oven about 1 1/2 hours or until golden brown.
- Cool in pan 30 minutes before removing.
- Drizzle cooled Cranberry Glaze over cake.
- Decorate with whole cranberries, if desired.
- Cranberry Glaze: In a saucepan, bring water and sugar to rapid boil.
- Simmer 10 minutes and add cranberries.
- Cook until cranberries pop, about 5 minutes.
- Remove cranberries with slotted spoon and discard or save for another use.
- Continue to cook syrup until thickened, about 20 minutes.
- Allow to cool before using.

Nutrition Information

- Calories: 622
- Total Fat: 26.4
- Sodium: 211.8
- Sugar: 63.9
- Total Carbohydrate: 90.4
- Saturated Fat: 15.7
- Fiber: 2.1
- Cholesterol: 202.6
- Protein: 8.1

95. Cranberry, Chocolate Chip And Coconut Cookies

Serving: 3 dozen cookies, 36 serving(s) | Prep: 10mins | Ready in:

Ingredients

- 1 cup butter, softened
- 1 cup brown sugar
- 1/2 cup white sugar
- 2 eggs
- 1 teaspoon vanilla
- 1 cup rolled oats
- 1 1/2 cups flour
- 1 teaspoon baking soda
- 1 teaspoon baking powder
- 1 cup dried coconut
- 1 cup dried cranberries
- 1 cup chocolate chips

Direction

- Preheat oven to 350 degrees.
- Cream butter and sugars. Add eggs and vanilla and mix to combine. In a separate bowl, combine dry ingredients. Add into wet ingredients gradually.
- Drop spoonfuls onto cookie sheets. Bake for 10 minutes until edges are crisp and center is slightly gooey. Let rest on cookie sheet for a few minutes before moving to cooling rack to cool completely.

Nutrition Information

- Calories: 147.6
- Fiber: 0.9
- Cholesterol: 25.3
- Protein: 1.6
- Total Fat: 7.9
- Saturated Fat: 5
- Sodium: 95.2
- Sugar: 12.5
- Total Carbohydrate: 18.8

96. Cream Cheese Almond Bars

Serving: 2 1/2 dozen | Prep: 20mins | Ready in:

Ingredients

- 1/2 cup butter, softened
- 2 teaspoons sugar
- 2 tablespoons milk
- 1/2 teaspoon grated lemon rind
- 1 1/3 cups all-purpose flour
- 2 (8 ounce) packages cream cheese, softened
- 1 cup sugar
- 1 large egg, lightly beaten
- 1 teaspoon grated lemon rind
- 1 cup chopped toasted almond
- 1 cup sifted powdered sugar
- 1 tablespoon water
- 1 teaspoon ground cinnamon
- garnish toasted sliced almonds

Direction

- Combine first 4 ingredients; beat at medium speed with an electric mixer until creamy.
- Gradually add flour, beating well.
- Press dough into a lightly greased 9-inch square pan. Set aside.
- Combine cream cheese, 1 cup sugar, egg, and 1 teaspoons lemon rind; beat at medium speed until smooth.

- Stir in almonds; spoon mixture over prepared dough.
- Bake at 300F for 1 hour and 10 minutes or until set.
- Combine powdered sugar, water, and cinnamon, stirring well.
- Dollop topping onto uncut warm bars.
- Let stand 1 minute; spread evenly.
- Cool in pan on a wire rack.
- Cover and chill 3 to 4 hours.
- Cut into bars.

Nutrition Information

- Calories: 2080.4
- Cholesterol: 383.5
- Protein: 36.1
- Total Fat: 132.4
- Saturated Fat: 66.4
- Sodium: 835.3
- Fiber: 8.9
- Sugar: 133.8
- Total Carbohydrate: 199.2

97. Creamy Pineapple Peach Dessert

Serving: 10-12 serving(s) | Prep: 20mins | Ready in:

Ingredients

- 1 cup orzo pasta
- 1 (5 1/3 ounce) packagegiant ladyfingers
- 1 (14 ounce) can crushed pineapple, well drained, reserving 1/3 cup juice
- 1 (28 ounce) cansliced peaches, drained and rinsed under cold water
- 1 cup ricotta cheese
- 1 3/4 cups cold milk
- 1 package instant vanilla pudding (4 serving size)
- 2 cups Cool Whip or 2 cups whipping cream, whipped

Direction

- In a large pot of boiling water, cook pasta for about 6 minutes or until tender but firm.
- Drain, rinse under cold water and drain again
- Set aside.
- Meanwhile, line an 11 by 7 inch baking dish with lady fingers.
- Cut lady fingers if necessary to cover bottom of dish.
- Brush lady fingers with reserved pineapple juice.
- Reserve about 8 slices of the peaches for garnish.
- Layer remaining peaches over lady fingers.
- Sprinkle with pineapple.
- Place ricotta cheese in a large bowl.
- Whisk until smooth.
- Add milk and instant pudding mix.
- Whisk for about 2 minutes until slightly thickened.
- Stir in cooked orzo pasta.
- Pour mixture over pineapple layer.
- Refrigerate for about 20 minutes.
- Cover pasta layer with Cool Whip (or whipping cream).
- Garnish with reserved peach slices.
- Refrigerate for 1 hour.

Nutrition Information

- Calories: 327.5
- Sugar: 29.3
- Protein: 9
- Total Fat: 10.5
- Saturated Fat: 6.9
- Sodium: 211.5
- Fiber: 2.2
- Total Carbohydrate: 50.8
- Cholesterol: 73.8

98. Crock Pot Bread Pudding

Serving: 6 serving(s) | Prep: 10mins | Ready in:

Ingredients

- 8 slices day old bread, cubed (raisin bread is especially good)
- 4 eggs
- 2 cups milk
- 1/4 cup sugar
- 1/4 cup melted butter or 1/4 cup margarine
- 1/2 cup raisins (use only 1/4 cup if using raisin bread)
- 1/2 teaspoon cinnamon
- Sauce
- 2 tablespoons butter or 2 tablespoons margarine
- 2 tablespoons flour
- 1 cup water
- 3/4 cup sugar
- 1 teaspoon vanilla

Direction

- Place bread cubes in greased slow cooker.
- Beat together eggs and milk.
- Stir in sugar, butter, raisins, and cinnamon.
- Pour over bread and stir.
- Cover and cook on high 1 hour.
- Reduce heat to low and cook 3-4 hours, or until thermometer reaches 160°.
- Make sauce just before pudding is done baking.
- Begin by melting butter in saucepan.
- Stir in flour until smooth.
- Gradually add water, sugar, and vanilla.
- Bring to boil.
- Cook, stirring constantly for 2 minutes, or until thickened.
- Serve sauce over warm bread pudding.

Nutrition Information

- Calories: 468.6
- Cholesterol: 182.9
- Sodium: 397.6
- Sugar: 42.3
- Total Carbohydrate: 66
- Total Fat: 19
- Saturated Fat: 10.4
- Fiber: 1.4
- Protein: 10.2

99. Crock Pot Peach Dump Dessert

Serving: 8 serving(s) | Prep: 5mins | Ready in:

Ingredients

- 2 cups frozen peaches, sliced (undrained)
- 1 tablespoon cornstarch
- 1/2 teaspoon vanilla
- 1/4 cup brown sugar
- 1/4-1/2 teaspoon cinnamon
- 1 -9 ounce Jiffy white cake mix (or 1/2 package of a 2-layer size cake mix)
- 4 tablespoons melted butter

Direction

- Lightly grease the slow cooker/Crock Pot; place peaches in the bottom.
- Sprinkle with cornstarch; toss.
- Drizzle with vanilla and sprinkle brown sugar over all.
- Sprinkle with cinnamon then cake mix.
- Drizzle melted butter evenly over cake mix.
- Cover and cook on high for 3 to 3 1/2 hours.

Nutrition Information

- Calories: 155.7
- Sugar: 22.5
- Sodium: 80.1
- Fiber: 1.2
- Total Carbohydrate: 25.5
- Cholesterol: 15.3
- Protein: 0.6
- Total Fat: 6.2
- Saturated Fat: 3.7

100. Crock Pot Rice Pudding

Serving: 8 serving(s) | Prep: 5mins | Ready in:

Ingredients

- 3/4 cup short-grain rice
- 1 (13 1/2 ounce) can evaporated milk (skim is fine, 385ml)
- 2 cups water
- 1/3 cup white sugar
- 1/2 cup raisins
- 1 1/2 teaspoons vanilla
- 3/4 teaspoon salt
- 1 (3 inch) cinnamon sticks

Direction

- Combine all ingredients in slow cooker; stir well.
- Cover and cook on Low for 4 to 5 hours or on High for 2 to 2-1/2 hours.
- Stir twice during cooking period.

Nutrition Information

- Calories: 192.8
- Total Fat: 3.8
- Sodium: 271.8
- Fiber: 0.9
- Total Carbohydrate: 35.2
- Saturated Fat: 2.2
- Sugar: 13.8
- Cholesterol: 13.9
- Protein: 4.8

101. Crunchy Cereal Bars

Serving: 20 serving(s) | Prep: 10mins | Ready in:

Ingredients

- 1/2 cup semi-sweet chocolate chips (Ghiradelli preferred)
- 2 tablespoons butter
- 4 cups crisp rice cereal
- 2 cups toasted oats cereal
- cooking spray
- 1/2-1 cup toasted almond (or other nut) (optional)

Direction

- Combine chocolate chips and butter on stovetop and gently melt, stirring frequently.
- Stir in cereals, and nuts, if desired.
- Spread mixture evenly into a 13x9x2-inch pan coated with cooking spray.
- Let cool and cut into bars.

Nutrition Information

- Calories: 50.7
- Sodium: 51.4
- Fiber: 0.3
- Cholesterol: 3
- Saturated Fat: 1.5
- Sugar: 2.7
- Total Carbohydrate: 7.5
- Protein: 0.6
- Total Fat: 2.5

102. Custard (Vanilla) Slice

Serving: 16 serving(s) | Prep: 20mins | Ready in:

Ingredients

- 2 sheets of thawed puff pastry
- 1 cup sugar
- 1 cup custard powder
- 4 cups milk
- 2 teaspoons vanilla

Direction

- Place piece greaseproof paper onto a flat biscuit tray and spray with cooking spray. Put a sheet of puff pastry on tray and pierce all over with a fork, but don't go all the way through pastry.
- Put in oven about 200°C until puffed up and golden.
- Let cool for a few minutes and gently push pastry down (I use a tea towel so my hands don't get burned) so it's flat. Take it off baking tray and remove paper.
- Put pastry into a square dish that has been greased and lined with greaseproof paper. If pastry too big trim the sides a little. It should be a snug fit.
- Bake second sheet of pastry, remove the paper and set pastry to one side until custard is done.
- For the custard, put the sugar and custard powder into a large saucepan and mix together with a wire whisk.
- Add the milk and mix to combine well.
- Put saucepan on stovetop and heat on medium high until mixture begins to thicken, then lower the heat until mixture is very thick and hard to stir. I find using the wire whisk until mix begins to thicken prevents lumps, then use a spoon to stir it.
- Add vanilla and mix well then pour into prepared dish.
- Smooth top so it's even and put 2nd pastry sheet on top.
- The icing amount depends on how thick a layer you want it, but I usually melt about 1 tablespoon of butter with 1 teaspoon boiling water. Then I add icing sugar, passionfruit pulp and a bit of water or lemon juice until it's the right consistency and amount--you don't want it too runny.
- Pour the icing on top and put in fridge for a few hours or overnight.
- Cut into squares and enjoy!

Nutrition Information

- Calories: 258.1
- Sodium: 106.5
- Sugar: 12.8
- Cholesterol: 8.5
- Protein: 4.2
- Saturated Fat: 4.3
- Fiber: 0.5
- Total Carbohydrate: 29.2
- Total Fat: 13.9

103. Custard/Pudding

Serving: 3 cups | Prep: 10mins | Ready in:

Ingredients

- 2 -3 tablespoons cornstarch
- 1/2 cup sugar
- 3 eggs
- 1 (12 ounce) can evaporated milk
- 1 cup skim milk
- 1 teaspoon vanilla

Direction

- Mix together the sugar and cornstarch, then add the eggs. Beat until the mixture is well combined and pale colored.
- In a large saucepan, bring the milk to a boil over medium-high heat. Stir frequently to keep it from sticking.
- Add a little of the hot milk to the egg mixture, and stir until combined. Then pour the egg mixture into the milk.
- Cook the mixture until it reaches desired thickness, stirring constantly.
- Stir in the vanilla.
- Remove from heat, and place plastic wrap on the surface of the pudding instead of just around the pot. This will prevent a skin from forming while it cools.

Nutrition Information

- Calories: 410.4

- Total Fat: 13.5
- Fiber: 0.1
- Cholesterol: 220.5
- Saturated Fat: 6.9
- Sodium: 240.5
- Sugar: 33.6
- Total Carbohydrate: 54.7
- Protein: 17.3

104. Daffodil Dessert

Serving: 1 cake | Prep: 30mins | Ready in:

Ingredients

- 1 jiffy yellow cake mix
- 8 ounces cream cheese, softened
- 1/2 cup milk
- 1 package instant vanilla pudding
- 1 1/2 cups milk
- 20 ounces crushed pineapple, drained
- 10 ounces Cool Whip
- chopped pecans

Direction

- Mix cake according to package directions.
- Bake in 9x13 pan for 20 minutes at 350.
- Cream cream cheese with fork; add 1/2 cup milk.
- Mix pudding according to package directions, except use 1 1/2 cups milk (instead of 2 cups).
- Combine cheese and pudding mixtures; spread over cooled cake.
- Cool until set.
- Spread pineapple over pudding.
- Spread Cool Whip over top; sprinkle with chopped pecans.

Nutrition Information

- Calories: 4982.6
- Saturated Fat: 132.3
- Fiber: 10.3
- Cholesterol: 328.3
- Protein: 62.1
- Total Fat: 230.5
- Sodium: 5856.3
- Sugar: 466.8
- Total Carbohydrate: 684.3

105. Dark Chocolate Cake

Serving: 1 cake | Prep: 0S | Ready in:

Ingredients

- 1 3/4 cups self-raising flour
- 1/2 teaspoon bicarbonate of soda
- 1/4 teaspoon salt
- 1/2 cup cocoa
- 1 1/4 cups sugar
- 125 g butter
- 1 cup milk
- 1 teaspoon vanilla
- 2 eggs
- Chocolate Icing
- 1 1/2 cups icing sugar
- 2 teaspoons cocoa
- 2 teaspoons butter
- 2 tablespoons water

Direction

- Sift dry ingredients into a large bowl; add sugar.
- Add melted butter gradually, mix well.
- Add milk and vanilla; beat well.
- Add lightly-beaten eggs gradually, beating well after each addition.
- Put mixture into greased and greased-paper lined deep 20cm round cake tin.
- Bake in a moderate oven 65 minutes or until cooked when tested.
- Top with Chocolate Icing when cold.
- Chocolate Icing: Sift together icing sugar and cocoa; mix in melted butter and water; beat until smooth.

Nutrition Information

- Calories: 3822
- Total Fat: 135.9
- Saturated Fat: 81.4
- Sugar: 428.7
- Total Carbohydrate: 629.6
- Sodium: 5030.5
- Fiber: 21.4
- Cholesterol: 744.5
- Protein: 52.5

106. Date Raisin Squares Microwave

Serving: 25 squares | Prep: 10mins | Ready in:

Ingredients

- Filling
- 1 1/2 cups dates, chopped
- 1 cup water
- 1/2 cup raisins
- 2 tablespoons lemon juice
- Crumbles
- 1 cup all-purpose flour
- 1 cup rolled oats
- 1 cup lightly packed brown sugar
- 1/2 teaspoon baking powder
- 1/4 teaspoon salt
- 1/2 cup butter, softened

Direction

- Filling------.
- Combine dates, water, raisins and lemon juice in 4 cup measure.
- Cover with vented plastic wrap and microwave at high 4-6 minutes or until boiling.
- Stir every 2 minutes.
- Dates should be soft.
- Let stand, covered, 5 minutes.
- Uncover and cool to lukewarm, stirring occasionally.
- Crumbles------.
- Combine first 5 dry ingredients in mixing bowl.
- Cut in butter until mixture is crumbly.
- Press half firmly into 8 inch square microwave baking dish.
- Spread with date filling.
- Sprinkle with remaining crumble mixture, patting down lightly.
- Microwave at medium high for 9 minutes, rotating every 3 minutes, (not necessary if you have a rotating plate) remove from microwave and cover with aluminum foil.
- Let stand covered directly on counter for 10 minutes.
- Uncover and cool completely on wire rack.
- Cut into small squares.

Nutrition Information

- Calories: 135.5
- Saturated Fat: 2.4
- Sodium: 61.1
- Sugar: 17
- Total Carbohydrate: 25
- Cholesterol: 9.8
- Total Fat: 4
- Fiber: 1.4
- Protein: 1.4

107. Delicious Healthy Truffles

Serving: 12 truffles | Prep: 15mins | Ready in:

Ingredients

- 1/2 cup pitted prunes
- 1/4 cup pitted dates
- 2 tablespoons peanut butter
- 1 1/2 tablespoons maple syrup
- 3 tablespoons unsweetened cocoa
- 1/2 cup unsweetened flaked coconut

Direction

- Chop dates and prunes into small pieces, then squish together with a fork (use a sturdy, large bowl).
- Add peanut butter and maple syrup and mix together.
- Add cocoa and mix thoroughly.
- Roll mixture into bite-size pieces and roll in coconut to cover.
- Refrigerate and eat!

Nutrition Information

- Calories: 59.1
- Sugar: 4.4
- Total Carbohydrate: 6.5
- Protein: 1.3
- Total Fat: 3.8
- Saturated Fat: 2.4
- Fiber: 1.5
- Sodium: 14.1
- Cholesterol: 0

108. Dessert Lovers Sweet Rice

Serving: 4 serving(s) | Prep: 15mins | Ready in:

Ingredients

- 1 cup long-grain basmati rice, soaked for 2 hours in
- 4 drops pineapple essence
- 4 cups water, to cook the rice
- salt
- 2-3 cinnamon sticks
- 1 cup sugar
- 4 tablespoons ghee, melted
- 1/2 cup warm water
- 1 teaspoon yellow food coloring
- 1/2 teaspoon cardamom powder
- 4-5 saffron strands
- 1 tablespoon raisins
- 1 tablespoon pistachios, sliced
- 1 tablespoon almonds, blanched and thinly sliced
- 4-5 slices pineapple, for garnishing (optional)

Direction

- Pour 4 cups of water and 1/2 tsp. of salt in a skillet.
- Add cinnamon sticks.
- Bring to a boil.
- Lower flame, add rice and stir well.
- Parboil rice until half cooked.
- Strain well.
- Keep aside.
- In a pot, heat ghee on medium flame.
- Add raisins, pistachios and almonds.
- Stir-fry for 2 minutes.
- Add sugar, food color, pineapple essence and warm water.
- Stir until sugar dissolves.
- Add saffron and 1/2 to 1 tsp. of cardamom powder.
- Mix in the strained rice.
- Cover the pot with a lid.
- Cook on simmer for 10-15 minutes (your kitchen will smell wonderful while this is cooking!) or until the rice is dry and fluffy, stirring every 5 minutes so that the rice does not stick to the bottom of the pan.
- Transfer to a serving tray.
- Garnish with pineapple slices, if desired and serve.

Nutrition Information

- Calories: 508
- Saturated Fat: 8.4
- Cholesterol: 32.8
- Total Fat: 16.1
- Sodium: 16.2
- Fiber: 2.2
- Sugar: 52.1
- Total Carbohydrate: 88.8
- Protein: 4.7

109. Dimple Icing

Serving: 2 1/2 cups | Prep: 10mins | Ready in:

Ingredients

- 2 cups packed brown sugar
- 3/4 cup light cream
- 1 tablespoon butter
- 1 teaspoon vanilla

Direction

- Bring cream and sugar to boil.
- Cook for 8-10 min or until soft ball stage.
- Remove from heat.
- Add butter and vanilla.
- Beat just until spreadable.
- Spread on cake quickly before icing hardens.
- If you are having trouble and it is not turning thick and creamy add some icing sugar.

Nutrition Information

- Calories: 849.5
- Total Fat: 18.5
- Saturated Fat: 11.6
- Sodium: 130.3
- Fiber: 0
- Protein: 2
- Sugar: 169.7
- Total Carbohydrate: 174.2
- Cholesterol: 59.7

110. Dolly Parton's Green Tomato Cake

Serving: 1 cake, 12 serving(s) | Prep: 20mins | Ready in:

Ingredients

- 1 cup raisins
- hot water
- 3 cups all-purpose flour
- 1 teaspoon salt
- 1 teaspoon baking powder
- 1 teaspoon ground cinnamon
- 1/2 teaspoon ground nutmeg
- 2 1/4 cups granulated sugar
- 1 cup butter, melted
- 3 eggs
- 2 teaspoons vanilla extract
- 1 cup chopped walnuts
- 1 1/4 lbs green tomatoes, cored, seeded, and diced small
- 1 cup unsweetened flaked coconut
- Cream Cheese Frosting
- 1 lb chilled cream cheese (two 8-oz packages)
- 8 tablespoons butter, at room temperature
- 1 tablespoon vanilla extract
- 4 cups powdered sugar, sifted
- 1 pinch ground cinnamon, to taste

Direction

- Preheat oven to 350 degrees F. Butter two 9-inch cake pans and lightly dust them with flour.
- Place the raisins in a bowl and add hot water to cover; set aside. (Note from Julesong: you can use warm rum or other liquor, if you like.).
- Sift the flour into a medium bowl, then add the salt, baking powder, cinnamon, and nutmeg; stir to combine.
- In another large bowl, whisk together the sugar, melted butter, eggs, and vanilla. Gradually add the flour mixture, stirring, until a smooth batter forms.
- Drain the raisins in a sieve.
- Stir the walnuts, drained raisins, cored/diced tomatoes, and coconut flakes into the batter.
- Pour an equal amount of batter into each prepared cake pan and spread evenly with a spatula.
- Bake in preheated 350 degree F oven for about 60 minutes or until a toothpick inserted into center comes out clean. When done, remove from oven and let cake cool in pans on wire racks.

- When cake is cool to the touch, slide a knife or icing spatula around the inside rim of each pan to loosen edges and carefully flip the cake layers onto the wire racks to continue cooling. (You can use an inverted plate on top of the pan, flip, and carefully transfer to racks, if you like.).
- If you want to frost the cake, make the cream cheese frosting while layers are cooling.
- To make the frosting, in a medium bowl beat together the cream cheese and butter with an electric or hand mixer until well blended.
- Add the vanilla and beat until incorporated.
- Gradually add the powdered sugar while continuing to beat until smooth.
- Beat in cinnamon until incorporated. Use to frost the cake.
- To frost cake: when cake is completely cooled place one layer on serving plate and, using a spatula, frost all over with half the frosting. Place second layer on top. Frost second layer with remaining frosting.

Nutrition Information

- Calories: 932.2
- Total Carbohydrate: 117.8
- Cholesterol: 155.5
- Protein: 10.8
- Total Fat: 48.9
- Saturated Fat: 28
- Sodium: 528.5
- Fiber: 3.8
- Sugar: 87

111. Donut Pudding With Quick Easy Zabaglione

Serving: 1 Pan, 12 serving(s) | Prep: 15mins | Ready in:

Ingredients

- 16 plain doughnuts, stale
- 1/2 cup unsalted butter, at room temperature
- 1 cup sugar
- 5 large eggs, lightly beaten
- 2 cups light cream or 2 cups half-and-half
- 1 1/2 teaspoons cinnamon
- 1 tablespoon pure vanilla extract
- raisins

Direction

- Preheat oven to 350°. Lightly butter a 9 by 13-inch baking dish.
- In a food processor combine butter and sugar just until it forms into a ball. Add eggs, cream, cinnamon, and vanilla, and process until blended.
- Break the donuts into 1-inch pieces and spread them in the prepared pan. Scatter the raisins over the top, and pour the egg mixture over all.
- Set aside to soak for 5 to 10 minutes, pushing the donut pieces down into the custard to ensure even coverage.
- Cover with foil and bake 35 to 40 minutes. Remove foil and bake for additional 10 minutes to brown the top.
- Donut pudding is done when the custard is set, but still soft.
- For zabaglione:
- Microwave ice cream for 20 seconds. Stir with a wooden spoon to loosen and then stir in Marsala wine.
- Cut pudding into squares and serve topped with zabaglione.

Nutrition Information

- Calories: 567.2
- Sodium: 320
- Sugar: 36
- Protein: 8.9
- Total Fat: 35.7
- Saturated Fat: 15
- Fiber: 1.1
- Total Carbohydrate: 54.1
- Cholesterol: 139.7

112. Double Cherry Crumble

Serving: 8 serving(s) | Prep: 10mins | Ready in:

Ingredients

- 1 (21 ounce) can cherry pie filling
- 1 (16 ounce) canpitted dark sweet cherries, drained
- 2/3 cup quick oats
- 1/2 cup Bisquick baking mix
- 1/2 cup packed brown sugar
- 1/4 cup chopped nuts (optional)
- 1/4 cup butter or 1/4 cup margarine
- 1 teaspoon cinnamon

Direction

- Preheat oven to 375F degrees.
- Mix pie filling cherries in an ungreased 8x8 baking pan.
- Combine oats, baking mix, brown sugar, nuts, butter cinnamon until crumbly; sprinkle over fruit.
- Bake uncovered until fruit is hot bubbly, and topping is golden brown, approximately 45 minutes.

Nutrition Information

- Calories: 273.3
- Protein: 2.5
- Total Fat: 7.5
- Fiber: 2.3
- Total Carbohydrate: 50.4
- Sugar: 20
- Cholesterol: 15.4
- Saturated Fat: 4
- Sodium: 156.2

113. Double Frosted Bourbon Brownies

Serving: 16 brownies | Prep: 20mins | Ready in:

Ingredients

- 3/4 cup all-purpose flour
- 1/4 teaspoon baking soda
- 1/4 teaspoon salt
- 1/2 cup sugar
- 1/3 cup shortening
- 2 tablespoons water
- 1 cup semi-sweet chocolate bit
- 1 teaspoon vanilla extract
- 2 large eggs
- 1 1/2 cups of chopped walnuts
- 1/4 cup Bourbon
- WHITE FROSTING
- 1/2 cup butter or 1/2 cup margarine
- 1 teaspoon vanilla extract
- 2 cups of sifted powdered sugar
- CHOCOLATE GLAZE
- 1 cup semi-sweet chocolate bit
- 1 tablespoon shortening

Direction

- Combine the first 3 ingredients in medium bowl; set aside.
- Combine the sugar, shortening, and water in medium saucepan.
- Bring to a boil over medium heat stirring constantly.
- Once it boils, remove from heat, and add the chocolate morsels and the vanilla, stirring until smooth.
- Add the eggs one at a time, stirring after each addition.
- Stir in the flour mixture and walnuts; stir well.
- Spoon into 9-inch square pan. Bake at 350°F for 30 minutes.
- Sprinkle bourbon evenly over the warm brownies.
- Cool completely in pan.

- Spread the white frosting on the brownies and pour warm chocolate glaze over the icing. Let stand until set. Cut into squares.
- WHITE FROSTING: Combine the butter and vanilla in large mixing bowl. Beat at medium speed with mixer until creamy. Gradually add the sugar and beat until smooth.
- CHOCOLATE GLAZE: Combine the chocolate morsels and shortening in top of double broiler. Bring the water to a boil. Reduce heat to low and cook until chocolate morsels melt, stirring occasionally.

Nutrition Information

- Calories: 437.2
- Saturated Fat: 10.2
- Sugar: 36.2
- Protein: 4.4
- Total Fat: 26
- Sodium: 107.1
- Fiber: 2.8
- Total Carbohydrate: 45.8
- Cholesterol: 42.5

114. Double Banana Pound Cake

Serving: 18 serving(s) | Prep: 25mins | Ready in:

Ingredients

- cooking spray
- 3 tablespoons dry breadcrumbs
- 3 cups all-purpose flour
- 1 teaspoon baking powder
- 1/4 teaspoon salt
- 1/4 teaspoon ground mace
- 1 cup mashed ripe banana
- 1/2 cup nonfat milk
- 1/2 cup banana liqueur
- 3/4 cup butter or 1/2 cup margarine, softened
- 2 cups granulated sugar
- 1 1/2 teaspoons vanilla extract
- 3 large eggs
- 1 tablespoon powdered sugar

Direction

- Preheat oven to 350°F.
- Coat a 10-inch tube pan with cooking spray; dust with breadcrumbs.
- Lightly spoon the flour into dry measuring cups, and level with a knife.
- Combine the flour, baking powder, salt, and mace in a bowl, and stir well with a whisk. (Very important step - flour needs to be whisked.)
- Combine the mashed banana, milk, and banana liqueur in a bowl.
- Beat the butter in a large bowl at medium speed of a mixer until light and fluffy.
- Gradually add the granulated sugar and vanilla extract, and beat the mixture until well-blended.
- Add the eggs, 1 at a time, beating well after each addition.
- Add the flour mixture to the sugar mixture alternately with the banana mixture, beating at low speed, beginning and ending with the flour mixture.
- Spoon the batter into prepared pan.
- Bake cake at 350° for 1 hour or until a wooden pick inserted in center comes out clean.
- Cool in pan 10 minutes on a wire rack; remove from pan.
- Cool completely on wire rack.
- Sift powdered sugar over top of cake.
- Note: To freeze extra pound cake, let cake cool completely on a wire rack; then cut into individual slices. Place unglazed slices in a heavy-duty zip-top plastic bag. Remove excess air from the bag; then seal and place it in your freezer for up to four months. To thaw, let it stand at room temperature.
- Note: You can use a 12 cup Bundt pan instead of the 10-inch tube pan. Just reduce the oven temperature to 325°.

Nutrition Information

- Calories: 259
- Total Fat: 8.8
- Protein: 3.8
- Saturated Fat: 5.2
- Sodium: 130.8
- Fiber: 0.8
- Sugar: 24.2
- Total Carbohydrate: 41.8
- Cholesterol: 55.7

115. Double Dark Mocha Drops

Serving: 4 1/2 dozen cookies, 54 serving(s) | Prep: 10mins | Ready in:

Ingredients

- 1/2 cup butter
- 1/3 cup granulated sugar
- 1/4 cup light brown sugar
- 1/2 teaspoon baking soda
- 1/2 teaspoon salt
- 1 tablespoon espresso powder
- 1/4 cup unsweetened dutch cocoa (or Dutch-process cocoa)
- 1 large egg
- 1 teaspoon vanilla
- 1 1/4 cups all-purpose flour
- 2 cups cappuccino chips (or a mixture) or 2 cups cinnamon baking chips (or a mixture) or 2 cups chocolate chips (or a mixture)

Direction

- Preheat the oven to 375°F Lightly grease two baking sheets, or line with parchment.
- Combine the butter, sugars, baking soda, salt, and espresso powder in a mixing bowl.
- Beat until the mixture is smooth.
- Add the egg and vanilla, and again beat till thoroughly combined. The mixture will look a bit grainy; that's OK.
- Beat in the cocoa.
- Add the flour, beating slowly to combine.
- Add the chips, mixing till they're well-distributed.
- Drop the dough by teaspoonfuls onto the prepared baking sheets. A teaspoon scoop works very well here. If the dough begins to stick, simply dip the scoop in cold water. Space the cookies at least 1" apart.
- Bake the cookies for 8 minutes; the cookies should seem barely done. If you attempt to pick an oven-hot cookie off the baking sheet, it'll fall apart.
- Allow the cookies to cool right on the baking sheet.

Nutrition Information

- Calories: 36.9
- Total Fat: 1.9
- Saturated Fat: 1.1
- Sugar: 2.2
- Total Carbohydrate: 4.7
- Protein: 0.5
- Sodium: 47.1
- Fiber: 0.2
- Cholesterol: 8.4

116. Dreamsicle Jello Salad

Serving: 10-12 serving(s) | Prep: 10mins | Ready in:

Ingredients

- 2 (3 ounce) packages instant vanilla pudding
- 1 (3 ounce) package orange Jell-O
- 1 1/2 cups boiling water
- 1 (22 ounce) can mandarin oranges (with juice)
- 1 (16 ounce) container Cool Whip

Direction

- Combine the pudding, Jell-O and boiling water and dissolve completely.

- Add the Mandarin Oranges (with juice).
- Fold in the Cool Whip.

Nutrition Information

- Calories: 273.8
- Saturated Fat: 10
- Fiber: 1.1
- Total Carbohydrate: 42.3
- Protein: 1.7
- Total Fat: 11.8
- Sodium: 298.1
- Sugar: 40.2
- Cholesterol: 0

117. Dump Cake (Only 3 Ingredients!)

Serving: 12-16 serving(s) | Prep: 3mins | Ready in:

Ingredients

- 2 (20 ounce) cans cherry pie filling
- 1 (18 1/2 ounce) box chocolate cake mix or 1 (18 1/2 ounce) box devil's food cake mix, unprepared
- 3/4 cup butter, melted

Direction

- Preheat oven to 350 degrees.
- Dump cherry pie filling into 13 x 9 inch cake pan.
- Spread out evenly in pan.
- Sprinkle cake mix evenly over filling.
- Drizzle butter over top.
- Bake for 1 hour.
- Serve in pan.

Nutrition Information

- Calories: 397.8
- Cholesterol: 30.5
- Protein: 3
- Total Carbohydrate: 58.4
- Total Fat: 18.4
- Saturated Fat: 8.7
- Sodium: 479.5
- Fiber: 1.6
- Sugar: 16.8

118. Eagle Brand Chocolate Sheet Cake

Serving: 16 serving(s) | Prep: 20mins | Ready in:

Ingredients

- 1 1/4 cups margarine or 1 1/4 cups butter
- 1/2 cup unsweetened cocoa
- 1 cup water
- 2 cups all-purpose flour
- 1 1/2 cups firmly packed brown sugar
- 1 teaspoon baking soda
- 1 teaspoon ground cinnamon
- 1/2 teaspoon salt
- 1 (14 ounce) caneagle brand sweetened condensed milk (Not evaporated milk)
- 2 eggs
- 1 cup coarsely chopped nuts
- 1 teaspoon vanilla extract
- 1 cup confectioners' sugar

Direction

- Preheat oven to 350. In small saucepan, melt 1 cup margarine; stir in 1/4 cup cocoa, then add water. Bring to a boil; remove from heat.
- In large mixing bowl combine flour, brown sugar, baking soda, cinnamon and salt. Add cocoa mixture; beat well. Stir in 1/3 cup Eagle Brand, eggs and vanilla.
- Pour into greased 15x10 inch jellyroll pan. Bake 15 minutes or until cake springs back when lightly touched.
- In small saucepan melt remaining 1/4 cup margarine; add remaining 1/4 cup cocoa and remaining Eagle Brand. Stir in confectioners' sugar and nuts. Spread on warm cake.

- (CHOCOLATE MOCHA SHEET CAKE: Add 1 tablespoon instant coffee with cocoa to cake; add 1 tablespoon instant coffee with cocoa to frosting.).

Nutrition Information

- Calories: 437.5
- Sugar: 41.2
- Cholesterol: 34.9
- Sodium: 424.4
- Fiber: 2.2
- Total Carbohydrate: 57
- Protein: 6.5
- Total Fat: 21.9
- Saturated Fat: 4.9

119. Easter Nests With Jelly Bean Eggs (Peanut Free)

Serving: 20 nests | Prep: 10mins | Ready in:

Ingredients

- 5 cups chow mein noodles
- 2 cups chocolate chips
- 1/2 cup Skor English toffee bit
- 1/2 cup sugar
- 1/2 cup golden syrup
- 60 jelly beans

Direction

- Break chow mein noodles into small pieces in a bowl.
- Place chocolate chips, skor bits, sugar and corn syrup in a pot and melt on low heat until thoroughly melted, combined and smooth.
- Pour mixture over noodles and toss until completely coated.
- Let cool very slightly until you are able to work with mixture, don't let it sit too long or it will harden too much to shape.
- In the palm of your hand, shape mixture into a small ball and press an indentation in the center of each ball so they look like bird's nests.
- Place each nest in a small muffin cup and let cool completely.
- Place three jelly beans in each nest.
- If desired, serve on a bed of green-tinted coconut for extra festive look.

Nutrition Information

- Calories: 176.5
- Saturated Fat: 3.7
- Sodium: 23.8
- Total Carbohydrate: 32.5
- Cholesterol: 2.1
- Protein: 0.8
- Total Fat: 6.3
- Fiber: 1.1
- Sugar: 24.6

120. Easy Ambrosia Parfait

Serving: 10 serving(s) | Prep: 10mins | Ready in:

Ingredients

- 1 (14 ounce) can pineapple chunks, drained
- 2 (6 ounce) cans mandarin oranges, drained
- 2 apples, cored and cut into chunks
- 2 pears, cored and cut into chunks
- 1 1/2 cups red grapes (go for seedless)
- 1 cup blueberries
- 2 cups frozen whipped topping, thawed (I use real whipped cream)
- 1 (2 ounce) jar marshmallow cream
- 1 cup shredded sweetened coconut

Direction

- In a large bowl, toss the pineapple chunks, mandarin oranges, apple and pear chunks, grapes and blueberries together.

- In a separate bowl, whisk the whipped cream into the marshmallow cream.
- Spoon 2 tablespoons of fruit into the bottom of 10 parfait glasses.
- Add the whipped marshmallow mixture and sprinkle with coconut.
- Keep repeating layers until the glass is full.

Nutrition Information

- Calories: 201.3
- Fiber: 3.5
- Saturated Fat: 5.4
- Sodium: 29.5
- Sugar: 29.9
- Total Carbohydrate: 37.6
- Cholesterol: 0
- Protein: 1.4
- Total Fat: 6.5

121. Easy Butterscotch Chip Chocolate Cookies

Serving: 36-42 cookies | Prep: 10mins | Ready in:

Ingredients

- 1 (18 1/2 ounce) package chocolate cake mix
- 1/2 cup vegetable oil
- 2 large eggs
- 2 cups butterscotch chips
- 1/2 cup chopped pecans

Direction

- Combine cake mix, oil and eggs in large bowl.
- Stir in chips and pecans.
- Chill for about an hour.
- Preheat oven to 350°.
- Roll dough into 1" balls and place on ungreased cookie sheets.
- Bake for 8-10 minutes or until centers are just about set.
- Let stand for a minute or so and remove to wire racks.

Nutrition Information

- Calories: 154.6
- Total Fat: 9.4
- Sodium: 132.5
- Cholesterol: 11.8
- Protein: 1.6
- Saturated Fat: 3.3
- Fiber: 0.5
- Sugar: 12
- Total Carbohydrate: 17.2

122. Easy Chocolate Chip Oatmeal Cookies

Serving: 50 cookies | Prep: 15mins | Ready in:

Ingredients

- 1 cup margarine or 1 cup butter
- 3/4 cup brown sugar
- 1/4 cup white sugar
- 1 teaspoon vanilla
- 1 1/2 cups flour
- 1/3 cup water
- 1 teaspoon baking soda
- 2 cups oats
- 1 cup chocolate chips

Direction

- Cream together butter and sugar in a bowl, then mix in vanilla.
- Add flour and mix well.
- Mix together baking soda and water, and then add to the batter.
- Stir in the oats and chocolate chips.
- Drop by spoonfuls onto a cookie sheet (no need to grease it), and bake at 350° for 12-15 minutes.

Nutrition Information

- Calories: 103.1
- Total Fat: 5.1
- Saturated Fat: 1.4
- Cholesterol: 0
- Protein: 1.6
- Sodium: 69.3
- Fiber: 1
- Sugar: 6
- Total Carbohydrate: 13.4

123. Easy Chocolate Dipped Apricots (Apricot Chanukah Gelt)

Serving: 48 pieces | Prep: 30mins | Ready in:

Ingredients

- 1 lb dried apricot
- 1 lb bittersweet chocolate, chopped
- aluminum foil, candy wrappers (optional)

Direction

- Line two baking sheets with parchment paper.
- Heat chocolate over a double-boiler. Allow the water in the boiler to get hot but not fully boil. Use a plastic spatula to scrape chocolate away from the sides. Remove from heat as soon as the chocolate is melted. If you prefer to use a microwave, melt the chocolate in a glass bowl in short intervals, stirring well with spatula.
- Immediately add all the apricots to the pot melted chocolate, and stir gently until they are all coated fully. Carefully lift each piece out of the pot with a fork, allowing some of the excess chocolate to drip off. For a more sophisticated look, you can also try holding each apricot by one end with your fingers and dipping only half of it into the chocolate.
- Place carefully on parchment-lined baking sheet. Refrigerate until the chocolate has become firm (20-30 minutes). Optionally, you can wrap individually in foil wrappers to give as gifts. Store in the refrigerator - If refrigerated, they can last up to a week (though they are best if eaten within 3 days).

Nutrition Information

- Calories: 22.8
- Cholesterol: 0
- Sodium: 0.9
- Fiber: 0.7
- Total Carbohydrate: 5.9
- Protein: 0.3
- Total Fat: 0.1
- Saturated Fat: 0
- Sugar: 5.1

124. Easy Lemon Pudding

Serving: 6 serving(s) | Prep: 6mins | Ready in:

Ingredients

- 2/3 cup sugar
- 1 1/3 cups water
- 5 teaspoons cornstarch
- 1/4 cup lemon juice
- 1/4 teaspoon lemon extract
- 1/4 teaspoon salt
- 3 egg yolks

Direction

- On med-hi heat, bring sugar and water to a boil.
- Mix cornstarch, lemon juice and lemon extract.
- Stir into boiling mixture.
- Beat the egg yolks and stir about 1/4 cup of the hot mixture into them.
- Quickly stir this into the hot mix.
- Spoon into dessert cups.
- Chill.
- If you prefer you can put the mix into a baked pie shell, and cover with meringue.

Nutrition Information

- Calories: 122.2
- Total Fat: 2.1
- Fiber: 0.1
- Sugar: 22.6
- Cholesterol: 83
- Protein: 1.2
- Saturated Fat: 0.7
- Sodium: 102.7
- Total Carbohydrate: 25.3

125. Easy Rhubarb Upside Down Cake

Serving: 1 9x13 cake, 12 serving(s) | Prep: 20mins | Ready in:

Ingredients

- 1 (18 ounce) package lemon cake mix or 1 (18 ounce) package white cake mix
- 3 eggs (or as called for by your cake mix) or 3 egg whites (or as called for by your cake mix)
- 1/3 cup oil (or as called for by your cake mix)
- 1 teaspoon lemon extract
- 1 1/3 cups water (or as called for by your cake mix)
- 4 cups rhubarb, cut up 1/2 inch pieces
- 6 teaspoons minute tapioca
- 1 1/2 cups sugar
- 1 (3 ounce) package strawberry Jell-O gelatin dessert or 1 (3 ounce) package raspberry Jell-O gelatin

Direction

- Preheat oven to 350 degrees.
- Grease 9x13inch pan.
- Mix together Rhubarb, tapioca, sugar and package of DRY Jell-O (NO WATER) and pour into prepared pan.
- Prepare cake mix according to package directions (adding the lemon extract to the wet ingredients) and pour over Rhubarb mixture.
- Bake 1 hour.
- Serve with whipped cream or ice cream.

Nutrition Information

- Calories: 396.2
- Total Fat: 12.3
- Sodium: 343.3
- Saturated Fat: 1.9
- Fiber: 1.2
- Sugar: 51.4
- Total Carbohydrate: 68.6
- Cholesterol: 47.4
- Protein: 4.4

126. Easy Rocky Road Brownies

Serving: 12 brownies, 12 serving(s) | Prep: 15mins | Ready in:

Ingredients

- 1 (16 ounce) package refrigerated brownie bar dough, NESTLE TOLL HOUSE Refrigerated Mini Brownie Bites Bar Dough
- 1/2 cup semisweet chocolate morsel, divided
- 1 cup miniature marshmallow
- 1/4-1/2 cup walnuts, chopped

Direction

- PREHEAT oven to 350°F Grease 8-inch-square baking pan.
- PLACE whole brownie bar in prepared pan. Allow to soften for 5 to 10 minutes. Using fingertips, pat dough gently to fill pan.
- BAKE for 24 to 26 minutes or until wooden pick inserted in centre comes out slightly sticky.

- SPRINKLE 1/4 cup morsels over hot brownie. Let stand for 5 minutes or until morsels are shiny; spread evenly over brownie. Top with marshmallows, remaining morsels and nuts; press down lightly.
- BAKE for an additional 5 minutes or just until marshmallows just begin to puff. Cool in pan on wire rack for 20 to 30 minutes. Cut into bars with wet knife. Serve warm.

Nutrition Information

- Calories: 78.2
- Total Carbohydrate: 10
- Cholesterol: 0.3
- Saturated Fat: 1.6
- Sodium: 3.7
- Fiber: 0.8
- Sugar: 7.5
- Protein: 0.9
- Total Fat: 4.1

127. Easy Snickers Bar Pie

Serving: 2 pies, 16 serving(s) | Prep: 10mins | Ready in:

Ingredients

- 8 ounces cream cheese, softened
- 1 1/2 cups powdered sugar
- 1/2 cup creamy peanut butter or 1/2 cup chunky peanut butter
- 3 regular sized Snickers candy bars, chopped
- 16 ounces Cool Whip, thawed
- 2 (6 ounce) chocolate cookie pie crust or 2 (6 ounce) graham cracker pie crust

Direction

- In a large mixing bowl, beat cream cheese, sugar and peanut butter until creamy.
- Stir in chopped candy bars.
- Gently fold in the Cool Whip just until mixed.
- Pour into crusts and refrigerate overnight.

Nutrition Information

- Calories: 390.8
- Saturated Fat: 12.2
- Sodium: 259.4
- Total Fat: 25.3
- Fiber: 1.1
- Sugar: 28.9
- Total Carbohydrate: 38.1
- Cholesterol: 17.2
- Protein: 5.1

128. Edinburgh Gingerbread

Serving: 1 gingerbread loaf, 8 serving(s) | Prep: 10mins | Ready in:

Ingredients

- 8 ounces plain flour
- 1 teaspoon baking soda
- 2 teaspoons ground ginger
- 1 teaspoon cinnamon
- 1 pinch salt
- 6 ounces unsalted butter
- 6 ounces molasses
- 4 ounces packed brown sugar
- 6 tablespoons milk
- 2 large eggs
- 2 ounces sultanas (golden raisins)
- 2 ounces almonds, flaked

Direction

- Sift the flour, spices, salt and baking soda, and then stir in the fruit and nuts.
- Melt the butter with the molasses and sugar on a low heat.
- The mixture should remain somewhat cool but the sugar should be dissolved.
- Add the milk and stir in the eggs.

- Pour the warm mixture into a well in the centre of the dry ingredients and mix thoroughly to form a batter.
- Pour into a greased and lined 2 lb loaf tin.
- Bake at 325°F/160°C/gas mark 3 for 1¼ hours.
- This is a fairly heavy recipe and may sink on cooling.

Nutrition Information

- Calories: 471
- Saturated Fat: 11.9
- Sodium: 242.7
- Fiber: 2.2
- Sugar: 30.2
- Total Fat: 23.3
- Total Carbohydrate: 60.9
- Cholesterol: 100.2
- Protein: 7.2

129. Elsie's Pineapple Oatmeal Bars

Serving: 24 serving(s) | Prep: 15mins | Ready in:

Ingredients

- 1 (20 ounce) can crushed pineapple (Do NOT drain)
- 1 cup sugar
- 3 1/2 tablespoons cornstarch
- 1 3/4 cups oatmeal
- 1/4 teaspoon salt
- 1 cup brown sugar
- 1 1/2 cups flour
- 1 teaspoon baking powder
- 3/4 cup butter or 3/4 cup margarine, softened

Direction

- For the filling, combine the sugar and cornstarch in a saucepan and mix well. Add the pineapple and its juice, and cook over medium heat until thickened, stirring constantly. Cool.
- For the crust, combine oatmeal, salt, brown sugar, flour, and baking powder together. Work in butter until mixture is uniform.
- Reserve 1 1/4 cup of crumb mixture, and press the rest into an ungreased 9 x 13 pan, working up edges just slightly to help hold filling off of the edge of the pan.
- Pour filling over oatmeal mixture and spread evenly.
- Sprinkle reserved crumbs evenly over filling.
- Bake at 350 for 20 minutes. Cool and cut into bars.

Nutrition Information

- Calories: 187.5
- Sugar: 20.7
- Total Carbohydrate: 32.1
- Cholesterol: 15.2
- Saturated Fat: 3.7
- Fiber: 1
- Protein: 1.8
- Total Fat: 6.2
- Sodium: 93.5

130. Emz Luscious Lemon Slice

Serving: 6-8 serving(s) | Prep: 15mins | Ready in:

Ingredients

- for the base
- 125 g flour
- 90 g sugar
- 75 g butter, cold and chopped into small pieces
- 1 1/2 teaspoons lemon zest
- for the filling
- 4 eggs
- 225 g sugar
- 1/2-3/4 cup lemon juice, freshly squeezed

- 2 tablespoons flour

Direction

- To make the base put all base ingredients in a food processor and wizz until the mixture forms a ball.
- Roll out and press into the base of a 23cm buttered springfoam tin.
- Bake at 180 degrees C for about 20 mins until just turning golden.
- Meanwhile, for the filling, beat together the eggs and sugar until creamy.
- Fold in the lemon juice and flour.
- Pour this mixture over the crust and bake at 180 degrees C for a further 15 minutes.
- Lower the heat to 150 degrees C and bake for a further 30 mins, until the lemon mix is set.
- Cool and dust with icing sugar.
- Enjoy!

Nutrition Information

- Calories: 431.9
- Sugar: 53.3
- Total Carbohydrate: 72.5
- Saturated Fat: 7.5
- Sodium: 118.9
- Fiber: 0.8
- Cholesterol: 167.7
- Protein: 6.8
- Total Fat: 13.6

131. English Blackberry Cobbler

Serving: 1 yummy pie, 6 serving(s) | Prep: 25mins | Ready in:

Ingredients

- 2 lbs blackberries, washed and sorted
- 4 ounces sugar
- 1 tablespoon plain flour
- 1/2 lb self raising flour
- 3 ounces granulated sugar, plus extra for sprinkling
- 2 ounces butter
- 1 egg
- milk, to mix

Direction

- First put the fruit in a large pie dish with the sugar mixed with the tablespoon of plain flour.
- Cover with foil and bake in a very slow oven until the juice runs and the fruit is tender.
- Then take it out of the oven and turn up the heat to 220°C/ 425°F/ Gas Mark 7.
- Sieve the self-rising flour and the granulated sugar together.
- Rub in the butter.
- Add the beaten egg and a little milk and mix to a light dough.
- Roll out to fit the pie dish, and then cut squares about 4 cm (1½ inches) across.
- Place these on top of the fruit, put the whole dish in the oven and bake for 10 minutes.
- Sprinkle the top with granulated sugar and bake for a further 5 minutes at 190°C/ 375°F/ Gas Mark 5.

Nutrition Information

- Calories: 415
- Total Fat: 9.6
- Sugar: 40.5
- Total Carbohydrate: 77.5
- Protein: 7.3
- Saturated Fat: 5.2
- Sodium: 81.9
- Fiber: 9.1
- Cholesterol: 51.3

132. FUDGY Peanut Butter Bars

Serving: 36 bars | Prep: 20mins | Ready in:

Ingredients

- Crust
- 1 1/2 cups flour
- 3/4 cup finely chopped dry roasted peanuts
- 1/2 cup packed brown sugar
- 1/2 cup butter, softened
- Topping
- 2 cups semi-sweet chocolate chips
- 3/4 cup creamy peanut butter or 3/4 cup chunky peanut butter
- 1/3 cup powdered sugar

Direction

- Combine flour, peanuts, brown sugar and butter in ungreased 13 x 9 inch pan; press into bottom of pan.
- Bake in 375 degree oven for 10 to 12 minutes until light brown around edges.
- Melt chips and peanut butter together until smooth.
- Add powdered sugar and stir vigorously until smooth.
- Spread over hot cookie base.
- Chill just until chocolate is no longer shiny and cut into bars.
- Serve at room temperature.

Nutrition Information

- Calories: 161.3
- Sugar: 9.8
- Total Carbohydrate: 16
- Total Fat: 10.5
- Saturated Fat: 4.2
- Sodium: 83.6
- Fiber: 1.4
- Cholesterol: 6.8
- Protein: 3.4

133. Fabulous Fat Free Pineapple Cake

Serving: 12 serving(s) | Prep: 20mins | Ready in:

Ingredients

- CAKE
- 4 egg whites or 1/2 cup egg substitute
- 2 cups sugar
- 2 cups flour
- 2 teaspoons baking soda
- 1 (20 ounce) can crushed pineapple, undrained
- 1 teaspoon vanilla extract
- FROSTING
- 1 (8 ounce) package fat free cream cheese, softened
- 1 1/2 cups confectioners' sugar
- 1/4 teaspoon vanilla extract

Direction

- Preheat oven to 350°F
- Spray 13 x 9 x 2-inch baking pan with nonstick cooking spray.
- CAKE: Beat egg whites and sugar until blended.
- In another bowl, combine flour and baking soda.
- Beat into wet ingredients.
- Add pineapple and vanilla extract.
- Pour batter into prepared pan.
- Bake for 40 minutes, or until it tests done when a toothpick inserted in the center comes out clean.
- Cool for 10 minutes.
- FROSTING: Gradually whisk in confectioners' sugar into cream cheese and vanilla.
- Frost cake with a knife, or by pouring it on if the frosting is thin.

Nutrition Information

- Calories: 318.4
- Sodium: 362.3

- Total Carbohydrate: 73.2
- Protein: 6.5
- Total Fat: 0.5
- Saturated Fat: 0.2
- Fiber: 0.9
- Sugar: 56
- Cholesterol: 2.3

134. Fantasy Ribbon Fudge

Serving: 1 pan, 16-20 serving(s) | Prep: 10mins | Ready in:

Ingredients

- 1 (7 ounce) jar marshmallow cream
- 1 (11 1/2 ounce) package chocolate chips
- 2/3 cup unsweetened evaporated milk
- 3/4 cup peanut butter
- 2 teaspoons vanilla
- 3 cups sugar
- 12 tablespoons butter

Direction

- Mix 1 1/2 cups sugar, 1/3 cup milk, and 6 tablespoons of butter in pan, stirring on medium heat to boil. Reduce heat to med-low, set timer for 4 minutes stir continuously.
- Immediately remove from heat and add 1 teaspoon vanilla and quickly add 1/2 jar of marshmallow.
- Add 3/4 bag of chocolate chips; mix vigorously until creamy and there are no hints of marshmallow.
- Pour into 9 x 13-inch pan for thin fudge and an 8x8 pan for thick fudge.
- Repeat instructions listed, adding the peanut butter, in place of the chocolate chips.
- Pour over chocolate fudge let cool completely and keep refrigerated.
- Hint: Make sure that your butter, sugar, milk are at a rolling boil before setting your timer.
- Add vanilla, fluff, then the chips or peanut butter in that order.

- And, share.

Nutrition Information

- Calories: 445.7
- Total Fat: 21.7
- Sugar: 55.6
- Protein: 4.8
- Cholesterol: 25.9
- Saturated Fat: 10.8
- Sodium: 140.2
- Fiber: 1.9
- Total Carbohydrate: 63.6

135. Fast, Easy Apple Cobbler

Serving: 1 cobbler, 6 serving(s) | Prep: 10mins | Ready in:

Ingredients

- 20 ounces apple pie filling
- 1 cup baking mix (Bisquick or other)
- 2 tablespoons all-purpose flour
- 1 teaspoon baking powder (fresh!)
- 3 tablespoons sugar, divided
- 1 egg, beaten
- 1/2 teaspoon salt
- 7/8 cup whole milk
- 1/2 teaspoon canola oil
- 1/2 teaspoon vanilla extract
- cooking spray

Direction

- Preheat the oven to 350-degrees F.
- In a mixing bowl, whisk together the baking mix, the flour, baking powder, 2 tablespoons of the sugar, the beaten egg, the salt, the canola oil, the vanilla, and the milk. The batter will be pretty thin.
- Spray a 9" x 9" baking dish with the cooking spray and spread the apple pie filling in the bottom. Pour the batter over it and place into the preheated oven.

- After 25 minutes, remove the cobbler from the oven and sprinkle the remaining sugar (1 tablespoon) and the cinnamon over the top. Return it to the oven right away and bake for 15-20 more minutes until it is light brown on top. You can test the top with a toothpick at the end of this time to see if it comes out clean. If so, it's done. If not, bake for a few more minutes.
- NOTE: You can also substitute cherry or blueberry pie filling for this recipe!

Nutrition Information

- Calories: 253.6
- Sodium: 577.4
- Cholesterol: 39.2
- Protein: 4.2
- Total Fat: 5.6
- Saturated Fat: 1.8
- Fiber: 1.4
- Sugar: 23.8
- Total Carbohydrate: 47.7

136. Fat Free Gingersnaps

Serving: 8 serving(s) | Prep: 5mins | Ready in:

Ingredients

- 3/4 cup applesauce
- 1 teaspoon cinnamon
- 1 cup brown sugar
- 1/2 teaspoon clove
- 1 egg
- 1/4 cup molasses
- 2 cups flour
- 2 teaspoons baking soda
- 1/2 teaspoon salt
- 1 teaspoon ginger

Direction

- Spray cookie sheet with Pam cooking spray.
- Bake at 375* for 10 minutes.

Nutrition Information

- Calories: 277.3
- Sodium: 491.1
- Sugar: 32.5
- Total Carbohydrate: 63.8
- Cholesterol: 26.4
- Total Fat: 1
- Fiber: 1.4
- Protein: 4.1
- Saturated Fat: 0.3

137. Five Flavor Pound Cake

Serving: 1 Bundt cake, 12 serving(s) | Prep: 20mins | Ready in:

Ingredients

- Cake
- 1 cup butter, softened
- 1/2 cup shortening
- 3 cups granulated sugar
- 5 eggs, beaten
- 3 cups all-purpose flour
- 1/2 teaspoon baking powder
- 1 pinch salt
- 1 cup milk
- 1 teaspoon coconut extract
- 1 teaspoon lemon extract
- 1 teaspoon rum extract
- 1 teaspoon butter flavor extract
- 1 teaspoon vanilla extract
- Glaze
- 1/2 cup white sugar
- 1/4 cup water
- 1/2 teaspoon coconut extract
- 1/2 teaspoon rum extract
- 1/2 teaspoon butter flavor extract
- 1/2 teaspoon lemon extract
- 1/2 teaspoon vanilla extract

Direction

- Preheat oven to 325°F.
- Grease a 10-inch tube or Bundt cake pan.
- In small bowl, combine flour, baking powder and salt; set aside.
- In a measuring cup, combine the milk and 1 teaspoon of each of the 5 extracts; set aside.
- In mixing bowl, cream butter, shortening and 3 cups of sugar until light and fluffy.
- Add eggs one at a time and beat until smooth.
- Beat in flour mixture alternately with milk mixture, beginning and ending with flour mixture.
- Spoon mixture into prepared pan.
- Bake for 1 1/2 hours, or until cake tests done.
- Let cake cool for 5 minutes and then pour 1/2 of glaze over cake (while still in pan).
- Let sit for another 5 minutes and then turn cake out of pan onto wire rack (with waxed paper under rack to catch drippings).
- Slowly spoon remaining glaze onto top of hot cake.
- Cool completely before serving.
- To make the Five Flavor Glaze: In saucepan, combine 1/2 cup sugar, water and 1/2 teaspoon of each of the 5 extracts.
- Bring to a boil, stirring until sugar is dissolved.
- Variations: Six Flavor Cake/Glaze: Add 1 teaspoon of almond extract to Five Flavor Cake ingredients and 1/2 teaspoon almond extract to Five Flavor Glaze ingredients.
- Seven Flavor Cake/Glaze: Add 1 teaspoon pineapple flavored extract to Six Flavor Cake and 1/2 teaspoon pineapple flavored extract to Six Flavor Glaze.

Nutrition Information

- Calories: 600.6
- Cholesterol: 121
- Total Fat: 26.9
- Sugar: 58.6
- Total Carbohydrate: 83.5
- Protein: 6.7
- Saturated Fat: 13
- Sodium: 204.2
- Fiber: 0.8

138. Fresh Peach Crumble

Serving: 10 serving(s) | Prep: 12mins | Ready in:

Ingredients

- 6 cups peeled sliced ripe peaches
- 1/4 cup packed brown sugar
- 3 tablespoons flour
- 1 teaspoon lemon juice
- 1/2 teaspoon lemon zest, grated
- 1 teaspoon cinnamon
- TOPPING
- 1 cup flour
- 1 cup sugar
- 1 teaspoon baking powder
- 1/4 teaspoon salt
- 1/4 teaspoon nutmeg
- 1 egg, beaten
- 1/2 cup butter, melted and cooled

Direction

- Heat oven to 375*.
- Put peach slices in greased, shallow 11x7 baking dish.
- Mix brown sugar, flour, lemon juice, peel, and cinnamon.
- Sprinkle over the peaches.
- Mix flour, sugar, baking powder, salt, and nutmeg.
- Stir in egg until mixture is coarse crumbs.
- Sprinkle over peaches.
- Drizzle butter evenly over topping.
- Bake for 38 minutes.

Nutrition Information

- Calories: 278.2
- Total Carbohydrate: 46
- Cholesterol: 43

- Total Fat: 10.1
- Saturated Fat: 6
- Sodium: 184.7
- Fiber: 1.9
- Sugar: 33.1
- Protein: 3.1

139. Fruit Custard Pizza

Serving: 12 serving(s) | Prep: 30mins | Ready in:

Ingredients

- 1/2 cup cream-style cottage cheese, small curd
- 1/4 cup butter or 1/4 cup margarine, softened
- 1 cup all-purpose flour
- 1/2 cup quick-cooking rolled oats
- 1 teaspoon finely shredded lemon, rind of
- 1/4 teaspoon salt
- 1 (2 1/8 ounce) envelope vanilla pudding mix
- 2 cups milk
- 1/2 cup apricot jam
- 1 banana, sliced
- 1 small orange, peeled and sectioned
- 1 (8 1/4 ounce) can pineapple slices, drained
- 1 (8 3/4 ounce) can peach slices, drained

Direction

- In bowl combine cottage cheese and butter and beat till smoothen and well blended.
- In large bowl stir together flour, rolled oats, lemon peel and salt.
- Add cottage cheese mixture to dry ingredients and mix well.
- Form into ball and with hands, press evenly into greased 12 inch pizza pan, forming rim about 1/2 inch above edge; crimp edge.
- Bake in 400 degree oven for 15 to 20 minutes; cool.
- In saucepan prepare pudding mix according to pkg., using the 2 cups milk.
- Cover surface with clear plastic wrap and chill.
- Spread in prepared crust.
- Heat jam till melted.
- Arrange fruit atop pudding; brush with melted jam.
- Chill.

Nutrition Information

- Calories: 193.3
- Saturated Fat: 3.7
- Fiber: 1.4
- Sugar: 12.8
- Total Carbohydrate: 31.4
- Protein: 4.5
- Total Fat: 6.2
- Sodium: 174.7
- Cholesterol: 17.2

140. Fruit Jello Delight

Serving: 4 serving(s) | Prep: 10mins | Ready in:

Ingredients

- 1 (5/8 ounce) package Jello gelatin (sugar-free, any flavor)
- 1 cup boiling water
- 1 cup cold water
- 1 banana (chopped)
- 1 apple (diced or chopped)
- 1 cup grapes (or any other small fruit of your choice)

Direction

- Boil the one cup of water and add it to the Jello in a bowl or container.
- Stir for about 2 minutes, until completely dissolved.
- Add one cup cold water, stir.
- Put 1 cup chopped banana into bottom of the bowl.
- Chill in refrigerator for about 1-2 hours, or until a thick jelly-like consistency.
- Add other fruit into Jello, spread evenly.

- Place back into refrigerator for about 2-3 more hours.
- Enjoy!

Nutrition Information

- Calories: 92.2
- Protein: 1
- Fiber: 2.2
- Sugar: 17.8
- Saturated Fat: 0.1
- Sodium: 24.9
- Total Carbohydrate: 23.7
- Cholesterol: 0
- Total Fat: 0.2

141. Fruit Salad For A Crowd

Serving: 20 serving(s) | Prep: 15mins | Ready in:

Ingredients

- 4 medium golden delicious apples, unpeeled, diced
- 4 medium Red Delicious apples, unpeeled, diced
- 2 cups green seedless grapes, halved
- 2 cups red seedless grapes, halved
- 1 (20 ounce) can pineapple chunks, drained
- 1 (11 ounce) can mandarin oranges, drained
- Dressing
- 1 (3 ounce) package cream cheese, softened
- ½ cup sour cream
- ½ cup mayonnaise
- ½ cup sugar

Direction

- Combine all the fruit in a large bowl.
- In a mixing bowl, beat dressing ingredients until smooth.
- Pour over fruit; toss gently to coat.
- Serve immediately.

Nutrition Information

- Calories: 129
- Fiber: 2.5
- Sugar: 23.3
- Cholesterol: 7.7
- Protein: 1
- Saturated Fat: 1.5
- Sodium: 20.2
- Total Fat: 2.8
- Total Carbohydrate: 27.4

142. Fruity Vanilla Cupcakes

Serving: 20 cupcakes | Prep: 20mins | Ready in:

Ingredients

- 2 egg whites
- 2 cups granulated sugar
- 2 cups flour
- 2 teaspoons baking soda
- 1 (20 ounce) can crushed pineapple (if you don't have crushed, sliced works fine)
- 1 teaspoon vanilla extract

Direction

- Heat the oven to 350 degrees F.
- Prepare cupcake cups.
- Beat eggs and sugar together well (the recipe says with an electric mixer, but I just beat the heck out of it with a wire whisk).
- Mix in the flour and baking soda.
- If the pineapple is not pre-crushed use your wire whisk to press down into the can over and over again until the pineapple is in small chunks.
- Then add the whole can (juice and all) to the mixture.
- Stir very well.
- Add vanilla.
- Stir well.
- Pour into cake cups and place in oven.
- Cooking time really depends on your oven.

- Check them every couple minutes until lightly browning on the tops.

Nutrition Information

- Calories: 142.2
- Protein: 1.8
- Saturated Fat: 0
- Sodium: 131.9
- Fiber: 0.6
- Total Carbohydrate: 34
- Cholesterol: 0
- Total Fat: 0.1
- Sugar: 24.2

143. Fudge Macaroons

Serving: 24 cookies | Prep: 20mins | Ready in:

Ingredients

- 1 tablespoon margarine
- 2/3 cup evaporated milk
- 3/4 cup sugar
- 1 teaspoon vanilla
- 1 (6 ounce) package chocolate chips
- 1 1/4 cups desiccated coconut
- 2 cups corn flakes
- 1/2 cup chopped nuts

Direction

- Combine first three ingredients and bring to a boil.
- Cook, stirring for 2 minutes then remove from heat.
- Stir in vanilla and chips until they melt.
- Add remaining ingredients, stir and drop quickly onto wax paper.
- Chill till firm.

Nutrition Information

- Calories: 115.9
- Sodium: 59.6
- Total Carbohydrate: 16.1
- Protein: 1.6
- Total Fat: 5.8
- Saturated Fat: 3
- Sugar: 12.2
- Cholesterol: 2
- Fiber: 0.9

144. Fudgy Chocolate Layer Cake

Serving: 8 serving(s) | Prep: 20mins | Ready in:

Ingredients

- 3/4 cup butter
- 2 ounces unsweetened chocolate
- 2 1/4 cups flour
- 2 cups sugar
- 1/4 cup cocoa
- 2 teaspoons baking soda
- 1 teaspoon salt
- 1 3/4 cups buttermilk
- 2 eggs (at room temperature)
- 3/4 cup whipping cream
- 1 1/2 cups chocolate chips (I use semi-sweet)

Direction

- Heat oven to 350*; grease and flour 2 9inch cake pans.
- In sm saucepan, melt butter and chocolate, stirring, over low heat.
- Mix flour, sugar, cocoa, baking soda and salt in lg mixer bowl.
- Add melted chocolate, buttermilk and eggs.
- Beat on low to combine; beat on high until light and fluffy, about 2 minutes.
- Pour into cake pans.
- Bake for 25 minutes, or until cakes test done.
- Cool in pan 5 minutes; invert onto wire rack.
- Frosting: Bring cream JUST to a boil.
- Remove from heat and stir in chocolate chips.

- Stir until frosting is smooth and starts to thicken.
- Place 1/3 cup on bottom layer.
- Top with second layer; frost top and sides.

Nutrition Information

- Calories: 787
- Saturated Fat: 24.7
- Sodium: 846.1
- Fiber: 4.5
- Total Carbohydrate: 103.8
- Cholesterol: 125
- Total Fat: 40.9
- Protein: 10.3
- Sugar: 69.9

145. Ginger Chocolate Shortbread

Serving: 40-50 cookies | Prep: 1hours10mins | Ready in:

Ingredients

- 1 cup butter (at room temperature)
- 1/2 cup superfine sugar (also known as fruit sugar)
- 2 cups all-purpose flour
- 1/2 cup finely chopped preserved gingerroot (not candied, but the type preserved in syrup)
- 3 ounces semisweet chocolate (chopped)

Direction

- Please note that this recipe calls for preserved ginger, which is the ginger typically sold in jars or in bulk stores (where I buy mine) that is in a sweet syrup; the type of ginger that is candied and sugared is NOT the type of ginger to use.
- Place soft butter and superfine sugar in a mixing bowl and, using an electric mixer, blend butter and sugar together until fluffy.
- Slowly stir in flour, then chopped ginger, then chopped chocolate.
- The mixture will be crumbly.
- Divide the dough in half and shape each half into a log about 1-1/2 inches in diameter; wrap logs tightly in plastic wrap and refrigerate until firm, about one hour.
- Dough keeps well in the fridge for several days, so there's no need to bake the whole batch up at one time if you're pressed for time.
- When ready to bake, preheat oven to 300°F.
- Cut logs of cookie dough into slices about 3/8-inch thick (I found a sharp serrated steak knife worked better for me than my chef's knife); arrange about two inches apart on ungreased cookie sheet and bake in center of oven for 18 to 20 minutes.
- Cool cooked cookies on a wire rack; do not store until completely cool.

Nutrition Information

- Calories: 83.8
- Saturated Fat: 3.6
- Protein: 1
- Total Fat: 5.8
- Fiber: 0.5
- Sugar: 2.5
- Total Carbohydrate: 7.9
- Cholesterol: 12.2
- Sodium: 33.3

146. Ginger Lemon Cookies

Serving: 28 cookies | Prep: 10mins | Ready in:

Ingredients

- 1/2 cup unsalted butter, at room temperature
- 1 cup sugar, divided
- 1 egg
- 2 3/4 teaspoons grated fresh lemon rind
- 1/2 teaspoon vanilla extract
- 1 cup flour, plus

- 2 tablespoons flour
- 1 1/2 teaspoons baking powder
- 1 teaspoon ground ginger
- 1/4 teaspoon salt
- extra flour, for shaping (Andrea Gordon(she won!)

Direction

- Set the oven at 325 degrees.
- Line 2 baking sheets with parchment.
- In an electric mixer, cream the butter with the 3/4 cup plus 1 tablespoon sugar.
- When the mixture is smooth, beat in the egg, lemon rind, and vanilla.
- Sift the flour, baking powder, ginger, and salt.
- With the mixer set on its lowest speed, add the dry ingredients to the batter.
- Scrape down the sides of the bowl, cover with plastic wrap, and refrigerate at least 1 hour or until well chilled.
- With floured hands, using heaping teaspoons of the dough to form balls, roll them until smooth.
- Arrange them 2-inches apart on the baking sheets.
- Put the remaining 3 tablespoons of sugar in a bowl.
- Dip the bottom of a glass first in cold water, then in sugar and press the balls to flatten them to a 1/3-inch thickness.
- Bake the cookies for 18 minutes or until the edges are golden brown.
- Cool on wire racks.
- Store in an airtight container.

Nutrition Information

- Calories: 78.2
- Fiber: 0.2
- Sugar: 7.2
- Protein: 0.8
- Total Fat: 3.5
- Saturated Fat: 2.1
- Sodium: 43.4
- Total Carbohydrate: 11.1
- Cholesterol: 15.4

147. Gingersnaps!

Serving: 30-60 cookies, 30 serving(s) | Prep: 30mins | Ready in:

Ingredients

- 1 1/2 cups soft whole wheat flour
- 1 cup soft unbleached flour
- 1 cup dark brown sugar (I use Sucanat)
- 1 1/2 teaspoons baking soda
- 3 teaspoons ground ginger
- 2 teaspoons ground cinnamon
- 1/2 teaspoon ground nutmeg
- 1/4 teaspoon ground cloves
- 1/2 teaspoon salt
- 1/2 cup light molasses, warmed
- 1/3 cup vegetable oil
- 1/3 cup water

Direction

- Sift the dry ingredients together in a large bowl.
- Warm the molasses, and mix the molasses, oil and water.
- If the molasses is not warm enough to dissolve into the water, they can all be warmed a little together- the microwave is fine for this.
- Mix the wet ingredients into the dry ingredients.
- The dough should be quite stiff, and not particularly sticky.
- If it is too soft and sticky, add a little more flour.
- Preheat the oven to 350°F.
- Roll out the dough to about 1/4" thick, and cut out with cookie cutters.
- Place cookies on cookie trays which have been lined with parchment paper, or lightly oiled.
- Re-roll and cut the scraps, until the dough is gone.

- Bake for 10 to 14 minutes, until lightly browned and set- they will harden up as they cool.

Nutrition Information

- Calories: 102.1
- Saturated Fat: 0.4
- Fiber: 1
- Sugar: 10.2
- Protein: 1.3
- Total Fat: 2.6
- Sodium: 107.2
- Total Carbohydrate: 19.1
- Cholesterol: 0

148. Graham Cracker Oatmeal Crust

Serving: 1 pie crust | Prep: 10mins | Ready in:

Ingredients

- 11 whole graham crackers (yield approx. 1 1/3 cups crumbs)
- 5 tablespoons unsalted butter, melted
- 1/2 cup old fashioned oats
- 3 tablespoons firmly packed dark brown sugar
- 1 teaspoon pure vanilla extract
- 1/8 teaspoon salt

Direction

- Preheat oven to 350°.
- Process crackers in food processor until finely ground.
- You can also place crackers in plastic bag and grind down using rolling pin.
- Combine crumbs, butter, oats, brown sugar, vanilla and salt, stirring until crumbs are moistened.
- Press mixture evenly across 9-inch pie plate.
- Bake crust until crisp, about 7 minutes.
- Let cool completely before filling.

- Crust may also be wrapped tightly in plastic and frozen up to one month.

Nutrition Information

- Calories: 1484.2
- Saturated Fat: 39.3
- Sodium: 1248.3
- Sugar: 88.9
- Total Carbohydrate: 186.3
- Total Fat: 75.7
- Fiber: 8.3
- Cholesterol: 152.7
- Protein: 17.7

149. Gramma's Old Fashioned Cinnamon Sweet Rolls

Serving: 2 13x9 pans, 24 serving(s) | Prep: 15mins | Ready in:

Ingredients

- 1 1/2 cups warm milk or 1 1/2 cups water
- 1 tablespoon yeast
- 1 teaspoon yeast
- 1/2 cup sugar
- 1/4 cup melted butter
- 2 eggs
- 1/2 teaspoon salt
- 5 1/2 cups flour

Direction

- In a liquid measuring cup, heat milk/water to "wrist-warm" (do NOT boil; just warm).
- Add yeast and 2 tablespoons of the sugar (you'll use the rest in the next step). Stir the yeast and sugar; let this "work" for about 5 or 10 minutes. You should have some bubbly, frothy stuff in the cup when you return. (If not--your yeast is no good, dump it out and get better yeast.).

- Pour yeast-milk into mixing bowl, and add remaining sugar, butter, eggs, salt and 1 cup of the flour. Using beater, mix this mess for about a minute.
- Switch to the paddle (flat beater) or a dough hook, and add remaining flour one cup-at-a-time. The dough will form a ball, and feel slightly sticky. You may not need the entire 5 1/2 cups (depends on humidity, too).
- Fill medium glass bowl with hottest tap water. If your oven can be adjusted to 100 degrees, set it to 100 degrees. Also, if your oven has a light, turn it on; place the hot water on the bottom of the oven. Close the door.
- Grease a large, glass bowl. Remove dough from mixing bowl to a floured table/counter-top; knead for 1 minute; form into a ball and place in greased bowl, turning to get grease on all sides. Cover bowl loosely with a sheet of plastic wrap.
- Turn off 100 degree oven, place bowl of dough into oven; close the door. Set the timer for 1 hour.
- Clean up the mess BUT leave floured counter-top AS IS.
- At the end of one hour the dough should've risen to about double the size. If not, let it go for another 15 minutes (set the timer--it's easy to forget---out of sight, out of mind!).
- Gather filling ingredients: 1/4 cup of melted butter; cinnamon; brown sugar; raisins and/or chopped nuts (optional).
- Punch down the down; remove from bowl; with a large butcher knife, cut dough into two equal parts. Set one aside (cover with plastic wrap).
- Grease two 13x9-inch pans with BUTTER (no substitutes are allowed -- this is GRAMMA's recipe). :-) humor me, okay?
- On floured counter-top, lay dough and with a rolling pin, shape roll into large rectangle, oh about 8 x 16 inches or a bit larger, keep thickness consistent throughout.
- Pour HALF of the melted butter over this, and spread with a pastry brush, right out to the edges. Sprinkle generously with cinnamon (like 1-2 tablespoons), then a handful of brown sugar, spreading it evenly with fingers; right to the edges!
- Sprinkle some raisins and chopped nuts -- if using. Keep these closer to the long side closest to you.
- HERE's THE HARD PART: Starting at the side closest to you, LOOSELY roll away from you. Loosely is the KEY word. Tuck in any runaway raisins or nuts.
- Use that big knife to divide the roll in half in the middle. Then cut each half into SIX equal portions, for a total of 12 rolls.
- Starting in the middle of the roll (nicest shaped rolls) and working to the sloppy outside roll pieces, set them along the outside edges of the buttered pan, spacing evenly in the pan. Put the two end rolls in the very center of the pan. Set the cut side DOWN (so the top looks flat-ish). Set this pan on the stove for now.
- Repeat with remaining dough; vary the ingredients -- if you skipped raisins or nuts, maybe add some to this pan of rolls.
- Check if the water in the oven is still warm, if not dump out and start with fresh hot water. Put plastic wrap on both pans (re-use the other piece), and pop in the warm oven. Set the timer for 45 minutes. Go do something productive---clean the counter-top before all that stuff gets hard! :-D.
- When the rolls have risen to the top of the pan (or a smidgen over), remove them from the oven, preheat oven to 350. When it's warm bake them for 20 minutes; tops will be golden brown.
- Cool on a rack; then frost with a cream cheese/butter cream frosting (slather it on thick like Gramma does for the grandkids!).
- You have JUST entered the Pearly Gates!

Nutrition Information

- Calories: 155.2
- Total Fat: 3.2
- Total Carbohydrate: 27
- Cholesterol: 22.7
- Protein: 4.3

- Saturated Fat: 1.7
- Sodium: 79.7
- Fiber: 0.9
- Sugar: 4.2

150. Grammy's Famous Raspberry Jello Mold

Serving: 12 serving(s) | Prep: 20mins | Ready in:

Ingredients

- 1 cup hot water
- 2 (6 ounce) packages raspberry Jell-O gelatin
- 1 (18 ounce) jar applesauce
- 1 (8 ounce) package frozen raspberries

Direction

- Mix the hot water and Jello together. Stir very well.
- Add nearly the whole medium-sized jar of applesauce and the raspberries.
- Put in a circular mould (similar to a Bundt pan) and chill overnight to set.

Nutrition Information

- Calories: 160
- Saturated Fat: 0
- Sodium: 144.8
- Fiber: 1.4
- Sugar: 28.5
- Cholesterol: 0
- Total Fat: 0.1
- Total Carbohydrate: 39.1
- Protein: 2.4

151. Grandma Rampke's Easy Rhubarb Custard Pie

Serving: 1 pie, 4-6 serving(s) | Prep: 0S | Ready in:

Ingredients

- 1/2 pie crust
- 1 1/2 cups cut rhubarb, in 1 inch pieces
- 1/2 cup sugar
- 2 large eggs, beaten (extra large eggs are even better)
- 1/2 cup sugar (yes, another 1/2 cup)
- 1 cup whole milk (not skim milk)
- cinnamon

Direction

- Place 1/2 pie crust into pie plate.
- Put the rhubarb in the crust and cover with 1/2 cup sugar.
- Add the other 1/2 cup sugar to the milk and beaten eggs, and pour mixture over rhubarb.
- Sprinkle top with cinnamon.
- Bake at 350 degrees for 45 minutes; let cool before serving to allow custard to set.
- Note from Julie: this was my dad's favorite pie, and my mom got the recipe from his mother.
- Note, again: I've been on the 'net for a very, very long time, and this is one of the earliest recipes that I submitted to any search engines. What I can say: it's a tried and true recipe, one we've been using for well over 50 years. It's what my mom will be serving at Christmas this year... what else can I say?

Nutrition Information

- Calories: 391.6
- Fiber: 1.6
- Sugar: 50.5
- Cholesterol: 101.5
- Protein: 6.9
- Total Fat: 12.2
- Saturated Fat: 4.1
- Sodium: 184.6

- Total Carbohydrate: 65.3

152. Grandma's Jello Salad

Serving: 8 serving(s) | Prep: 20mins | Ready in:

Ingredients

- 2 (3 ounce) packages lime Jell-O gelatin
- 1 cup boiling water
- 1 pint sour cream
- 2 cups miniature marshmallows
- 1 (20 ounce) can crushed pineapple
- 1/2 cup walnuts, chopped
- 1/2 cup maraschino cherry, halved

Direction

- Stir boiling water into Jello to dissolve.
- Stir in sour cream until smooth.
- Add pineapple, marshmallows, nuts and cherries.
- Pour into a 9" glass loaf pan; chill overnight, until set.

Nutrition Information

- Calories: 334.2
- Protein: 5.1
- Saturated Fat: 8
- Fiber: 1.1
- Sugar: 36
- Total Carbohydrate: 44
- Cholesterol: 25.3
- Total Fat: 16.9
- Sodium: 141.1

153. Grandma's Spaghetti And Cheese Pudding

Serving: 12 serving(s) | Prep: 10mins | Ready in:

Ingredients

- 500 g spaghetti (better use whole wheat spaghetti, it's healthier this way)
- 200 g low fat cottage cheese
- 200 g feta cheese
- 3 eggs
- 1 tablespoon olive oil
- sea salt, to taste
- white pepper, to taste

Direction

- Boil the pasta following the instructions on the package. (10-12 minutes).
- Preheat your oven at 392.
- Coat the oven tray with some olive oil.
- Drain the spaghetti and put them in a large bowl.
- Whisk the eggs with salt and pepper and pour them over the pasta.
- Using a fork, blend cheeses together and when they have a paste-like consistency add them over the spaghetti.
- *Add sliced/mashed garlic. (Optional).
- Mix well, then put them in the oven tray.
- Place the tray in the oven and cook for about 30-35 minutes, until golden and crispy. You can use the grill for the last 10 minutes to create a lovely crust on top.

Nutrition Information

- Calories: 262.4
- Total Fat: 7
- Saturated Fat: 3.3
- Sodium: 261.6
- Fiber: 1.5
- Total Carbohydrate: 36.9
- Cholesterol: 63
- Sugar: 2.6
- Protein: 12.1

154. Granny's Banana Cream Pie

Serving: 6-8 serving(s) | Prep: 45mins | Ready in:

Ingredients

- 3/4 cup sugar
- 1/3 cup all-purpose flour
- 1/4 teaspoon salt
- 2 cups milk
- 3 egg yolks, lightly beaten
- 2 tablespoons butter or 2 tablespoons margarine
- 1 teaspoon vanilla extract
- 3 medium firm bananas
- 1 (9 inch) pie shells, baked
- whipped cream or Cool Whip
- sliced banana

Direction

- In a saucepan, combine sugar, flour, and salt; stir in milk and mix well.
- Cook over medium heat, stirring constantly, until the mixture thickens and comes to a boil; boil for 2 minutes.
- Remove from the heat.
- Stir a small amount of cream mixture into egg yolks; return all to saucepan.
- Cook for 2 minutes, stirring constantly; remove from the heat.
- Add butter and vanilla; mix well; allow to cool slightly.
- Slice the bananas and place evenly in pastry shell; pour cream mixture over bananas.
- Cool; before serving, garnish with whipped cream or Cool Whip and bananas.
- Refrigerate any leftovers.

Nutrition Information

- Calories: 438.8
- Total Carbohydrate: 61.6
- Cholesterol: 104.6
- Saturated Fat: 7.6
- Fiber: 2.8
- Sugar: 32.4
- Total Fat: 19.1
- Sodium: 331.1
- Protein: 7.1

155. Grape Salad With A Twist

Serving: 12 serving(s) | Prep: 25mins | Ready in:

Ingredients

- 2 cups red seedless grapes
- 2 cups green seedless grapes
- 8 ounces cream cheese
- 8 ounces sour cream
- 1/2 cup sugar
- 4 butterfinger candy bars, crushed
- 1/4-1/2 cup pecans, crushed

Direction

- Wash grapes.
- Cream together cream cheese, sour cream and sugar then fold in the grapes.
- Put mixture into a 9 X 13 dish.
- Sprinkle top with crushed butterfingers then top off with crushed pecans.
- Press and Chill.

Nutrition Information

- Calories: 277.7
- Saturated Fat: 8
- Sodium: 123.8
- Fiber: 1.1
- Sugar: 26.7
- Protein: 3.2
- Total Carbohydrate: 33.7
- Cholesterol: 31.2
- Total Fat: 15.9

156. Guiness Ginger Cupcakes

Serving: 12 cupcakes, 12 serving(s) | Prep: 15mins | Ready in:

Ingredients

- 1/2 cup stout beer, such as Guinness
- 1/2 cup mild-flavored molasses
- 1/2 cup vegetable oil
- 1/4 teaspoon baking soda
- 3/4 cup packed light brown sugar
- 1 1/3 cups all-purpose flour
- 1 1/4 teaspoons baking powder
- 2 tsp.ground ginger
- 1 teaspoon ground cinnamon
- 1/4 teaspoon ground cloves
- 1/2 teaspoon table salt
- 2 large eggs
- 1/2 cup finely minced candied ginger
- 4 tablespoons unsalted butter
- 1 1/2 cups confectioners' sugar, sifted
- 2 1/2 tablespoons freshly squeezed lime juice
- 1 tablespoon whole milk

Direction

- Make the cupcakes:
- Preheat the oven to 350°F Line a standard 12-cup muffin tin with cupcake liners.
- To make the cupcakes, in a very large saucepan, bring the stout, molasses, and oil to a boil over medium-high heat. Remove from the heat and whisk in the baking soda until dissolved. (The mixture will foam up, then settle down.) Stir in the brown sugar, then let cool until tepid.
- Into a small bowl, sift together the flour, baking powder, ginger, cinnamon, cloves, and salt.
- Whisk the eggs into the stout mixture, then whisk in the flour mixture just until incorporated. Don't over mix. Gently stir in the minced candied ginger.
- Divide the batter among the cupcake liners and bake until the cupcakes feel just set in the centre, 22 to 24 minutes. Let cool completely.
- Make the frosting:
- In a stand mixer fitted with the paddle attachment, beat the butter on high speed until smooth, about 10 seconds. Decrease the speed to low and, with the mixer running, gradually add half of the confectioners' sugar. Stop the mixer and scrape down the bowl as needed to make sure the ingredients are being incorporated. Add the lime juice, then add the remaining confectioners' sugar. Once the sugar is incorporated, add the milk. Beat the frosting on high speed until completely smooth and fluffy, about 3 minutes. Taste, and add a few more drops of lime juice, if desired.
- Transfer the frosting to a pastry bag fitted with a star tip. Remove the cupcakes from the muffin tin. Pipe rosettes of frosting in the centre of each cupcake. (If you don't have a pastry bag, you can spoon a mound of frosting decoratively in the centre.) Garnish each with strips of candied citrus peel or a piece of candied ginger.

Nutrition Information

- Calories: 334.6
- Protein: 2.6
- Total Fat: 14
- Saturated Fat: 3.9
- Sodium: 185.2
- Fiber: 0.5
- Sugar: 35.9
- Total Carbohydrate: 50.5
- Cholesterol: 45.5

157. Gujiya Or Perakiya(Indian Pastry Sweet)

Serving: 15-16 gujiyas, 2-3 serving(s) | Prep: 1hours | Ready in:

Ingredients

- 1 cup all-purpose flour

- 3 tablespoons ghee or 3 tablespoons unsalted butter
- 1 pinch salt
- 1/2 liter oil (for frying)
- 1 cup khoya or 1 cup reduced milk
- 1/2 cup sugar
- 3 almonds
- 3 raisins
- 1/2 teaspoon cardamom powder
- 1 tablespoon poppy seed

Direction

- In a mixing bowl combine the salt, flour and ghee. Rub in well. Gradually add water and knead to form a firm dough. Cover with wet cloth and set aside.
- How to prepare Khoya: Take about 2 liters of milk. Heat the Milk in a solid non - stick pan in low heat, stir continuously make sure that the milk doesn't stick to the bottom.
- Let the milk reduce this process may take several minutes, stir continuously with medium low heat. Stir until the milk becomes semi solid. Then take them out and place them out in usable sizes. They can be stored in the freezer and can be defrosted and used later.
- For the stuffing: Mix khoya, sugar, chopped almonds and raisins, cardamom powder, and poppy seeds (optional) till the milk evaporates.
- Divide the dough into 20-25 sections, roll them out into flat round pancakes. Place a spoon of stuffing at the center and fold the pancake in half. Use a cutter to create the fluted crescent border and cut off excess dough. You can seal the edges by applying a little milk and pressing down hard.
- After all the gujiyas are stuffed, fry them in very hot oil for 2-3 minutes or till golden brown, remove onto paper towels and allow to cool.
- The gujiyas can last for 7-8 days if stored in an air tight container.

Nutrition Information

- Calories: 2636.6
- Fiber: 2.5
- Cholesterol: 49.1
- Total Carbohydrate: 100.1
- Protein: 7.8
- Total Fat: 249.9
- Saturated Fat: 41.7
- Sodium: 87.5
- Sugar: 51.3

158. Gwyn's Orange Jello Salad

Serving: 12 serving(s) | Prep: 30mins | Ready in:

Ingredients

- 2 (6 ounce) packages orange Jell-O
- 2 cups boiling water
- 1 (6 ounce) canun-diluted frozen orange juice
- 2 (8 ounce) cans crushed pineapple, undrained
- 1 (15 ounce) can mandarin oranges, drained
- 8 ounces Cool Whip
- 1 (3 ounce) package instant lemon pudding
- 1 cup shredded cheddar cheese

Direction

- Boil water and stir in orange jello until dissolved.
- Add the 6 oz. can of frozen orange juice and stir until dissolved.
- Add the pineapple and mandarin oranges to the jello mixture and stir.
- Pour into a 9 x 13 pan and chill until firm.
- Prepare instant lemon pudding according to package directions, then stir in cool whip.
- Layer on top of chilled jello and sprinkle with grated cheddar cheese.
- Chill until ready to serve.

Nutrition Information

- Calories: 260.7

- Saturated Fat: 4.1
- Sodium: 234.4
- Total Carbohydrate: 53.3
- Cholesterol: 0
- Total Fat: 5
- Fiber: 1.1
- Sugar: 43.6
- Protein: 3.3

159. Halo Halo Hawaiian Filipino Dessert

Serving: 240 oz, 40 serving(s) | Prep: 1hours | Ready in:

Ingredients

- 2 quarts vanilla ice cream
- 2 bananas, sliced and quartered
- 1 honeydew melon, balled
- 1 cantaloupe, balled
- 1 papaya, balled
- 1 young shredded coconut (fresh or frozen)
- 1/2 cup tapioca (large or small pearl)
- 1 (3 ounce) package strawberry Jell-O gelatin dessert
- 8 cups crushed ice

Direction

- Cook tapioca until pearls become translucent (add tapioca to boiling water, lower heat to medium, watch for 15 minutes or more, stirring occasionally).
- Rinse tapioca in cool water (careful, it's sticky) and set aside.
- Prepare Jell-O using half of the water called for and refrigerate until stiff.
- Put the fruit (except bananas) and coconut into drink cooler (for party) or large bowl (to serve with a meal).
- Cut Jell-O into 1/2" squares.
- Add bananas, tapioca, and Jell-O to fruit mixture.
- Prepare ice cream by emptying container into a large bowl and smoothing into paste (i.e. use potato masher, hands, etc.) Scoop ice cream into fruit mixture.
- Cover fruit mixture with crushed ice.
- If using cooler, cover with lid.
- Wait 30 minutes and stir to combine all ingredients (including ice) well.
- Serve with ladle in paper cups with spoons.
- (Last 5 hours in cooler--stir before each serving).
- Leftovers can be refrigerated for the next day.

Nutrition Information

- Calories: 99.4
- Saturated Fat: 1.8
- Sodium: 42
- Fiber: 1.1
- Total Carbohydrate: 17.3
- Total Fat: 3
- Sugar: 13.4
- Cholesterol: 11.6
- Protein: 1.5

160. Ham Swiss Bread Pudding I

Serving: 9 serving(s) | Prep: 30mins | Ready in:

Ingredients

- 1/4 cup butter, melted, divided
- 3 tablespoons butter, melted, divided
- 18 slices day-old French bread, divided (3/4 inch thick)
- 1/2 cup stone ground mustard
- 1 1/2 cups cubed fully cooked ham
- 1 cup sliced fresh mushrooms
- 2 garlic cloves, minced
- 1/4 cup chopped green onion
- 2 cups shredded swiss cheese
- 8 eggs

- 4 cups heavy whipping cream
- 1/2 teaspoon salt
- 1/2 teaspoon pepper
- 2 tablespoons minced fresh parsley
- warm maple syrup (optional)

Direction

- Pour 1/4 cup butter into a 13-in. x 9-in. baking dish; set aside. Spread both sides of bread with mustard. Arrange nine slices in baking dish.
- In a large skillet, sauté the ham, mushrooms and garlic in remaining butter until mushrooms are tender. Add the onions; cook 1 minute longer or until onions are crisp-tender. Spoon over bread; sprinkle with cheese. Arrange remaining bread on top. In a large bowl, beat the eggs, cream, salt and pepper. Stir in parsley; pour over bread.
- Place dish in a larger baking pan. Fill larger pan with hot water to a depth of 1 inches Bake at 325° for 50-60 minutes or until a knife inserted near the center comes out clean. Let stand for 5 minutes before serving. Drizzle with maple syrup if desired.

Nutrition Information

- Calories: 998.7
- Total Fat: 64.8
- Saturated Fat: 37
- Total Carbohydrate: 72.8
- Protein: 31.7
- Sodium: 1631.5
- Fiber: 4.5
- Sugar: 1.7
- Cholesterol: 390.9

161. Hardee's Peach Cobbler Copycat

Serving: 1 8 x 8 inch pan, 6-8 serving(s) | Prep: 10mins | Ready in:

Ingredients

- 1 (16 ounce) can peach pie filling, the large can
- 1 frozen pie crust, thawed
- 1/4 cup butter, cut into pats
- 1 dash cinnamon
- 1 dash sugar

Direction

- Preheat oven to 375 degrees F.
- Spread the pie filling into a square baking pan. Put the slices of butter on top of the pie filling, placing them as evenly as possible.
- Carefully remove the pie crust from the pan it is in, and place it carefully on top of the pie filling and butter. You will need to cut off the edges that hang over and make them fit on the square pan. Sprinkle liberally with cinnamon and sugar. Bake for about 20 to 25 minutes, until pie crust is lightly browned.
- Serve with a scoop of vanilla ice cream.

Nutrition Information

- Calories: 199.6
- Total Fat: 15.2
- Sodium: 185.5
- Cholesterol: 20.3
- Saturated Fat: 7.2
- Fiber: 0.7
- Sugar: 0
- Total Carbohydrate: 14
- Protein: 1.9

162. Hawaiian Pie

Serving: 8 serving(s) | Prep: 20mins | Ready in:

Ingredients

- 1 (5 1/8 ounce) box instant vanilla flavor pudding and pie filling
- 1 (20 ounce) can crushed pineapple, undrained
- 1 (8 ounce) container sour cream

- 1 (9 inch) graham cracker crust

Direction

- In large bowl, combine vanilla pudding mix (dry) undrained pineapple, and sour cream; stir until well blended.
- Pour mixture into pie crust.
- Cover and chill 2 hours before serving.

Nutrition Information

- Calories: 316
- Sodium: 455.9
- Saturated Fat: 5.1
- Fiber: 1
- Sugar: 39.5
- Total Carbohydrate: 48.3
- Cholesterol: 15.6
- Protein: 2.2
- Total Fat: 13.5

163. Hawaiian Sweet Rolls (Bread Machine)

Serving: 12 rolls, 12 serving(s) | Prep: 2hours | Ready in:

Ingredients

- 1/2 cup milk (*)
- 2 eggs
- 1 egg yolk
- 3 tablespoons butter
- 1 potatoes, mashed or 6 ounces prepared mashed potatoes
- 1/3 cup sugar
- 3/4 teaspoon salt
- 3 1/2 cups flour
- 2 teaspoons yeast

Direction

- Prepare the bread machine: Combine ingredients as recommended by your machine's manufacturer. Use the dough setting.
- After the cycle, turn out onto a floured surface and preheat the oven to 350.
- Stretch dough into a log and with a sharp knife cut into 12 pieces.
- Use a 9x13x2 greased baking pan. Let it rise for an hour to 90 minutes.
- Brush with milk and bake at 350 degrees x20 minutes.
- Cover with aluminum foil after 10 minutes to prevent burning**.
- Note on directions:
- **One baker used a glass Pyrex dish, like you would use for lasagna, lined it, ungreased, with waxed paper. Raised and baked it as directed, and it did not require the aluminum to prevent burning. I make these in a lower oven shelf and also haven't needed to cover them up.

Nutrition Information

- Calories: 218.1
- Fiber: 1.5
- Total Carbohydrate: 37.3
- Total Fat: 4.8
- Sodium: 185.2
- Protein: 6
- Saturated Fat: 2.5
- Sugar: 5.9
- Cholesterol: 60

164. Hazelnut Chocolate Pastries

Serving: 26 cookies | Prep: 10mins | Ready in:

Ingredients

- 13 ounces premade puff pastry
- 8 tablespoons chocolate hazelnut spread (Neutella)
- 1/2 cup toasted hazelnuts

- 5 teaspoons sugar

Direction

- Preheat oven to 425F.
- Lightly grease a cookie sheet.
- On a lightly floured surface, roll out the puff pastry into a rectangular shape by about 15 x 9 inches in size. Spread the chocolate hazelnut spread evenly over the top and sprinkle with the hazelnuts.
- Roll both on the long ends so that they meet at the center of the dough.
- Where the pieces meet, dampen the edges with a little water to join them together.
- Using a sharp knife, cut into thin slices.
- Place on the prepared cookie sheet and flatten slightly with a spatula.
- Sprinkle with the sugar Bake for 10-15 minutes, or until golden.
- When done, transfer to a wire rack to cool before serving.

Nutrition Information

- Calories: 128.3
- Sodium: 37.6
- Fiber: 0.8
- Total Carbohydrate: 11.2
- Cholesterol: 0
- Saturated Fat: 1.8
- Sugar: 4.2
- Protein: 1.7
- Total Fat: 8.7

165. Healthy Apple Pear Cake

Serving: 24 serving(s) | Prep: 30mins | Ready in:

Ingredients

- 2 cups flour
- 1/2 cup white sugar
- 1 tablespoon baking powder
- 1/2 teaspoon baking soda
- 1/2 teaspoon salt
- 2 teaspoons cinnamon
- 1/2 cup pecans, Chopped
- 1 cup milk
- 3 medium apples, Peeled, Cored and Chopped
- 3 medium pears, Peeled Cored and Chopped
- 1 tablespoon brown sugar
- 2 teaspoons powdered sugar, for dusting

Direction

- Pre-heat oven to 350.
- Spray 9 x 13 Glass Baking Dish with Pam.
- Put first 6 ingredients in a large bowl and use a whisk to mix together.
- Add milk and mix.
- Stir in Pecans, Apples and Pears.
- Pour into prepared 9 x 13 Baking Dish and spread out evenly.
- Using your fingers sprinkle Brown Sugar on top.
- Bake at 350 degrees for 30 minutes.
- Test with toothpick to see if it is done.
- Let it cool for 15 minutes and then dust with powdered sugar.
- Enjoy.

Nutrition Information

- Calories: 104.8
- Cholesterol: 1.4
- Total Fat: 2.2
- Fiber: 1.9
- Sugar: 9.6
- Total Carbohydrate: 20.6
- Protein: 1.8
- Saturated Fat: 0.4
- Sodium: 125.9

166. Healthy Chocolate No Bake Oatmeal Cookies

Serving: 30-35 cookies | Prep: 12mins | Ready in:

Ingredients

- 2 cups sugar
- 3 tablespoons carob powder
- 1/2 cup butter
- 1 teaspoon vanilla
- 1/2 cup milk
- 1/2 cup peanut butter
- 3 cups old-fashioned oatmeal
- 1/4 cup flax seed, ground
- 1/4 cup coconut
- 1/4 cup nutritional yeast
- 1/8 cup spirulina

Direction

- Prepare oats, flax, coconut, nutritional yeast, and spirulina in a large (preferably metal) bowl, mix well. Prepare flat surface equal to 2 large cookie sheets with wax paper.
- Place sugar, carob powder, butter and milk in 2 or 3 quart heavy pan on medium heat, stirring frequently to mix and help melt ingredients together.
- When mixture comes to a rolling boil, let boil 3 minutes, without stirring, take off heat, add vanilla and peanut butter and mix well.
- Add to prepared oat mixture and place on wax paper by teaspoonful. Mixture may take several hours to dry solid depending on humidity.

Nutrition Information

- Calories: 155
- Total Carbohydrate: 21
- Cholesterol: 8.7
- Fiber: 1.9
- Sugar: 13.9
- Protein: 3.5
- Total Fat: 7
- Saturated Fat: 3
- Sodium: 45.3

167. Healthy Sorbet

Serving: 2-10 serving(s) | Prep: 5mins | Ready in:

Ingredients

- 1 cup cut fresh fruit
- 1/4 cup soymilk or 1/4 cup fruit juice
- honey (optional)

Direction

- Add ingredients to a blender and Liquify.
- Pour into containers, cover and freeze.
- Eat with a spoon!
- Combination Suggestions:
- Apple, Banana, Pear.
- Mixed Berries.
- Strawberry, Banana, Blueberry.
- Mango, Pear, Apple.
- Pineapple, Raspberry, Banana.
- Notes: This is a great way to cut down on sugar because fruit is naturally sweet when ripe.
- If you are an absolute sweetaholic, you can mix approximately 1/4- to 1/2-teaspoon of honey (uncooked) for each 1-cup serving of sorbet.
- Or, you can add a banana.
- You can make a thinner sorbet with more soymilk or juice or add chopped ice to the mixture.
- Sometimes I prefer a thinner mixture if I am using grainy berries (e. g., blueberries, raspberries).
- You can make sorbet cubes in ice trays with mini-bamboo skewers (you can cut long skewers with a scissors to fit).
- You can purchase low-cost, disposable, small containers with lids for easy travel and cook-out fun.
- You may even find Popsicle trays in your supermarket!

- You can cover dishes with plastic wrap, if you wish to serve sorbet in decorative bowls.
- This makes a wonderful dessert for parties.
- Sorbet is an excellent way to use over-ripe fruit.
- When blended together and frozen, the fruit is quite delicious.
- Be creative with your recipes and please feel free to share them with me!

Nutrition Information

- Calories: 16.4
- Total Fat: 0.5
- Saturated Fat: 0.1
- Cholesterol: 0
- Sodium: 15.5
- Fiber: 0.2
- Sugar: 1.2
- Total Carbohydrate: 1.9
- Protein: 1

168. Hg's Bananarama Wafer Puddin' Ww Points = 3

Serving: 6 serving(s) | Prep: 10mins | Ready in:

Ingredients

- 2 cups nonfat milk, at fridge temperature
- 1 (3 1/2 ounce) box fat-free sugar-free instant vanilla pudding mix, 4-serving size box
- 2 medium bananas, sliced
- 24 reduced-fat vanilla wafers
- Optional
- fat-free whipped topping (optional)

Direction

- Combine pudding mix and milk in a bowl. Beat with a whisk for 2 minutes or until thoroughly blended. Set aside.
- In a medium bowl or casserole dish, arrange a layer of wafers and then top with a layer of banana slices. Continue alternating layers until all wafers and banana slices are in the dish.
- Top dish with the pudding and let it seep down in between the wafer and banana layers. Refrigerate 2 to 3 hours. If desired, add whipped topped before serving.

Nutrition Information

- Calories: 188.9
- Total Fat: 2.9
- Sodium: 779.8
- Protein: 4.2
- Saturated Fat: 0.8
- Fiber: 1.5
- Sugar: 15.1
- Total Carbohydrate: 37.6
- Cholesterol: 9.8

169. Homemade Banana Pudding

Serving: 6-8 serving(s) | Prep: 10mins | Ready in:

Ingredients

- 5 eggs, separated (6 or 7 if small)
- 1 1/2 cups sugar
- 3 - 3 1/2 cups milk
- 1 pinch salt
- 1 -2 teaspoon banana flavoring
- 3 tablespoons cornstarch
- 1 box vanilla wafer
- 2 -3 bananas

Direction

- Beat yolks with sugar, milk, salt, banana flavor, and corn starch. Heat on medium heat. Stir constantly (I prefer using a double boiler). Don't let it burn.

- Line the bottom and sides of a baking dish with vanilla wafers. When pudding thickens pour about half of it over the wafers.
- Lay a layer of banana slices on this and top with another layer of wafers then another layer of pudding. Use the egg whites for your meringue if so desired.

Nutrition Information

- Calories: 384.7
- Total Carbohydrate: 68.6
- Protein: 9.7
- Saturated Fat: 4.1
- Sodium: 144.7
- Fiber: 1.1
- Sugar: 55.1
- Total Fat: 8.7
- Cholesterol: 193.3

170. Honey Apple Noodle Kugel

Serving: 8 serving(s) | Prep: 10mins | Ready in:

Ingredients

- 12 ounces wide egg noodles, cooked
- 6 eggs
- 1/2 cup sugar
- 1 cup raisins
- 1/2 cup honey
- 1 (20 ounce) can apple pie filling
- 2 teaspoons lemon juice

Direction

- Preheat oven to 350F and lightly spray your 13 x 9 baking pan with cooking spray.
- Mix everything together.
- Bake for 1 hour.

Nutrition Information

- Calories: 458.7
- Total Fat: 5.8
- Saturated Fat: 1.7
- Sodium: 95.8
- Fiber: 2.8
- Sugar: 51.6
- Cholesterol: 194.5
- Total Carbohydrate: 93.9
- Protein: 11.5

171. Honey Bun Cake 1st Umc

Serving: 1 13x9 pan, 24 serving(s) | Prep: 30mins | Ready in:

Ingredients

- Cake
- 18 ounces butter recipe cake mix, less 1/2 cup for filling
- 1 cup butter or 1 cup margarine, softened
- 4 eggs
- 1 (8 ounce) carton sour cream
- Filling
- 1/2 cup dry cake mix, reserved
- 1/2 cup brown sugar, packed
- 1/3 cup chopped pecans
- 2 teaspoons cinnamon
- Topping
- 1 cup powdered sugar
- 3 tablespoons milk, divided
- 1 teaspoon vanilla

Direction

- Preheat oven to 350 degrees. Grease bottom only of 13x9 in pan.
- Remove 1/2 cup dry cake mix and reserve in small bowl.
- Make cake: Beat remaining cake mix with butter, eggs and sour cream on medium speed for two minutes. Spread only half of the batter into 13x9 pan. It will be thicker than usual cake batter.

- Make filling: Stir together reserved dry cake mix, brown sugar, pecans and cinnamon. Sprinkle over batter in 13x9 pan.
- Carefully spread remaining batter over pecan mixture.
- Bake 30-33 minutes or until deep golden brown. Remove cake and place on wire rack.
- Make topping: In small bowl, stir powdered sugar, 1 tablespoon milk and vanilla together. Add additional milk - 1 tablespoon at a time - until icing is thin enough to drizzle.
- Poke top of warm cake with fork and spread icing over top.

Nutrition Information

- Calories: 263.2
- Saturated Fat: 7
- Cholesterol: 60.7
- Fiber: 0.5
- Sugar: 21.3
- Total Carbohydrate: 30.8
- Protein: 2.8
- Total Fat: 14.8
- Sodium: 246

172. Honey Lime Fruit Toss

Serving: 7 serving(s) | Prep: 5mins | Ready in:

Ingredients

- 1 (20 ounce) can pineapple chunks, drain and reserve 1/4 cup juice
- 1 (11 ounce) can mandarin oranges, drained
- 1 banana, sliced
- 1 cup strawberry, sliced
- 1 kiwi fruit, sliced
- 1/4 teaspoon grated lemon, rind of
- 2 tablespoons lime juice
- 1 tablespoon honey

Direction

- Combine first 6 ingredients.
- For dressing, stir reserved pineapple juice with last three ingredients.
- Toss fruit and dressing.

Nutrition Information

- Calories: 110.7
- Protein: 1.2
- Saturated Fat: 0.1
- Sodium: 2.6
- Fiber: 2.7
- Sugar: 23
- Total Carbohydrate: 28.5
- Cholesterol: 0
- Total Fat: 0.4

173. Hot Sweet Potato Salad

Serving: 4 cups, 4 serving(s) | Prep: 40mins | Ready in:

Ingredients

- 5 cups sweet potatoes, peeled and cut into 1-inch cubes
- 1 tablespoon sugar
- 1 tablespoon vegetable oil
- 1 teaspoon kosher salt
- 1/2 teaspoon red pepper flakes
- 3 slices thick bacon, chopped
- 1/2 cup red onion, slivered
- 1/4 cup apple jelly
- 2 tablespoons apple cider vinegar
- 1/4 cup pecans, toasted and chopped
- 2 tablespoons fresh lime juice
- 2 tablespoons scallions, thinly sliced
- salt, to taste

Direction

- Preheat oven to 425.
- Toss sweet potatoes with sugar, oil, salt, and red pepper flakes.
- Roast 25-30 minutes.

- While potatoes are roasting, sauté bacon in a skillet over medium heat until crisp.
- Pour off fat, leaving bacon in pan.
- Add onions and sauté 3 minutes.
- Add jelly and vinegar, stirring until jelly melts.
- Remove sweet potatoes from oven and put in large bowl.
- Add bacon mixture, pecans, lime juice, and scallions to potatoes and toss.
- Season with salt.

Nutrition Information

- Calories: 328.7
- Saturated Fat: 1.8
- Fiber: 6.4
- Total Carbohydrate: 55.2
- Protein: 4.3
- Total Fat: 11.2
- Sodium: 585.6
- Sugar: 22.2
- Cholesterol: 4.1

174. Impossible Peanut Butter Cookies

Serving: 18 cookies | Prep: 15mins | Ready in:

Ingredients

- 1 cup peanut butter (your choice, smooth or chunky)
- 1 cup granulated sugar
- 1 large egg
- sugar, for rolling (optional)

Direction

- Mix peanut butter, sugar, and egg together until smooth.
- Drop by teaspoon onto cookie sheet two inches apart. If desired, roll in extra sugar before placing on cookie sheet.
- Press with fork; press again in opposite direction.
- Bake 10 to 12 minutes at 350 degrees Fahrenheit.
- Do not brown; do not over bake.

Nutrition Information

- Calories: 131.2
- Cholesterol: 10.3
- Fiber: 0.9
- Sugar: 12.4
- Total Carbohydrate: 13.9
- Total Fat: 7.5
- Saturated Fat: 1.6
- Sodium: 69.8
- Protein: 4

175. Impossibly Easy Pumpkin Pie (Bisquick...too Easy :)

Serving: 6 serving(s) | Prep: 10mins | Ready in:

Ingredients

- 1 cup canned pumpkin (not pumpkin pie mix)
- 1/2 cup original Bisquick baking mix
- 1/2 cup sugar
- 1 cup evaporated milk
- 1 tablespoon butter or 1 tablespoon margarine, softened
- 1 1/2 teaspoons pumpkin pie spice
- 1 teaspoon vanilla
- 2 eggs
- whipped topping, if desired

Direction

- Heat oven to 350°F.
- Grease 9-inch pie plate.
- Stir all ingredients except whipped topping until blended.
- Pour into pie plate.

- Bake 35 to 40 minutes or until knife inserted in center comes out clean.
- Cool 30 minutes.
- Refrigerate about 3 hours or until chilled.
- Serve with whipped topping.
- Store covered in refrigerator.

Nutrition Information

- Calories: 222.4
- Total Fat: 8.5
- Sodium: 307.8
- Total Carbohydrate: 31
- Cholesterol: 88
- Saturated Fat: 4.1
- Fiber: 1.5
- Sugar: 19.4
- Protein: 6.2

176. Incredible Ice Cream Sandwich Sundae Dessert

Serving: 12-15 serving(s) | Prep: 30mins | Ready in:

Ingredients

- 19 ice cream sandwiches (regular "or" neopolitan)
- 1 (12 ounce) container frozen whipped topping, thawed
- 1 (12 ounce) jar chocolate fudge topping
- 0.5 (12 ounce) jar strawberry ice cream topping (optional)
- 0.5 (12 ounce) jar butterscotch sundae sauce (optional) or 0.5 (12 ounce) jar caramel ice cream topping (optional)
- 1 cup of chopped walnuts (or 1 jar of wet nuts ice cream topping)
- 1 (10 ounce) jar maraschino cherries
- banana, sliced (optional)

Direction

- Cut one ice cream sandwich in half.
- Put one whole and one-half ice cream sandwich along the short side of a 9" x 13" baking dish.
- Arrange eight ice cream sandwiches in opposite direction evenly in bottom of pan.
- Spread with half of the whipped topping.
- Drizzle or dollop most of fudge topping on top of whipped topping (save a couple tablespoons).
- Drizzle optional toppings (if using) and nuts on top, reserving a couple tablespoons of each.
- Repeat another layer of ice-cream sandwich.
- Top with remaining whipped topping.
- Fancily drizzle remaining hot fudge, butterscotch and strawberry toppings on top, along with walnuts or wet nuts.
- Cover and freeze for up to 2 months.
- Remove from freezer 20-30 minutes before serving.
- Cut into squares and top with a few maraschino cherries.
- Serve slices bananas on the side for people who are in a banana split mood and want to top theirs with bananas!
- YUM YUM YUM!

Nutrition Information

- Calories: 292.8
- Total Fat: 16.2
- Saturated Fat: 8
- Sodium: 106.4
- Fiber: 2.2
- Sugar: 25.5
- Total Carbohydrate: 35.7
- Cholesterol: 0.6
- Protein: 3.2

177. Incredibly Easy Amazing Strawberry Shortcake

Serving: 10-12 serving(s) | Prep: 20mins | Ready in:

Ingredients

- Cake
- 1 (18 ounce) box white cake mix or 1 (18 ounce) box yellow cake mix
- 1 (1 1/3 ounce) envelope Dream Whip, unprepared
- 4 eggs
- 1 cup cold water
- Topping and Filling
- 1 cup ice cold milk
- 1 (3 1/2 ounce) box vanilla pudding mix
- 1 (12 ounce) container Cool Whip, thawed
- 2 pints strawberries, hulled and sliced (Leave 5 or 6 nice looking berries whole)

Direction

- Preheat oven to 350 degrees.
- Combine all cake ingredients in a large mixing bowl and beat 4 minutes at medium speed.
- Pour into a greased and floured tube pan and bake for about 50 minutes or into 2- 8 or 9 inch greased and floured pans and bake for about 30 minutes, or until cake test done.
- Cool completely.
- Topping and Filling: Mix milk, pudding mix and whipped topping in a large bowl and beat until peaks form.
- If not using right away, keep in the refrigerator.
- Put it together: Cut tube pan cake in half lengthwise.
- Frost bottom with half of filling and layer with sliced strawberries.
- Place top half of cake on and frost with remaining filling.
- Decorate with whole berries.

Nutrition Information

- Calories: 453.8
- Saturated Fat: 10.8
- Sodium: 469
- Fiber: 1.9
- Sugar: 49
- Total Fat: 18.9
- Total Carbohydrate: 65.8
- Cholesterol: 88
- Protein: 6.8

178. Irish Apple Crumble

Serving: 8 serving(s) | Prep: 25mins | Ready in:

Ingredients

- pastry dough, to fit an 8-inch pie pan
- 4 medium granny smith apples or 4 medium Red Delicious apples, peeled, cored, and coarsely chopped
- 3/4 cup sugar, plus
- 1 tablespoon sugar
- 1/2 teaspoon cinnamon
- 1/2 cup all-purpose flour
- 4 tablespoons unsalted butter, softened

Direction

- Preheat the oven to 350°F.
- Line an 8-inch pie pan or heatproof baking dish with the pie dough; prick the dough with the tines of a fork.
- In a bowl, mix together the apples, ¼ cup of the sugar, and ¼ teaspoon of the cinnamon.
- In a second bowl, mix together the flour, ½ cup of the sugar, and the unsalted butter; work these ingredients together with a fork until you have a crumbly mixture.
- Fill the pie crust with the apple mixture and smooth over the surface.
- Spoon the crumble over the apple mixture so that the apples are completely covered.
- Sprinkle the remaining tablespoon of sugar and ¼ teaspoon of cinnamon over the crumble.
- Bake for 25 minutes.

Nutrition Information

- Calories: 194.2
- Saturated Fat: 3.7

- Total Carbohydrate: 35.9
- Total Fat: 6
- Fiber: 1.9
- Sugar: 27.5
- Cholesterol: 15.3
- Protein: 1.1
- Sodium: 1.7

179. Jack Daniels Bread Pudding

Serving: 48 pieces, 48 serving(s) | Prep: 45mins | Ready in:

Ingredients

- Pudding
- 15 cups sourdough French bread, cubed and toasted
- 5 cups milk
- 8 eggs
- 12 tablespoons salted butter
- 2 cups sugar
- 1 teaspoon nutmeg (I use a bit more of both the nutmeg and cinnamon)
- 1 teaspoon cinnamon
- 1 teaspoon vanilla
- 2 pinches salt
- 1 cup raisins
- Jack Daniels Sauce
- 1 lb brown sugar
- 1 cup salted butter
- 1 cup heavy whipping cream
- 1 pinch salt
- 1/2 cup Jack Daniels Whiskey (I use more because I like to be able to REALLY taste this)

Direction

- Pudding:
- Lightly grease deep dish casserole pans.
- Fill with toasted bread cubes and raisins mixed together.
- Heat milk and butter in pan over medium heat.
- Whisk sugar, eggs, nutmeg, cinnamon, vanilla, and salt. Add 1 cup of the heated milk mixture to this, then mix this into the hot milk mixture. Pour over the bread and raisins. Put your casserole dish (I use two 9x13 inch casseroles and bake one at a time) with the pudding into a deeper pan that has at least an inch of water in it, and cover with foil.
- Bake at 350°F for one hour. Remove foil and place back in oven for an additional 15 minutes, or until nicely browned. Pour cream sauce over the pudding and keep warm in oven until time to serve.
- Cream Sauce (I make this while the pudding is cooking):
- Combine all ingredients into a large saucepan and heat to boiling. Turn heat down to low and allow to reduce to consistency of your liking.
- I double the sauce recipe so I can have some to pour over the pudding and ice cream when I serve it.
- Serve hot with both ice cream and extra sauce or with heavy cream drizzled over it.

Nutrition Information

- Calories: 393.5
- Fiber: 1.9
- Sugar: 21.2
- Cholesterol: 59.1
- Total Fat: 11.6
- Total Carbohydrate: 61.5
- Protein: 10.5
- Saturated Fat: 6.6
- Sodium: 462.3

180. Julia Child's Cherry Clafouti

Serving: 4 for breakfast, 6-8 serving(s) | Prep: 10mins | Ready in:

Ingredients

- 1 1/4 cups milk
- 2/3 cup sugar, divided
- 3 eggs
- 1 tablespoon vanilla
- 1/8 teaspoon salt
- 1/2 cup flour
- 3 cups cherries, pitted
- powdered sugar, for garnish

Direction

- Preheat oven to 350 degrees F.
- Using a blender, combine the milk, 1/3 cup sugar, eggs, vanilla, salt and flour, and blend.
- Lightly butter an 8-cup baking dish, and pour a 1/4-inch layer of the blended mixture over the bottom. Set remaining batter aside.
- Place dish into the oven for about 7-10 minutes, until a film of batter sets in the pan but the mixture is not baked through. Remove from oven (but don't turn the oven off, yet).
- Distribute the pitted cherries over the set batter in the pan, then sprinkle with the remaining sugar. Pour the remaining batter over the cherries and sugar.
- Bake in the preheated oven for 45 to 60 minutes, until the clafouti is puffed and brown and a knife inserted into the center comes out clean.
- Sprinkle with powdered sugar and serve warm.
- Servings: 6-8 for dessert, 4 for breakfast.

Nutrition Information

- Calories: 247
- Protein: 6.7
- Total Fat: 4.5
- Saturated Fat: 2
- Sodium: 109.5
- Fiber: 1.9
- Total Carbohydrate: 45.3
- Cholesterol: 100.1
- Sugar: 32.5

181. Kids' Fruit Salad

Serving: 3 cups, 6 serving(s) | Prep: 10mins | Ready in:

Ingredients

- 16 ounces fruit cocktail, drained (I also rinsed mine to get rid of the syrupy taste)
- 2 medium bananas, sliced
- 1 cup miniature marshmallow
- 1/2 cup sour cream
- 2 tablespoons sugar
- 1/2 teaspoon vanilla

Direction

- In large bowl, combine all ingredients and stir gently to combine.
- Refrigerate until serving time.
- Store in refrigerator.

Nutrition Information

- Calories: 159.2
- Sugar: 25.1
- Total Carbohydrate: 31.9
- Protein: 1.3
- Total Fat: 4
- Saturated Fat: 2.3
- Sodium: 27
- Fiber: 1.8
- Cholesterol: 10

182. Kiwi And Cream Pie

Serving: 6-8 serving(s) | Prep: 15mins | Ready in:

Ingredients

- 1 cup heavy cream, chilled
- 1/4 cup confectioners' sugar
- 1/3 cup sour cream
- 1 prepared 9 inch shortbread pie crust
- 4 kiwi fruits, peeled and cut into 1/8 inch rounds

Direction

- Combine heavy cream and sugar in a medium size bowl, using an electric mixer with a whisk attachment, beat until soft peaks form.
- Add sour cream and beat again until soft peaks form.
- Pour into pie shell and smooth with a spatula.
- Arrange kiwi slices over the filing in overlapping circles, cover and chill until serving time.

Nutrition Information

- Calories: 300.2
- Saturated Fat: 12.6
- Fiber: 1.7
- Total Carbohydrate: 22.3
- Protein: 2.5
- Total Fat: 23.1
- Sodium: 131.2
- Sugar: 10.2
- Cholesterol: 60

183. Kumara / Sweet Potato Buns

Serving: 12 buns, 12 serving(s) | Prep: 5mins | Ready in:

Ingredients

- 3 cups mashed sweet potatoes
- 1 cup milk
- 1 cup self-rising flour
- 1 teaspoon cinnamon
- 1 teaspoon lemon juice

Direction

- Peel the sweet potatoes and boil them for 20 minutes or until mashable. Drain and mash, and let cool in a large bowl.
- Add the milk to the mashed sweet potatoes after they cooled off enough.
- Sprinkle in the lemon juice and cinnamon, and any additional spices you'd like and add the flour in bit by bit to make a firm dough.
- Shape the dough into egg-size balls, and place in a greased pie pan or cookie sheet.
- Bake at 450F or 220C for 15-25 minutes or until set. Cool then serve.

Nutrition Information

- Calories: 112.8
- Total Fat: 1
- Sugar: 4.7
- Protein: 2.8
- Saturated Fat: 0.5
- Sodium: 164.4
- Fiber: 2.4
- Total Carbohydrate: 23.4
- Cholesterol: 2.9

184. Layered Ice Cream Candy Cake!

Serving: 12 serving(s) | Prep: 10mins | Ready in:

Ingredients

- 24 ice cream sandwiches
- 8 ounces Cool Whip
- 1 (11 3/4 ounce) chocolate syrup
- 1 (11 3/4 ounce) butterscotch syrup or 1 (11 3/4 ounce) caramel syrup
- 4 Snickers candy bars (or your favorite candy bar)
- 1/2 cup peanuts (optional)

Direction

- Layer 12 ice cream sandwiches in a 9x13 pan.
- Spread half of the Cool Whip on top then 1/2 of the caramel and chocolate toppings and sprinkle with half of the candy and half of the peanuts.
- Repeat, then freeze!

Nutrition Information

- Calories: 321.3
- Saturated Fat: 7
- Fiber: 1.5
- Sugar: 23.7
- Cholesterol: 3
- Total Fat: 11.8
- Sodium: 243.8
- Total Carbohydrate: 51.9
- Protein: 3.4

185. Lemon Cake With Crackly Caramel Glaze

Serving: 10 serving(s) | Prep: 3hours30mins | Ready in:

Ingredients

- CAKE
- 6 large eggs, separated
- 1/2 teaspoon cream of tartar
- 1 1/2 cups sugar
- 2 1/4 cups cake flour
- 1 tablespoon baking powder
- 1/2 teaspoon salt
- 3/4 cup water
- 1/2 cup pure olive oil
- 2 teaspoons pure vanilla extract
- 2 finely grated lemons, zest of
- LIMONCELLO SYRUP
- 1/4 cup water
- 1/4 cup sugar
- 2 tablespoons limoncello or 1/2 teaspoon lemon extract
- CARAMEL TOPPING
- 1 cup sugar
- 1/4 teaspoon cream of tartar
- 2 tablespoons water

Direction

- MAKE THE CAKE:
- Preheat the oven to 375°F
- Butter and flour a 12-cup Bundt pan. In a large bowl, using an electric mixer, beat the egg whites with the cream of tartar until soft peaks form.
- Gradually beat in 1/2 cup of the sugar.
- In a medium bowl, whisk the cake flour, baking powder and salt.
- In a large bowl, using an electric mixer, beat the 6 egg yolks with the water, olive oil, vanilla, lemon zest and the remaining 1 cup of sugar.
- Add the dry ingredients and beat until the batter is smooth.
- Using a spatula, fold in the beaten egg whites until no streaks remain.
- Spoon the batter into the prepared Bundt pan.
- Bake the cake for 35 to 40 minutes, until springy to the touch.
- Let cool for 20 minutes, then invert the cake onto a rack to cool completely.
- Lower the oven temperature to 350°.
- MAKE THE LIMONCELLO SYRUP:
- In a small saucepan, simmer the water and sugar over moderate heat just until the sugar is dissolved, about 5 minutes.
- Let cool, then stir in the Limoncello.
- Brush the syrup all over the cake, allowing it to soak inches
- MAKE THE CARAMEL TOPPING:
- Line a large baking sheet with parchment paper.
- In a heavy saucepan, stir the sugar with the cream of tartar and water until sandy.
- Wash down the side of the pan with a moistened pastry brush to remove any sugar crystals.
- Bring the mixture to a boil over moderately high heat and cook without stirring until a

deep honey-colored caramel forms, about 5 minutes.
- Remove from the heat.
- Carefully swirl the pan to cool the caramel slightly, then pour it onto the baking sheet in a rough round.
- Using an offset spatula, spread the caramel into a 13-inch round and let stand until slightly cooled but still pliable, about 5 minutes.
- Invert the caramel round over the cake and peel off the parchment paper.
- Gently press the caramel onto the cake before it hardens to help it conform.
- If the caramel hardens as you work, place the caramel-coated cake in the oven for 2 to 3 minutes, just to soften the caramel.
- When the caramel has hardened, serve with Lime-Yogurt Mousse (recipe to follow).

Nutrition Information

- Calories: 467.7
- Fiber: 0.5
- Sugar: 55.4
- Protein: 6.3
- Saturated Fat: 2.5
- Sodium: 268.8
- Total Carbohydrate: 79.8
- Cholesterol: 126.9
- Total Fat: 14.1

186. Lemon Frosted Golden Raisin Buns

Serving: 18 buns | Prep: 10mins | Ready in:

Ingredients

- 1 cup water
- 1/2 cup butter
- 1 teaspoon sugar
- 1/4 teaspoon salt
- 1 cup flour
- 4 eggs
- 1/2 cup golden raisin (soaked 5 minutes in hot water, then drained well)
- Frosting
- 1 tablespoon butter, melted
- 1 1/2 tablespoons cream or 1 1/2 tablespoons canned milk
- 1 cup sifted icing sugar
- 1 teaspoon lemon juice
- 1/2 teaspoon vanilla

Direction

- Heat oven to 375f degrees.
- Bring water, butter, sugar and salt to boil.
- Add flour and beat until mixture leaves sides of pan.
- Remove from heat and beat 2 minutes to cool.
- Add eggs one at a time, beating until smooth and satiny after each addition.
- Add raisins and mix well.
- Drop by measuring tablespoons full onto greased cookie sheet.
- Bake 30 to 35 minutes.
- Ice while warm.
- Frosting: Combine ingredients in order given.

Nutrition Information

- Calories: 135.5
- Sodium: 90.1
- Total Carbohydrate: 15.5
- Cholesterol: 63.6
- Protein: 2.3
- Saturated Fat: 4.2
- Fiber: 0.3
- Sugar: 9.3
- Total Fat: 7.3

187. Lemon Krisp Cookies

Serving: 48 cookies | Prep: 5mins | Ready in:

Ingredients

- 1 (18 1/4 ounce) box lemon cake mix
- 1 cup Rice Krispies
- 1/2 cup butter, melted
- 1 large egg, beaten
- 1 teaspoon grated lemon, rind of

Direction

- Preheat oven to 350 degrees.
- Combine all ingredients in a large mixing bowl until well mixed.
- Shape into 1 inch balls and place 2 inches apart on ungreased cookie sheets.
- Bake for 10 to 12 minutes.
- Leave on cookie sheets for a minute or two and then cool completely on wire racks.

Nutrition Information

- Calories: 67.4
- Total Fat: 3.3
- Saturated Fat: 1.4
- Protein: 0.7
- Sodium: 92.6
- Fiber: 0.1
- Sugar: 4.7
- Total Carbohydrate: 8.9
- Cholesterol: 9.2

188. Lemon Meringue Cake With Strawberries

Serving: 9 serving(s) | Prep: 25mins | Ready in:

Ingredients

- 1 pint strawberry, sliced (2 cups)
- 1/4 cup sugar
- 1 1/4 cups all-purpose flour
- 1 cup sugar
- 1/4 cup margarine, softened
- 1/2 cup skim milk
- 1 1/2 teaspoons baking powder
- 1 1/2 teaspoons grated lemons, rind of
- 1 teaspoon vanilla
- 1/4 teaspoon salt
- 2 egg whites or 1/4 cup egg substitute
- 2 egg whites
- 1/2 cup sugar

Direction

- Mix strawberries and 1/4 cup sugar.
- Cover and refrigerate until serving.
- Heat oven to 350 degrees F.
- Spray square pan, 9×9×2 inches, with cooking spray.
- Beat flour, 1 cup sugar, the margarine, milk, baking powder, lemon peel, vanilla, salt and 2 egg whites in large bowl with electric mixer on low speed 30 seconds, scraping bowl constantly.
- Beat on high speed 2 minutes, scraping bowl occasionally.
- Pour into pan.
- Bake 25 to 30 minutes or until toothpick inserted in centre comes out clean.
- Cool slightly.
- Increase oven temperature to 400 degrees F.
- Beat 2 egg whites in medium bowl on high speed until foamy.
- Beat in 1/2 cup sugar, 1 tablespoon at a time; continue beating until stiff and glossy.
- Spread over cake.
- Bake 8 to 10 minutes or until meringue is light brown.
- Cool completely.
- Top each serving with strawberries.

Nutrition Information

- Calories: 286.6
- Saturated Fat: 0.9
- Fiber: 1.3
- Protein: 4.3
- Total Fat: 5.4
- Sodium: 217.4
- Sugar: 40.9
- Total Carbohydrate: 56.4
- Cholesterol: 0.3

189. Lemon Pastry Shell

Serving: 1 "9 inch pastry shell" | Prep: 10mins | Ready in:

Ingredients

- 1 cup sifted flour
- 1/2 teaspoon salt
- 1/3 cup shortening
- 1 egg, beaten
- 1 tablespoon lemon juice concentrate

Direction

- Preheat oven to 400 degrees.
- Combine flour and salt; cut in shortening until crumbly.
- In a small bowl mix egg and lemon juice.
- Stir into flour mixture until it forms a ball.
- On a floured surface, roll out (1/8-inch thick) and line a 9-inch pie plate.
- Flute edges.
- Prick bottom with fork.
- Bake 12 to 15 minutes or until golden brown.

Nutrition Information

- Calories: 1134.4
- Sodium: 1238.4
- Fiber: 3.4
- Total Fat: 74.4
- Saturated Fat: 18.8
- Total Carbohydrate: 96.7
- Cholesterol: 211.5
- Protein: 19.3
- Sugar: 1.1

190. Lemon Raspberry Cheesecake Squares

Serving: 20 serving(s) | Prep: 35mins | Ready in:

Ingredients

- 3/4 cup shortening
- 1/3 cup packed brown sugar
- 1 1/4 cups all-purpose flour
- 1 cup rolled oats
- 1/4 teaspoon salt
- 1/2 cup seedless raspberry jam
- Filling
- 4 (8 ounce) packages cream cheese, softened
- 1 1/2 cups sugar
- 1/4 cup all-purpose flour
- 4 eggs
- 1/3 cup lemon juice (I use fresh squeezed)
- 4 teaspoon lemons, rind of, grated

Direction

- In a mixing bowl, cream shortening and brown sugar.
- Combine flour, oats, and salt; gradually add to creamed mixture.
- Press dough into a greased 13x9 inch baking dish.
- Bake at 350°F for 15-18 minutes or until golden brown.
- Spread with jam.
- Beat cream cheese, sugar and flour until fluffy.
- Add the eggs, lemon juice and peel just until blended.
- Carefully spoon over jam.
- Bake at 350°F for 30-35 minutes or until center is almost set.
- Cool on a wire rack.
- Cover and store in the refrigerator.

Nutrition Information

- Calories: 385.7
- Sodium: 181.7
- Protein: 6.3

- Total Fat: 24.8
- Fiber: 0.8
- Sugar: 22.7
- Total Carbohydrate: 35.6
- Cholesterol: 92.2
- Saturated Fat: 12.2

191. Lennie's Special Shortbread

Serving: 4-5 dozen | Prep: 10mins | Ready in:

Ingredients

- 1 cup butter, cold
- 1/2 cup icing sugar
- 1/2 cup cornstarch
- 1 1/2 cups flour
- 1/2 teaspoon vanilla

Direction

- Chop cold butter into chunks.
- In Cuisinart fitted with metal blade, process butter with icing sugar until well creamed, about one minute; you may have to scrape down the sides.
- Add remaining ingredients and process with several on/off turns, just until dough is well mixed and begins to gather together in a ball around the blade.
- What I do now is wrap this dough in wax paper and put it in the fridge, and make up a second batch with the remaining 1/2 pound of butter (1 cup butter= 1/2 pound); I then put that dough in the fridge and proceed with the first batch I made.
- Raw dough keeps well in the fridge for several days.
- Shape rounded teaspoonfuls of dough into small balls.
- Place on an ungreased cookie sheet (shiny is best) and flatten, using a fork dipped in icing sugar, cookie press dipped in icing sugar, or a cherry or nut (halved).
- I often put coloured sprinkles or coloured sugars on top of cookies before baking.
- Bake at 350 degrees for 12-15 minutes, watching carefully; edges should be very lightly browned.
- Yield: 40-50 cookies.

Nutrition Information

- Calories: 698.3
- Sugar: 14.9
- Total Carbohydrate: 65.4
- Cholesterol: 122
- Total Fat: 46.5
- Saturated Fat: 29.2
- Fiber: 1.4
- Protein: 5.4
- Sodium: 407.9

192. Light Fresh Peach Cobbler

Serving: 8 serving(s) | Prep: 18mins | Ready in:

Ingredients

- 6 medium peaches, sliced
- 6 1/3 tablespoons sugar
- 1 tablespoon cornstarch
- 1 teaspoon fresh lemon juice
- 1/2 teaspoon ground cinnamon
- 1 cup all-purpose flour
- 1 1/2 teaspoons baking powder
- 1/2 teaspoon table salt
- 3 tablespoons reduced-calorie margarine
- 1/2 cup nonfat milk

Direction

- Preheat oven to 375°F.
- In a large saucepan, combine peaches, 1/3 cup of the sugar (5 1/3 tablespoons), cornstarch, lemon juice, and cinnamon; toss to coat peaches.

- Set pan over medium heat and bring to a boil.
- Cook until mixture thickens, about 1 minute.
- Remove from heat and transfer mixture to an 8-inch square baking pan.
- To make the topping, in a large bowl, combine flour, remaining tablespoon of sugar, baking powder and salt.
- Work in margarine with a fork until mixture resembles coarse crumbs.
- Add milk and stir until flour mixture is evenly moistened.
- Drop 8 tablespoons of topping mixture onto peach mixture.
- Bake until topping is golden brown and filling is bubbly, about 20 to 25 minutes.
- Cut into 8 pieces and serve.

Nutrition Information

- Calories: 173
- Total Fat: 3.1
- Saturated Fat: 0.9
- Sodium: 252.2
- Fiber: 2.2
- Total Carbohydrate: 34.7
- Cholesterol: 4
- Sugar: 20.2
- Protein: 3.2

193. Light Pineapple Pudding

Serving: 6 serving(s) | Prep: 5mins | Ready in:

Ingredients

- 1 (3 1/2 ounce) package instant vanilla pudding or 1 (3 1/2 ounce) package vegetarian instant vanilla pudding mix
- 1 (19 ounce) can crushed pineapple
- 1 cup plain low-fat yogurt

Direction

- If you buy your pineapple in metric-sized tins, you want the 540mL tin of crushed pineapple.
- In a mixing bowl, whisk together pudding mix and undrained pineapple.
- Whisk in yogurt.
- Spoon into serving dishes and chill until serving time (needs only 30 minutes at the most in the fridge before they're ready to eat).
- These look particularly attractive when garnished with a few fresh berries-- try blueberries or raspberries.
- If taking to a potluck, don't spoon it into individual dishes but rather leave it in the bowl.

Nutrition Information

- Calories: 140.1
- Saturated Fat: 0.5
- Sodium: 260.7
- Total Carbohydrate: 31.9
- Sugar: 30.8
- Cholesterol: 2.5
- Protein: 2.5
- Total Fat: 0.8
- Fiber: 0.7

194. Light And Tasty Pumpkin Cheesecake Bars

Serving: 20 serving(s) | Prep: 15mins | Ready in:

Ingredients

- CRUST
- 2 cups graham cracker crumbs
- 1/4 cup sugar
- 1/4 cup land o' lakes stick light butter
- FILLING
- 3 (8 ounce) packages fat free cream cheese
- 1 (15 ounce) can solid-pack pumpkin
- 2 tablespoons all-purpose flour
- 3/4 teaspoon pumpkin pie spice

- 3/4 teaspoon vanilla extract
- 2 eggs, lightly beaten
- 10 walnuts, halved

Direction

- Preheat oven to 325°; spray PAM over the inside of a 13X9 pan.
- Combine crust ingredients and press onto the bottom of the 13X9 pan; cover and chill NO less than 15 minute.
- In a large mixing bowl, beat together the cream cheese and sugar until smooth; Beat in the canned pumpkin, the pie spice and vanilla.
- Add eggs and beat on low speed until JUST combined; our over the chilled crust; Bake in the preheated oven for 35-45 minutes or until the center is ALMOST set.
- Cool on a wire rack for 1 hour; then cover and chill for NO less than 8 hours or even overnight.
- Cut into 20 bars, topping each with a walnut half before serving.

Nutrition Information

- Calories: 121.9
- Sugar: 5.7
- Protein: 6.8
- Saturated Fat: 1.7
- Fiber: 0.5
- Cholesterol: 26.9
- Total Fat: 4.8
- Sodium: 256.6
- Total Carbohydrate: 13.3

195. Lil's Chocolate Cookies (Wheaties)

Serving: 24 squares | Prep: 15mins | Ready in:

Ingredients

- 1/2 cup butter, maybe a little more
- 1/2 cup sugar
- 1 cup self raising flour
- 1 cup cereal (I use Wheaties, or cornflakes)
- 1/2 cup coconut
- Icing
- 1 cup icing sugar
- 1 tablespoon cocoa
- milk, just a little to bind

Direction

- Mix butter and sugar to a cream, add flour, coconut and Wheaties, this is a very thick mixture.
- Press into slab tin and bake 20 mins at 200degC (400degF).
- Mix icing ingredients and ice whilst hot and cut into squares.

Nutrition Information

- Calories: 101
- Fiber: 0.5
- Sugar: 9.2
- Total Carbohydrate: 13.7
- Protein: 0.7
- Total Fat: 5.1
- Saturated Fat: 3.5
- Sodium: 28.1
- Cholesterol: 10.2

196. Limoncello Cream Cupcakes

Serving: 18 Cupcakes, 18 serving(s) | Prep: 8mins | Ready in:

Ingredients

- Cupcakes
- 18 1/4 ounces super moist white cake mix (I used Betty Crocker)

- 1/2 cup frozen lemonade concentrate, thawed (put the rest in the freezer you can use it for other recipes and this one!)
- 1 cup sour cream
- 3 ounces cream cheese, room temperature
- 3 egg whites
- 2 tablespoons lemon zest (no pith)
- Frosting
- 1 (12 ounce) canwhipped cream frosting (I used Betty Crocker) or 1 (12 ounce) canyour favorite white frosting
- 2 tablespoons limoncello
- Garnish
- lemon zest

Direction

- Preheat oven to 350.
- In a large bowl combine cake mix, lemonade concentrate, sour cream, cream cheese and egg whites. Beat with mixer until blended. Stir in zest.
- Spoon batter into paper lined muffin pan or muffin pans sprayed well with Pam Baking spray.
- I actually used those new foil liners - no pan necessary.
- Bake at 350 for 20 minutes or until tester comes out of the centre of a cupcake clean. Immediately do next step.
- While cupcakes are baking scrape all the frosting out of the can with a spatula into a medium bowl. Add two tablespoons Limoncello and stir till creamy. Taste. Do you need more? Go ahead then -- add more!
- Refrigerate while you wait.
- Cool cupcakes completely and then frost and sprinkle with zest.

Nutrition Information

- Calories: 264.1
- Total Fat: 10.6
- Sugar: 31.5
- Total Carbohydrate: 40.1
- Cholesterol: 10.8
- Protein: 2.7
- Saturated Fat: 3.8
- Sodium: 257.4
- Fiber: 0.3

197. Linda's Peanut Butter Cookies

Serving: 36-48 cookies | Prep: 10mins | Ready in:

Ingredients

- 1 cup soft shortening or 1 cup margarine
- 1 cup sugar
- 3/4 cup brown sugar
- 2 eggs
- 1 cup peanut butter
- 2 cups flour
- 1/2 teaspoon salt
- 2 teaspoons baking soda
- 1 cup rolled oats

Direction

- Place shortening and sugars in bowl.
- Beat until light and fluffy.
- Add eggs and beat well.
- Blend in peanut butter.
- In a separate bowl, sift together flour, salt and baking soda.
- Stir into the peanut butter mixture.
- Stir in the oats.
- Form small balls and place on ungreased cookie sheet or drop by spoonfuls.
- Press with a fork.
- Bake at 350 degrees for about 12 minutes.

Nutrition Information

- Calories: 169.2
- Fiber: 0.8
- Cholesterol: 11.8
- Protein: 3.2
- Saturated Fat: 2.3

- Sodium: 141
- Sugar: 10.7
- Total Carbohydrate: 18.2
- Total Fat: 9.8

- Fiber: 0.7
- Cholesterol: 3.7
- Protein: 1.2
- Total Fat: 6.6
- Sodium: 13.2
- Sugar: 17
- Total Carbohydrate: 18.4

198. Louisiana Caramel Pralines

Serving: 36 serving(s) | Prep: 5mins | Ready in:

Ingredients

- 2 cups granulated sugar
- 1 cup evaporated milk
- 1 cup granulated sugar
- 1 1/2 teaspoons vanilla
- 2 1/2 cups pecans (chopped, may use plain or toasted)
- 2 tablespoons butter

Direction

- Place 2 cups sugar milk in an lrg saucepan. Cook slowly, stirring often.
- At the same time, put other cup of sugar in a 2nd saucepan on low heat stir till melted.
- Pour 2nd mixture slowly into the sugar milk that should be read to boil stir while adding.
- Cook slowly till a firm ball forms when dropped into cold water (238°) remove from heat.
- Add vanilla, pecans butter. Stir till mixture begins to thicken.
- To avoid sticking as experienced by the 1st reviewer using waxed paper which was given as an option -- drop by spoonfuls in desired size onto a lightly sprayed baking sheet or buttered cookie sheet (candies should set up immediately).

Nutrition Information

- Calories: 132.3
- Saturated Fat: 1.2

199. Low Fat Noodle Kugel

Serving: 12 serving(s) | Prep: 20mins | Ready in:

Ingredients

- 1 (16 ounce) package wide egg noodles
- 1 cup reduced fat margarine
- 1/2 cup fat free sour cream
- 1 1/2 cups egg substitute
- 2 cups white sugar
- 1 teaspoon lemon juice
- 1 teaspoon vanilla extract
- 8 ounces jars applesauce
- 1/4 cup raisins
- 1/4 cup graham cracker crumbs (optional)
- 1 teaspoon ground cinnamon, to taste

Direction

- Preheat oven to 350 degrees F (175 degrees C).
- Coat a 9x13 baking dish with cooking spray.
- Bring a large pot of lightly salted water to a boil.
- Add pasta and cook for 8 to 10 minutes or until al dente; drain.
- Mix together margarine, sour cream, egg substitute, sugar, lemon juice, vanilla extract, and applesauce.
- Stir in noodles and raisins.
- Spread graham cracker crumbs on bottom of prepared pan.
- Pour noodle mixture over crumbs.
- Sprinkle top with cinnamon.
- Bake at 350 degrees F (175 degrees C) for 45 to 60 minutes, or until set.
- Cover with foil if it browns too quickly.

Nutrition Information

- Calories: 359.2
- Total Carbohydrate: 69.1
- Sugar: 37.2
- Cholesterol: 32.9
- Total Fat: 5.8
- Saturated Fat: 1.1
- Sodium: 228
- Fiber: 1.7
- Protein: 9

200. Low Fat Pumpkin Cake

Serving: 20 serving(s) | Prep: 25mins | Ready in:

Ingredients

- 3/4 cup Egg Beaters egg substitute
- 2 cups canned pumpkin
- 3/4 cup sugar-free applesauce, canned
- 1 teaspoon salt
- 1 teaspoon cinnamon
- 1/2 teaspoon baking powder
- 1 3/4 cups sugar
- 1/4 cup canola oil
- 2 1/4 cups all-purpose flour
- 1 teaspoon allspice
- 1 1/4 teaspoons baking soda
- Cream Cheese Frosting Ingredients
- 8 ounces fat free cream cheese, softened
- 1 teaspoon vanilla extract
- 2 cups powdered sugar

Direction

- Preheat oven to 350°F.
- Spray a 13x9-inch pan with non-stick cooking spray.
- In small bowl combine all dry ingredients.
- Set aside.
- In large mixing bowl, whip egg beaters with electric mixer until fluffy.
- Blend in sugar, pumpkin, oil, and applesauce until smooth.
- Gradually add dry mixture to egg mixture. Blend until smooth.
- Pour into prepared pan.
- Bake at 350°F for 35-40 minutes or until wooden pick inserted into center comes out clean.
- Edges will appear golden brown.
- Cool cake completely before frosting with fat-free whip or fat-free cream cheese frosting.
- Cream Cheese Frosting Directions:
- Beat cream cheese until smooth.
- Add vanilla and mix.
- Gradually add powdered sugar mixing in sugar until you get to the consistency you desire.

Nutrition Information

- Calories: 214.1
- Total Fat: 3.1
- Saturated Fat: 0.4
- Sodium: 325.6
- Sugar: 31.1
- Cholesterol: 0.9
- Fiber: 1.3
- Total Carbohydrate: 44.1
- Protein: 3.4

201. Low Fat Triple Fruit Pizza

Serving: 16 serving(s) | Prep: 40mins | Ready in:

Ingredients

- 1 (18 ounce) package refrigerated sugar cookie dough, softened
- 1 teaspoon flour
- 1 (8 ounce) package fat free cream cheese, softened
- 2 teaspoons powdered sugar

- 1/2 teaspoon vanilla
- 3/4 cup peach preserves
- 3 peaches, peeled and chopped
- 1 1/2 cups fresh strawberries, chopped
- 3 kiwi, peeled and chopped
- 2 teaspoons grated lemons, zest of

Direction

- Preheat oven to 350 degrees.
- Shape dough into a ball and place on cookie sheet.
- Flatten slightly, sprinkle with flour and roll into a 12 inch circle.
- Bake 18-20 minutes.
- In a small bowl, combine cream cheese, powdered sugar and vanilla until smooth.
- Spread evenly over cookie.
- Spread preserves over cream cheese.
- Top cookie with chopped fruit.
- Sprinkle with lemon zest.
- Immediately cut into wedges and serve.

Nutrition Information

- Calories: 216.8
- Protein: 3.9
- Total Carbohydrate: 35.3
- Cholesterol: 10.4
- Total Fat: 7
- Saturated Fat: 1.8
- Sodium: 217.2
- Fiber: 1.4
- Sugar: 18

202. Lox Mousse

Serving: 2 cups apprx. | Prep: 15mins | Ready in:

Ingredients

- 2 ounces lox
- 1 lb cream cheese
- 2 tablespoons onions, finely minced
- 2 teaspoons fresh lemon juice
- 1/4 cup black olives, sliced
- pepper

Direction

- Blend together lox cream cheese.
- Add onion, lemon juice pepper.
- Fold in the olives.
- Serve with crisp crackers or small toasts, garnish with black olives or a small piece of lox.

Nutrition Information

- Calories: 834.6
- Total Fat: 80.8
- Fiber: 0.7
- Sugar: 7.8
- Total Carbohydrate: 11.6
- Cholesterol: 256.4
- Protein: 18.9
- Saturated Fat: 44.3
- Sodium: 1420.3

203. Loz (Almond Sweetmeats)

Serving: 40 Loz | Prep: 15mins | Ready in:

Ingredients

- 8 ounces ground almonds
- 4 ounces icing sugar
- 4 -6 tablespoons orange blossom water
- 4 ounces pistachio nuts, peeled and finely chopped
- 1 ounce caster sugar
- 4 ounces extra icing sugar
- 4 ounces extra pistachio nuts, peeled, see note below

Direction

- Combine the finely chopped pistachio nuts and caster sugar, and set aside.
- Combine the ground almonds and icing sugar with enough orange-blossom water to form a stiff paste.
- Knead until smooth and allow to rest for about 10 minutes.
- Shape the paste into small balls the size of a walnut, and using a teaspoon handle, make a small hole in each ball and fill it with the combined pistachio nuts and caster sugar; close the hole over the filling and reshape to a round shape.
- Roll the balls in icing sugar and place in small paper cups or on a serving plate. Decorate the top of each ball with a peeled pistachio nut.
- Serve with coffee.
- Note: To peel pistachio nuts, simmer for 3 minutes, drain and slip off skins; dry on a paper towel before use.

Nutrition Information

- Calories: 89.4
- Sodium: 0.2
- Sugar: 7
- Total Carbohydrate: 9.1
- Protein: 2.4
- Total Fat: 5.4
- Saturated Fat: 0.5
- Fiber: 1.3
- Cholesterol: 0

204. M. Cunningham's Almond Butter Cake

Serving: 1 cake | Prep: 10mins | Ready in:

Ingredients

- The cake batter
- 3/4 cup butter
- 1 1/2 cups sugar
- 2 large eggs
- 1/2 teaspoon salt
- 1 1/2 teaspoons almond extract
- 1 teaspoon vanilla extract
- 1 1/2 cups all-purpose white flour
- 2 teaspoons soft butter or 2 teaspoons nonstick cooking spray (for greasing the cake pan)
- Topping
- 1 tablespoon sugar
- 4 ounces sliced almonds (3/4 cup)

Direction

- Preheat oven to 350-degrees.
- Melt the butter in a small saucepan over medium-low heat, stirring regularly.
- Pour the melted butter and 1 1/2 cups sugar into a large bowl and stir until smooth.
- Crack the eggs right into the same bowl and mix until the batter is creamy and all one color.
- Add the salt, almond extract, vanilla extract, and flour and stir briskly until the batter is smooth.
- Grease the bottom and sides of a 9-inch round cake pan with butter or nonstick cooking spray.
- Using a rubber spatula, scrape the batter from the bowl into the greased cake pan.
- Spread it evenly in the pan.
- Sprinkle the tablespoon of sugar, then the sliced almonds, over the top of the batter.
- Put the pan on the middle rack of the oven and set the timer for 35 minutes.
- When it rings, check to see if the cake is done.
- It should be light brown on top, and when you insert a toothpick in the center, it should have a few sticky crumbs adhering to it.
- If the cake is not browned enough and the toothpick comes out too wet, put the cake back in the oven and check it again in another 10 minutes.
- When the cake is done, remove it from the oven and let it cool on a heatproof counter for at least 30 minutes.
- Cut the cake into small wedges and serve with fresh fruit.

- This cake will stay fresh for about a week and will freeze indefinitely.
- Wrap it tightly in foil, or in a plastic bag you can seal with a zip or tie.
- Storing nuts: Whenever you have leftover nuts, freeze them in a plastic bag closed tightly.
- They will keep indefinitely in the freezer.

Nutrition Information

- Calories: 4012.8
- Total Fat: 214.9
- Saturated Fat: 100.1
- Protein: 57.6
- Sodium: 2343.2
- Fiber: 18.4
- Sugar: 320.5
- Total Carbohydrate: 480.2
- Cholesterol: 809.2

205. Maple Krispie Cookies

Serving: 3 dozen | Prep: 5mins | Ready in:

Ingredients

- 1 (18 ounce) package white cake mix
- 1 cup crisp rice cereal
- 1/2 cup butter, melted
- 1 large egg, beaten
- 1 teaspoon maple flavoring

Direction

- Preheat oven to 350°F degrees.
- In large bowl, mix all ingredients well (will be crumbly).
- Roll into 1-inch balls.
- Place 2 in apart on lightly sprayed cooking sheet.
- Bake for 10-12 minutes. Cool for 1 minute.
- Remove and cool completely.

Nutrition Information

- Calories: 1062.7
- Saturated Fat: 22.8
- Fiber: 1.6
- Cholesterol: 143.3
- Total Fat: 51.1
- Sodium: 1503.4
- Sugar: 94.2
- Total Carbohydrate: 141.9
- Protein: 10.8

206. Maple Pecan Squares

Serving: 24 squares | Prep: 20mins | Ready in:

Ingredients

- Base
- 1 cup all-purpose flour
- 1/4 cup packed brown sugar
- 1/2 cup butter, softened
- Topping
- 2/3 cup packed brown sugar
- 1 cup maple syrup (preferably dark maple syrup)
- 2 eggs, beaten
- 1/2 teaspoon pure vanilla extract
- 2 tablespoons all-purpose flour
- 1 cup pecan halves

Direction

- Preheat oven to 350F; have ready an ungreased 9-inch square cake pan.
- In a mixing bowl, combine flour and sugar, rub in butter to make coarse crumbs.
- Pat evenly and firmly into pan and bake for 5 minutes; remove from oven and set aside.
- Increase oven temperature to 425F.
- In a small saucepan, combine brown sugar and maple syrup and bring to a boil.
- Reduce heat and simmer gently for 5 minutes, then let cool for 10 minutes.

- Pour this syrup mixture into a mixing bowl and whisk in the eggs, vanilla and flour until smooth, then stir in pecans.
- Pour over base, return pan to oven, and bake for 10 minutes.
- Reduce heat to 350F and continue to bake until firm, about 15 more minutes.

Nutrition Information

- Calories: 156.7
- Total Fat: 7.3
- Sodium: 37.7
- Total Carbohydrate: 22.2
- Cholesterol: 27.8
- Saturated Fat: 2.8
- Fiber: 0.6
- Sugar: 16.3
- Protein: 1.6

207. Martin's Mum's Gingernuts

Serving: 54-60 crunchy cookies, 27-60 serving(s) | Prep: 2hours | Ready in:

Ingredients

- 1 lb self-raising flour
- 6 ounces unsalted butter
- 1/2 lb caster or 1/2 lb granulated sugar
- 1 large egg
- 1 teaspoon baking soda
- 1 teaspoon salt
- 4 teaspoons ground ginger
- 8 fluid ounces golden syrup or 8 fluid ounces light corn syrup (or, for variation, use molasses or maple syrup)

Direction

- Melt the butter and syrup and allow to cool slightly.
- Sift the dry ingredients thoroughly, add the egg and lastly the melted butter and syrup.
- Mix thoroughly, and then chill the dough until it is fairly stiff.
- Divide the mixture into pieces the size of a small walnut, place on a greased baking sheet and flatten very slightly.
- NOTE: Place them a few inches apart on the baking sheet (s) as they will expand during the baking process.
- Bake for 15 minutes at 175C/350F degrees.
- Store in a cookie tin at room temperature.

Nutrition Information

- Calories: 145.1
- Protein: 2
- Fiber: 0.5
- Sugar: 3.5
- Total Carbohydrate: 22.7
- Cholesterol: 20.4
- Total Fat: 5.5
- Saturated Fat: 3.3
- Sodium: 357.6

208. Mellow Yellow Jello Salad

Serving: 12 serving(s) | Prep: 10mins | Ready in:

Ingredients

- 2 cans crushed pineapple, drained
- 1 (6 ounce) box lemon Jell-O gelatin
- 2 cups 7-Up soda
- 2 cups pineapple juice
- 4 tablespoons flour
- 4 tablespoons butter
- 2 eggs
- 2 cups whipped topping

Direction

- Mix the pineapple, jello, and 7up.
- Pour into a 9x13 dish.

- Put into refrigerator to set.
- In saucepan, mix juice, flour, butter and eggs.
- Cook and stir, on med, bring to a boil.
- Boil for 1 minute.
- Allow to cool, while jello sets.
- Mix the cooked cooked mixture with the whipped topping.
- Spread over the jello.

Nutrition Information

- Calories: 173.8
- Sodium: 122.5
- Fiber: 0.1
- Sugar: 20.9
- Total Carbohydrate: 25.6
- Protein: 3
- Total Fat: 7
- Saturated Fat: 4.1
- Cholesterol: 53

209. Melting Moments

Serving: 1 small batch | Prep: 0S | Ready in:

Ingredients

- 4 ounces butter
- 1 ounce icing sugar
- 2 ounces flour
- 2 ounces cornflour
- 1/2 teaspoon baking powder

Direction

- Cream butter and sugar and work in other ingredients.
- Roll into small balls, place on greased trays, press down each biscuit with a fork (this mixture may be put through a biscuit forcer).
- Bake about 20 minutes at 350°F.
- Put together with your favourite icing.
- Cheers, Doreen Randal, Wanganui, New Zealand.

Nutrition Information

- Calories: 1335.7
- Total Fat: 94.7
- Saturated Fat: 58.6
- Sodium: 995.8
- Fiber: 5.7
- Sugar: 28.3
- Protein: 10.8
- Total Carbohydrate: 115.8
- Cholesterol: 243.8

210. Mile High Lemon Pie

Serving: 1 9inch deep dish pie, 10 serving(s) | Prep: 30mins | Ready in:

Ingredients

- 1 9 inch deep dish pie shell
- 1 envelope unflavored gelatin (I use Knox)
- 1 cup granulated sugar or 1 cup Splenda sugar substitute, for baking
- 1/2 teaspoon salt
- 2/3 cup fresh lemon juice
- 1 -2 teaspoon lemon, zest of
- 4 large eggs, separated
- 1 2/3 cups water
- 1/2 cup granulated sugar

Direction

- Bake pie shell according to package directions for a refrigerated pie.
- In saucepan, stir together gelatin, 1 cup sugar and salt.
- Beat together eggs yolks, lemon juice and water.
- Stir into gelatin mixture.
- Cook over medium heat, stirring constantly, until mixture just begins to boil.
- Remove from heat.

- Stir in lemon zest and chill, stirring occasionally, until partially set.
- NOTE: You can make this in two 8-inch regular pie shells.
- In mixing bowl, add egg whites and beat until soft peaks form.
- Gradually add 1/2 cup sugar, beating until stiff peaks form and sugar has dissolved.
- Fold the egg white mixture into the gelatin mixture until it becomes an even consistency.
- Pour into baked pie shell.
- Refrigerate and chill until firm (2 or more hours).
- Cut into small slices.
- If desired, dollop with whipped cream before serving.

Nutrition Information

- Calories: 216.8
- Fiber: 0.2
- Sugar: 31.1
- Total Carbohydrate: 37.8
- Cholesterol: 84.6
- Protein: 3.7
- Total Fat: 6.1
- Saturated Fat: 1.9
- Sodium: 228.1

211. Mini Chocolate Chip Cheese Pie

Serving: 1 pie | Prep: 5mins | Ready in:

Ingredients

- 1 (8 ounce) package cream cheese
- 1 (14 ounce) can sweetened condensed milk
- 1/3 cup lemon juice
- 1 teaspoon vanilla
- 1 cup miniature chocolate chip
- 1 chocolate cookie pie crust (bought or made)

Direction

- In large mixing bowl, using hand mixer, blend the first four ingredients until smooth.
- Fold in the mini-morsels.
- Pour filling into crust refrigerate until filling is set.

Nutrition Information

- Calories: 4055.1
- Sodium: 2694.2
- Sugar: 362.4
- Cholesterol: 386.7
- Protein: 67.5
- Saturated Fat: 117.3
- Total Carbohydrate: 460
- Total Fat: 234.9
- Fiber: 13.9

212. Mirj's Easy Sweet And Spicy Fat Free Curry Flavored Pumpkin

Serving: 3 serving(s) | Prep: 7mins | Ready in:

Ingredients

- 1 1/4 lbs pumpkin, cut into 3 inch dice
- 2 tablespoons tomato paste
- 2 tablespoons sweet chili sauce
- 1/2 teaspoon curry powder
- 1/2 teaspoon cinnamon
- salt and pepper, to taste

Direction

- Place the pumpkin dice in a large microwave-safe bowl.
- Add the rest of the ingredients and combine thoroughly.
- Nuke, covered and vented, for about 13 minutes on high, this will give you a crisp bite.
- For a mushier dish, nuke for about 18 minutes.

Nutrition Information

- Calories: 71.6
- Total Carbohydrate: 16.4
- Protein: 2.9
- Total Fat: 0.7
- Sodium: 153.2
- Fiber: 2
- Saturated Fat: 0.3
- Sugar: 4.1
- Cholesterol: 0.7

213. Mocha Butter Cupcakes With Mocha Butter Frosting

Serving: 30 cupcakes, 30 serving(s) | Prep: 19mins | Ready in:

Ingredients

- Mocha butter cupcakes
- 2 1/2 cups sifted cake flour
- 1 teaspoon baking powder
- 3/4 teaspoon salt
- 3/4 cup butter
- 1 tablespoon instant coffee powder
- 1/2 teaspoon vanilla extract
- 1 1/2 cups white sugar
- 3 eggs
- 1 cup whole milk
- Mocha butter frosting
- 1/2 cup butter
- 2 teaspoons instant coffee
- 1 1/2 teaspoons rum
- 3/4 cup sifted confectioners' sugar
- 1/2 cup all purpose cream (chilled)

Direction

- Mocha butter Cupcakes:
- Preheat oven to 350 F, line cupcake molders with paper baking cups.
- In a small bowl, sift together cake flour, baking powder and salt together.
- Using an electric mixer, cream butter together with sugar until light. Add vanilla extract and coffee powder. Add eggs one at a time, beating only until combined. Alternately add flour mixture and milk to the butter mixture, beating well after each addition. Start and end with the dry ingredients.
- Fill the batter 3/4 full into the cupcake molders.
- Bake for 25 minutes or until a toothpick inserted in the center comes out clean. Frost with mocha butter frosting. Makes 30 cupcakes.
- Mocha butter Frosting:
- Using an electric mixer, beat the butter until light.
- Mix the coffee and rum together until coffee dissolves. Add this to the butter. Put in the powdered sugar and continue beating until blended. Add cream one tablespoons at a time, while beating the mixture at medium speed, adding more cream only as soon as the butter mixture has absorbed all of the cream. After adding all the cream, continue beating mixture until smooth and fluffy.
- Use immediately to frost cooled cupcakes.
- You can top this with chocolate chips, marshmallows and candy sprinkles.

Nutrition Information

- Calories: 180.9
- Total Carbohydrate: 22.6
- Total Fat: 9.3
- Saturated Fat: 5.7
- Sodium: 136.9
- Fiber: 0.2
- Sugar: 13.4
- Cholesterol: 44.9
- Protein: 2

214. Mom's Infamous Mincemeat Pie

Serving: 1 pie, 8 serving(s) | Prep: 15mins | Ready in:

Ingredients

- 2 (9 ounce) packages mincemeat
- 1 large apple, diced very fine
- 1 cup raisins
- 2 1/2 cups water
- 1/2 cup brandy or 1/2 cup rum

Direction

- Break mincemeat into small pieces and put in saucepan.
- Add diced apples, raisins, water and liquor.
- Boil about 2 minutes; cool.
- When mincemeat mixture is cool, put into pastry lined 9" pie pan; cover with top crust.
- Prick top crust with folk.
- Bake at 425 degrees for 35 minutes or until crust is golden brown.

Nutrition Information

- Calories: 286.3
- Total Fat: 0.2
- Sugar: 44.4
- Protein: 0.9
- Total Carbohydrate: 61.9
- Cholesterol: 0
- Saturated Fat: 0
- Sodium: 24.3
- Fiber: 2

215. Most Incredible No Fail Pie Crust

Serving: 2 9-inch pie crusts, 8-16 serving(s) | Prep: 10mins | Ready in:

Ingredients

- 3 cups flour
- 1 cup shortening
- 1/2 teaspoon salt
- 1 large egg, beaten
- 5 tablespoons cold water
- 1 teaspoon vinegar

Direction

- Cut together flour, shortening and salt until it resembles small peas.
- Combine the egg, water and vinegar and gradually add to flour mixture.
- Stir just until moistened and a soft dough forms.
- Divide into 2 disks.
- Wrap and refrigerate until ready to use.
- Roll out and use with your favorite pie recipe!

Nutrition Information

- Calories: 406.2
- Protein: 5.6
- Saturated Fat: 6.7
- Sodium: 155.4
- Fiber: 1.3
- Sugar: 0.1
- Total Fat: 26.7
- Total Carbohydrate: 35.8
- Cholesterol: 23.2

216. My Grandma's Applesauce Spice Cake

Serving: 1 tube cake, 16-20 serving(s) | Prep: 20mins | Ready in:

Ingredients

- 2 cups raisins
- 2 cups applesauce
- 4 tablespoons melted butter
- 1/2 teaspoon salt
- 2 teaspoons cinnamon

- 2 teaspoons nutmeg
- 2 teaspoons allspice
- 3 1/2 cups all-purpose flour
- 2 teaspoons baking soda
- 2 cups sugar
- 1 cup walnuts, chopped (any kind of nut meat will work)

Direction

- Preheat oven to 325 degrees.
- Prepare a tube pan.
- Put raisins in a 1 quart pan and cover with water.
- Cook until almost dry.
- Meanwhile, combine dry ingredients.
- When raisins are done mix into dry ingredients with applesauce and melted butter.
- Bake in prepared tube pan for 1 1/2 hours.

Nutrition Information

- Calories: 350.9
- Total Fat: 8.2
- Sodium: 262.4
- Fiber: 2.5
- Cholesterol: 7.6
- Saturated Fat: 2.4
- Sugar: 36.1
- Total Carbohydrate: 68.1
- Protein: 4.6

217. My Mom's Oatmeal Cake

Serving: 8 pieces, 16 serving(s) | Prep: 30mins | Ready in:

Ingredients

- 1 1/2 cups water
- 1 cup quick oats
- 1/2-1 cup butter or 1/2-1 cup margarine
- 1 cup brown sugar
- 1 cup white sugar
- 2 well beaten eggs
- 1 1/3 cups flour
- 1 teaspoon baking soda
- 1 teaspoon cinnamon
- 1/2 teaspoon salt
- 1 teaspoon melted butter or 1 teaspoon melted margarine
- 1/2 cup canned cream or 1/2 cup canned milk
- 1 teaspoon vanilla
- 1 cup brown sugar

Direction

- Bring to a boil water and quick oats.
- Let stand 15 minutes.
- Cream together 1/2 cup butter or margarine, brown sugar, white sugar And 2 well beaten eggs. Mix with oatmeal.
- Sift together flour, baking soda, cinnamon, and salt
- Add to mix and beat well.
- Pour into a 13 X 9 in. baking pan.
- Bake 350 degrees F 30 to 35 minutes.
- FROSTING mix together melted butter or margarine, canned cream or milk, vanilla, and brown sugar.
- Spread on cake brown in oven for a few minutes.
- Can add raisins or coconut.

Nutrition Information

- Calories: 294.4
- Total Fat: 9.3
- Saturated Fat: 5.5
- Fiber: 0.8
- Sugar: 39.1
- Protein: 2.9
- Sodium: 216.8
- Total Carbohydrate: 51
- Cholesterol: 50.6

218. My Momma's Pear Salad

Serving: 1 yummy dessert, 12 serving(s) | Prep: 15mins | Ready in:

Ingredients

- 1 (3 ounce) package lemon Jell-O gelatin
- 1 (16 ounce) can pears
- 1 (8 ounce) package cream cheese, softened
- 1 (8 ounce) container Cool Whip

Direction

- Combine 1 c. juice from pears and pkg. Jell-O.
- Heat on stove till boiling.
- Chill until partially set (1/2-1 hour) Take pears and cream cheese and blend in blender till smooth (no chunks).
- Take out of blender and add Jell-O mixture and cool whip.
- Blend w/a spoon.
- Keep in refrigerator until set, about 3 hours.

Nutrition Information

- Calories: 175
- Sugar: 14.2
- Cholesterol: 20.8
- Total Fat: 11.4
- Saturated Fat: 8.3
- Sodium: 94.1
- Fiber: 1.2
- Total Carbohydrate: 17.1
- Protein: 2.4

219. My Sister's Sweet Potato Bread

Serving: 2 Standard Loaves | Prep: 10mins | Ready in:

Ingredients

- 2 cups white sugar
- 1 cup vegetable oil
- 3 eggs
- 2 cups mashed canned candied yams or 2 cups sweet potatoes
- 1 teaspoon vanilla
- 3 cups flour
- 1/4 teaspoon baking powder
- 1 teaspoon baking soda
- 1/2 teaspoon salt
- 1 teaspoon cinnamon
- 1 teaspoon ginger
- 1 teaspoon ground cloves
- 1 cup chopped walnuts

Direction

- Preheat oven to 325 degrees.
- In a large mixing bowl, combine sugar, oil, egg, sweet potatoes and vanilla.
- In a separate bowl, mix dry ingredients (except walnuts) together well and add to wet ingredients.
- Stir until just combined.
- Fold in walnuts.
- Pour into 2 standard loaf pans.
- Bake for 75 minutes or until thin knife inserted in center comes out clean.

Nutrition Information

- Calories: 2926.1
- Total Fat: 156.4
- Total Carbohydrate: 354.4
- Protein: 37.9
- Saturated Fat: 20.4
- Sodium: 1372.7
- Fiber: 10.2
- Sugar: 202.3
- Cholesterol: 279

220. Nana's Special Cookies

Serving: 6 dozen | Prep: 12mins | Ready in:

Ingredients

- 1 cup coconut
- 3/4 cup chopped pecans
- 1 cup butter, softened
- 1 1/2 cups packed brown sugar
- 1/2 cup sugar
- 2 eggs
- 2 cups flour
- 1 teaspoon baking soda
- 1/2 teaspoon salt
- 2 teaspoons vanilla
- 2 cups oats
- 2 cups chocolate chips

Direction

- Put coconut and pecans on a jelly roll pan and toast in the oven at 350* for 5 minutes, stirring often.
- Set aside to cool.
- In large mixing bowl, cream butter and sugars.
- Add eggs and beat well.
- Add dry ingredients and vanilla.
- Stir in oats, chips, coconut and pecans.
- Drop by rounded teaspoons on greased cookie sheets.
- Bake at 350* for 10-12 minutes, until just browned.

Nutrition Information

- Calories: 1381.5
- Protein: 20.1
- Saturated Fat: 39.5
- Fiber: 13.6
- Total Carbohydrate: 177.4
- Cholesterol: 151.8
- Total Fat: 72.1
- Sodium: 679.7
- Sugar: 102.1

221. Nicole's Punch Bowl Cake

Serving: 20 serving(s) | Prep: 35mins | Ready in:

Ingredients

- 1 (18 ounce) box yellow cake mix (butter or strawberry, these flavors work best, but you can use any flavor. I prefer butter flavor)
- 3 eggs (or as called for by your cake mix)
- 1/3 cup oil (or as called for by your cake mix)
- 1 1/3 cups water (or as called for by your cake mix)
- 2 (20 ounce) cans pineapple chunks, drained
- 2 (11 ounce) cans mandarin oranges, drained
- 2 (16 ounce) cans peach halves in syrup (I like to use spiced peaches, reserve the juice from both cans)
- 2 (16 ounce) jars maraschino cherries, drained
- 4 bananas, sliced into small pieces
- 2 (14 ounce) cans whipped cream
- 1 (3 1/2 ounce) box instant vanilla pudding
- 1 cup almonds (slices or slivers(or your favorite nut)
- 5 sugar ice cream cones, crushed (optional)
- chocolate syrup (optional)

Direction

- Reserve small amount of bananas, cherries, nuts and ice cream pieces for the top.
- Bake cake according to package directions.
- Make vanilla pudding, chill till needed.
- Tear cake into little pieces, set aside.
- If you don't premake you cake, make sure it is completely cooled before making this dessert.
- In a punch bowl or large serving bowl layer ingredients as follows.
- Thin layer of pudding to cover bottom of bowl.
- Small layer of cake pieces (1/4 pineapple, peaches, bananas, oranges and cherries).
- When spooning peaches, don't drain; you will use any leftover syrup at end.
- Small amount of nuts.
- Layer of whipped cream.

- Layer of crushed ice cream cone pieces.
- Follow the layers until you're done with fruit and pudding.
- May have some cake left over.
- Pour remaining syrup over last layer of cake.
- Top with remaining whipped cream, fruit, nuts and ice cream cone pieces.
- Drizzle chocolate sauce over the top.
- Chill till ready to serve. Best when cold.

Nutrition Information

- Calories: 414.8
- Saturated Fat: 2.7
- Fiber: 4.8
- Cholesterol: 38.6
- Protein: 4.9
- Total Fat: 13.2
- Sodium: 290.1
- Sugar: 57.1
- Total Carbohydrate: 73.5

222. Nigerian Fruit Salad

Serving: 10-12 serving(s) | Prep: 15mins | Ready in:

Ingredients

- 4 ripe papayas or 4 mangoes, peeled, seeded and cut into bite-size pieces
- 2 red apples, cored and chopped
- 2 ripe bananas, peeled and sliced
- 1 (16 ounce) can pineapple tidbits, well-drained
- 1 cup fresh orange juice
- 1 tablespoon granulated sugar
- 1/2 teaspoon ground cinnamon
- 1/3 cup sweetened flaked coconut

Direction

- In large bowl combine papayas, apples, bananas, pineapple, orange juice, sugar, and cinnamon. Toss to mix well. Cover and chill until ready to serve. To serve, sprinkle with shredded coconut.

Nutrition Information

- Calories: 136.6
- Sodium: 13
- Fiber: 4.4
- Sugar: 21.8
- Saturated Fat: 1.1
- Total Carbohydrate: 32.3
- Cholesterol: 0
- Protein: 1.6
- Total Fat: 1.5

223. Nutty Oatmeal Raisin Chews

Serving: 3-4 dozen cookies, 12 serving(s) | Prep: 10mins | Ready in:

Ingredients

- 2 cups uncooked old fashioned oats
- 1 cup packed brown sugar
- 1 cup all-purpose flour
- 1/4 teaspoon salt
- 1 cup light raisins or 1 cup dark raisin
- 1 cup walnut pieces
- 3 egg whites
- 1/2 cup oil
- 1 teaspoon vanilla

Direction

- Preheat oven to 375°.
- Place all ingredients in a large bowl, mix well.
- Spray a cookie sheet with non-stick spray.
- Drop 1 tablespoon full of batter, 2 inches apart on cookie sheet.
- Dampen fingers lightly with cold water and press batter to flatten into 2 inch rounds.
- Bake until cookies are light golden, but not brown, about 12 to 14 minutes.

- Cool on pan for 3 minutes, then transfer to a wire rack to cool completely.
- Store in an airtight container.

Nutrition Information

- Calories: 333.4
- Protein: 5.9
- Total Fat: 16.4
- Saturated Fat: 1.9
- Total Carbohydrate: 42.9
- Sugar: 23.1
- Cholesterol: 0
- Sodium: 71.3
- Fiber: 2.6

224. Oat N' Toffee Cookies

Serving: 48 cookies | Prep: 8mins | Ready in:

Ingredients

- 3/4 cup butter, softened (no subs)
- 1 cup packed brown sugar
- 3/4 cup sugar
- 2 eggs
- 3 teaspoons vanilla
- 2 1/4 cups flour
- 2 1/4 cups old fashioned oats
- 1 teaspoon baking soda
- 1 teaspoon baking powder
- 1/2 teaspoon salt
- 1 (10 ounce) package toffee pieces

Direction

- Cream butter and sugars.
- Add eggs, one at a time, beating well after each addition.
- Beat in vanilla.
- Mix flour, oats, baking soda, baking powder and salt.
- Gradually add to creamed mixture.
- Stir in toffee bits.
- Drop by rounded TBS onto ungreased baking sheets.
- Bake at 375* for 10-12 minutes, until light golden brown.
- Cool 1 minute before removing from pans to wire rack.

Nutrition Information

- Calories: 126.2
- Saturated Fat: 3
- Fiber: 0.6
- Cholesterol: 19.6
- Protein: 1.7
- Sodium: 102.2
- Sugar: 11.2
- Total Carbohydrate: 18.3
- Total Fat: 5.3

225. Oatmeal Apple Cookies

Serving: 30 cookies | Prep: 20mins | Ready in:

Ingredients

- 3/4 cup shortening
- 1 1/4 cups firmly packed brown sugar
- 1 large egg
- 1/4 cup milk
- 1 1/2 teaspoons vanilla
- 1 cup flour
- 1 1/4 teaspoons cinnamon
- 1/2 teaspoon salt
- 1/4 teaspoon baking soda
- 1/4 teaspoon nutmeg
- 3 cups quick oats (not instant or old fashioned)
- 1 cup peeled diced apple
- 3/4 cup raisins (optional)
- 3/4 cup coarsely chopped walnuts (optional)

Direction

- Preheat oven to 375° and grease cookie sheet.

- Combine shortening, sugar, egg, milk and vanilla in large bowl.
- Beat at medium speed until well blended.
- Combine flour, cinnamon, salt, soda and nutmeg in a small bowl and mix into creamed mixture at low speed until just blended.
- Stir in oats, apples, raisins and nuts.
- Drop rounded tablespoonfuls of dough about 2-inches apart onto prepared cookie sheets.
- Bake for 13 minutes or until just set.
- Cool for a minute or 2 on cookie sheets and then remove to a wire rack to cool completely.

Nutrition Information

- Calories: 132.8
- Sugar: 9.5
- Total Carbohydrate: 18.5
- Protein: 1.8
- Total Fat: 5.9
- Saturated Fat: 1.5
- Sodium: 55.8
- Fiber: 1.1
- Cholesterol: 6.5

226. Oatmeal Applesauce Cookies

Serving: 4 dozen | Prep: 10mins | Ready in:

Ingredients

- 1 3/4 cups quick-cooking oats
- 1 1/2 cups flour
- 1 teaspoon baking powder
- 1/2 teaspoon baking soda
- 1/2 teaspoon salt
- 1 teaspoon cinnamon
- 1/2 teaspoon nutmeg
- 1 cup packed light brown sugar
- 1/2 cup white sugar
- 1/2 cup butter, softened
- 1 large egg
- 3/4 cup applesauce
- 1 cup chocolate chips
- 1 cup raisins
- 1 cup chopped walnuts

Direction

- Set oven to 375°.
- Lightly grease a baking sheet.
- In a medium bowl mix the first 7 dry ingredients together.
- In a large bowl combine sugars with an electric mixer until combined.
- Add in butter and beat to form a grainy paste.
- Add in egg and applesauce; blend until smooth.
- Add in flour mixture; mix until combined.
- Add in the chocolate chips, nuts and raisins; mix until combined.
- Drop by tablespoonfuls onto prepared baking sheet leaving about 2-inches apart.
- Bake for 12-14 minutes, or until light brown.
- Immediately transfer to a cool flat surface to cool.

Nutrition Information

- Calories: 1373.4
- Fiber: 11.5
- Total Carbohydrate: 207.8
- Saturated Fat: 24.8
- Sodium: 766.3
- Sugar: 123.8
- Cholesterol: 113.9
- Protein: 19.8
- Total Fat: 59

227. Oh My D Lux Chocolate Chip Cookies

Serving: 90 cookies | Prep: 20mins | Ready in:

Ingredients

- 1 cup butter, softened
- 2 cups firmly packed brown sugar
- 2 large eggs
- 1 teaspoon vanilla
- 2 cups flour
- ½ teaspoon baking powder
- 2 cups Rice Krispies
- 1 -2 cup semi-sweet chocolate chips
- 1 cup sweetened flaked coconut
- 1 cup chopped walnuts or 1 cup pecans

Direction

- Preheat oven to 350°F.
- Cream butter and add sugar, beating at low speed until light and fluffy.
- Add eggs and vanilla and beat well.
- Combine flour and baking powder and add to creamed mixture until well combined.
- Stir in remaining ingredients.
- Drop by heaping teaspoonfuls (or roll into 1 inch balls) onto baking sheets.
- Bake for 10-12 minutes or until lightly browned.
- Cool on wire racks.

Nutrition Information

- Calories: 73.4
- Total Fat: 4
- Saturated Fat: 2.1
- Sodium: 28.9
- Fiber: 0.3
- Sugar: 6.3
- Total Carbohydrate: 9.3
- Cholesterol: 10.1
- Protein: 0.8

228. Old Fashioned Banana Pudding

Serving: 4-6 serving(s) | Prep: 30mins | Ready in:

Ingredients

- 1 cup sugar
- 4 egg yolks
- 2 tablespoons flour
- 2 cups milk
- 1 teaspoon vanilla
- 1 (12 ounce) package vanilla wafers
- 3 large ripe bananas, sliced
- 8 ounces whipped topping

Direction

- Mix together the sugar, egg yolks, flour and milk. Stir over medium heat until boiling. Remove from heat and add vanilla.
- Layer the bottom of a 2-quart dish with half of the vanilla wafers.
- Top with half of the sliced bananas.
- Pour half of the pudding over top.
- Repeat layers: vanilla wafers, bananas, then pudding.
- Refrigerate for 1 hour. Serve topped with whipped topping.

Nutrition Information

- Calories: 986.1
- Total Fat: 38.8
- Saturated Fat: 16.9
- Sodium: 407.5
- Sugar: 67.4
- Protein: 13.5
- Fiber: 4.5
- Total Carbohydrate: 150.7
- Cholesterol: 228.7

229. Old Fashioned GingerBread Cookies

Serving: 4 dozen(depending on size of cookie cutters or how t | Prep: 10mins | Ready in:

Ingredients

- 1 cup sugar
- 1 cup sorghum or 1 cup molasses
- 3/4 cup oil or 3/4 cup lard
- 1/2 cup hot water
- 2 eggs
- 1 teaspoon baking soda
- 1/2 teaspoon salt
- 2 teaspoons cinnamon
- 2 teaspoons ginger
- 6 -7 cups white flour

Direction

- Combine first four ingredients in large bowl.
- Add eggs.
- Mix dry ingredients together and add to wet.
- Mix well.
- Cover and refrigerate overnight.
- Roll dough out on Pam (or other non-stick cooking spray) covered surface (I roll mine out thick, I like a thicker cookie) Cut with desired shapes.
- Bake at 350 degrees for 10 minutes.
- These cookies freeze well and are softer and more flavorful after freezing.

Nutrition Information

- Calories: 1442
- Sodium: 648.4
- Sugar: 50.6
- Total Carbohydrate: 230.8
- Cholesterol: 93
- Protein: 28.1
- Total Fat: 46.7
- Saturated Fat: 6.6
- Fiber: 8.9

230. One Bowl Chocolate Mocha Cream Cake

Serving: 1 baking dish, 16 serving(s) | Prep: 15mins | Ready in:

Ingredients

- Cake
- 2 cups all-purpose flour
- 1 cup granulated sugar
- 1 cup dark brown sugar
- 3/4 cup unsweetened cocoa (I used Hershey's)
- 1 1/2 teaspoons baking soda
- 1 1/2 teaspoons baking powder
- 1/2 teaspoon salt
- 1 cup reduced-fat mayonnaise
- 3 tablespoons canola oil
- 1 cup hot strong brewed coffee (I used Cuban coffee)
- 2 teaspoons vanilla extract
- 1/3 cup semisweet chocolate morsel (I used a combination of Hershey's Netsle's)
- cooking spray
- Mocha Cream
- 1/4 cup boiling water
- 1 tablespoon instant coffee granules
- 1 (7 ounce) jar marshmallow creme
- 1 (8 ounce) container frozen light whipped dessert topping, thawed
- 1/3 cup light chocolate syrup (Hershey's Lite Syrup)
- almonds, toasted and chopped fine

Direction

- TO PREPARE CAKE:
- Preheat oven to 350°F.
- Combine flour and next 6 ingredients (through salt) in a large bowl.
- Add mayonnaise and oil beat with a mixer at low speed until well blended.
- Slowly add brewed coffee and vanilla, beat with a mixer at low speed 1 minute or until well blended.
- Stir in chocolate; pour batter into 9x13" baking dish coated with cooking spray.
- Bake for 30 minutes or until wooden pick inserted in center comes out clean.
- Cool completely in pan on wire rack.
- TO PREPARE MOCHA CREAM:
- Combine water and granules in a large bowl stir until granules dissolve.

- Add marshmallow creme; beat with a mixer at low speed until smooth.
- Fold in whipped topping.
- Spread mocha cream over top of cake; drizzle with chocolate syrup and sprinkle with nuts.

Nutrition Information

- Calories: 317.5
- Fiber: 2.1
- Sugar: 36.9
- Cholesterol: 5.4
- Total Fat: 9.6
- Saturated Fat: 2
- Total Carbohydrate: 57.1
- Protein: 2.9
- Sodium: 367.8

231. One Pan Fruit Brownies

Serving: 16 brownies, 16 serving(s) | Prep: 10mins | Ready in:

Ingredients

- 1/2 cup flour
- 1 cup sugar
- 6 tablespoons baking cocoa
- 1/2 cup butter, melted and cooled
- 2 eggs, beaten
- 1/2 cup raisins (or tart cherries or cranberries)

Direction

- Preheat oven to 350 degrees.
- Place flour, sugar and cocoa in an ungreased 8 x 8-inch baking pan. Stir with a fork until thoroughly combined; set aside.
- In a small bowl, blend butter and eggs well. Pour butter mixture into flour mixture. Stir with a fork, scraping corners and sides until wet and dry ingredients are completely combined.
- Stir in dried fruit.
- Bake for 25 minutes or until centre feels set when lightly touched. Cool and cut into squares.

Nutrition Information

- Calories: 140.8
- Total Fat: 6.7
- Fiber: 0.9
- Cholesterol: 41.7
- Sugar: 15.3
- Total Carbohydrate: 20.2
- Protein: 1.8
- Saturated Fat: 4
- Sodium: 50.6

232. Orange Dessert Squares

Serving: 12-14 | Prep: 20mins | Ready in:

Ingredients

- 2/3 cup sugar
- 1/2 cup butter, softened
- 2 eggs, separated
- 2 cups flour
- 3 teaspoons baking powder
- 1 teaspoon salt
- 3/4 cup milk
- 4 teaspoons finely grated orange peel
- Orange Sauce
- 2/3 cup sugar
- 1 tablespoon cornstarch
- 1/4 teaspoon salt
- 1 cup boiling water
- 1 teaspoon butter
- 4 teaspoons finely grated orange peel
- 1/2 cup fresh orange juice

Direction

- In a medium bowl beat sugar, butter, and egg yolks at medium speed until light and fluffy.

- Mix flour with baking powder and salt; add alternately to sugar mixture with milk at low speed, beginning and ending with flour mixture.
- Beat egg whites until stiff but not dry; fold egg whites and orange rind gently into the batter.
- Pour into greased and floured 13x9x2-inch baking pan.
- Bake at 375°F for 20-25 minutes or until golden brown.
- Cool, cut into squares, and serve with warm orange sauce. Enjoy!

Nutrition Information

- Calories: 263.6
- Total Fat: 9.6
- Saturated Fat: 5.7
- Fiber: 0.7
- Sugar: 23.2
- Total Carbohydrate: 41.2
- Protein: 3.9
- Sodium: 409.9
- Cholesterol: 58.6

233. Orange Honey Cake

Serving: 2 loaves, 20 serving(s) | Prep: 15mins | Ready in:

Ingredients

- 1 cup hot water
- 1 tablespoon instant coffee granules
- 1 (6 ounce) can frozen orange juice concentrate, thawed
- 1 teaspoon ground cinnamon
- 1 teaspoon ground allspice
- 1/4 teaspoon salt
- 2 teaspoons baking powder
- 2 teaspoons baking soda
- 3 1/2 cups all-purpose flour
- 4 large eggs
- 1/3 cup canola oil
- 1 1/4 cups sugar
- 1 cup honey

Direction

- Coat with nonstick spray or grease two 9 by 5-inch loaf pans.
- Line the bottom of each pan with a small piece of wax paper cut to fit; then spray or grease the paper.
- Set the pans aside.
- Preheat the oven to 325 degrees.
- Put the hot water into a 2-cup measuring cup or a small bowl.
- Add the instant coffee granules, and stir until they are dissolved.
- Stir in the orange juice concentrate to cool the coffee.
- Set aside.
- Measure out the cinnamon, allspice, salt, baking powder and baking soda, and place in a small custard cup or on a piece of wax paper.
- Set aside.
- Measure the flour by spooning it into the proper-size measuring cups, and leveling off the top.
- After measuring the flour, sift it onto a large piece of wax paper or into an extra bowl.
- (Sifting is necessary as tiny lumps may not beat out during the mixing process and will appear in the finished cake.) Put the eggs, oil, sugar, and honey into a large mixer bowl.
- With an electric mixer at medium speed, beat them together until completely combined, about 2 minutes.
- Add the spice mixture, and beat until combined.
- Beat in about a third of the flour, then a third of the orange-coffee mixture, repeating twice until all the ingredients are added.
- Beat on low speed until the flour is completely mixed in, scraping the bowl if necessary.
- Then beat the batter on high speed for 1 to 2 minutes or until it is very smooth.
- The batter will be thin.
- Pour the batter into the prepared pans, dividing it evenly.

- Bake the cakes at 325 degrees for about 60 to 70 minutes, or until a toothpick inserted into the center of each cake comes out completely clean (test both cakes).
- If there is a wet spot in the center of the top of a cake, bake it a few minutes longer.
- Remove the cakes from the oven, and let them cool for 1 hour in their pans on a wire rack.
- The sides of the cakes should shrink away from the pans a little.
- Run a knife around the sides of each cake to loosen it; then turn the cake out of its pan, and peel the wax paper from the bottom.
- Invert the cakes so the tops are facing upward.
- Cool the cakes completely on the wire rack.
- Wrap the cooled cakes well for storage (use sturdy plastic wrap and/or heavy-duty foil).
- If the wrapped cakes are allowed to "mellow" overnight, their taste and texture will improve, and they will be easier to slice (a serrated bread knife works best).
- The tightly wrapped loaves can be kept at room temperature for up to 4 days, or they may be frozen for several months.
- (Defrost, wrapped, at room temperature, before slicing and serving.) To serve, cut each loaf crosswise into slices, and arrange the slices, slightly overlapping, on a tray or platter.

Nutrition Information

- Calories: 244.7
- Cholesterol: 42.3
- Protein: 3.9
- Total Fat: 4.9
- Saturated Fat: 0.6
- Sodium: 207.1
- Fiber: 0.8
- Sugar: 30.5
- Total Carbohydrate: 47.7

234. Orange Mousse Dessert

Serving: 6-8 serving(s) | Prep: 10mins | Ready in:

Ingredients

- 1 (80 g) packet orange jelly powder
- 125 ml boiling water
- 200 g white sugar
- 375 ml fresh orange juice
- 1 (12 ounce) canice-cold evaporated milk
- fresh orange section (for decoration)
- stiffly beaten cream (for decoration)

Direction

- Dissolve jelly powder in the boiling water.
- Add sugar and juice and stir well while heating slightly if the sugar granules don't dissolve.
- Chill until jelly has the consistency of egg-white.
- Pour the milk into a deep bowl and beat it to a thick foam.
- Beat it gradually into the jelly and beat thoroughly mixed.
- Pour into a glass bowl and refrigerate until set.
- Decorate the dessert just before serving with the orange segments and cream.

Nutrition Information

- Calories: 106.5
- Total Fat: 4.4
- Saturated Fat: 2.6
- Fiber: 0.1
- Sugar: 5.8
- Cholesterol: 16.4
- Sodium: 61.2
- Total Carbohydrate: 12.8
- Protein: 4.3

235. Orange Walnut Bar Cake

Serving: 8 serving(s) | Prep: 30mins | Ready in:

Ingredients

- 125 g unsalted butter, softened
- 3/4 cup caster sugar
- 1 grated orange, rind of
- 1 grated lemon, rind of
- 2 eggs
- 1 1/2 cups self raising flour
- 1/2 cup walnut pieces
- 1/2 cup orange juice
- 3 tablespoons milk
- 2 teaspoons sugar
- Orange butter frosting
- 75 g soft unsalted butter
- 250 g icing sugar, sifted
- 1 grated orange, rind of
- 1/4 cup orange juice

Direction

- Preheat your oven to 180 degrees C.
- Grease a loaf or square cake tin well with some butter and line the base with baking paper.
- Cream the butter, sugar and grated rinds until light and fluffy.
- Add the eggs, one at a time, and beat in well.
- Fold through the sifted flour.
- Stir in the walnuts, followed by the orange juice and then the milk.
- Pour into the prepared tin and sprinkle with the 2 teaspoons sugar.
- Bake for about 50 minutes.
- Stand for a few minutes then cool on a wire rack.
- To make the frosting, cream the butter in a small mixing bowl until light.
- Beat in the icing sugar.
- Add the rind and juice then beat at high speed with electric mixer for a few minutes until frosting is stiff enough to shape easily but not too stiff to spread.
- If it's too thin add more sifted icing sugar.
- If too thick add some more juice or water.
- When the cake has cooled frost with the prepared frosting.

Nutrition Information

- Calories: 543.1
- Sodium: 24.2
- Fiber: 1.2
- Cholesterol: 107.4
- Total Fat: 26.8
- Saturated Fat: 13.9
- Sugar: 52.7
- Total Carbohydrate: 72.6
- Protein: 5.7

236. Orange Chocolate Ice Cream Sauce

Serving: 1 1/3 cups | Prep: 10mins | Ready in:

Ingredients

- 3/4 cup white sugar
- 1/2 cup cocoa
- 1/2 cup milk (use water if you want to cut down the dairy and/or the calories)
- 2 ounces bittersweet chocolate or 2 ounces semisweet chocolate, coarsely chopped
- 1/3 cup unsalted butter
- 2 tablespoons orange liqueur
- 1 teaspoon vanilla extract

Direction

- In a medium-sized saucepan, combine sugar and cocoa, then whisk in milk, then chopped chocolate.
- Turn heat to medium and cook, whisking constantly, for 5 minutes.
- Remove from the heat and stir in remaining ingredients until sauce is smooth.
- Serve either chilled or warmed, over vanilla ice cream.

- Store in the fridge, but this sauce will keep well in the freezer if your batch won't be gone within a week or two.

Nutrition Information

- Calories: 983.6
- Protein: 9.8
- Total Fat: 53.8
- Sodium: 58.1
- Sugar: 113.4
- Total Carbohydrate: 134.7
- Cholesterol: 134.7
- Saturated Fat: 33.8
- Fiber: 10.7

237.   Oreo Pudding

Serving: 10 serving(s) | Prep: 24hours | Ready in:

Ingredients

- 8 ounces cream cheese, room temperature
- 1 cup powdered sugar
- 3 cups milk
- 1 teaspoon vanilla
- 8 ounces Cool Whip
- 1 (1 lb) package Oreo cookies, crushed into chunks
- 4 tablespoons butter, room temperature
- 2 packages instant vanilla pudding (small size)

Direction

- In a large bowl, cream the cream cheese, butter and sugar with an electric mixer.
- Add the milk, vanilla and pudding mixes.
- Mix until all the lumps are gone.
- Fold in the Cool Whip.
- Put half of the cookies in the bottom of a large glass bowl.
- Cover with the entire pudding mixture.
- Top with remaining cookie chunks.
- Cover and refrigerate 8 hours or overnight.

Nutrition Information

- Calories: 446.3
- Total Fat: 24.6
- Saturated Fat: 15.2
- Fiber: 0.5
- Total Carbohydrate: 53
- Sodium: 533.2
- Sugar: 43.7
- Cholesterol: 47.5
- Protein: 5.1

238.   Our Family Fried Pies

Serving: 12-15 pies | Prep: 25mins | Ready in:

Ingredients

- 6 ounces dried apricots
- 1 tablespoon cinnamon (more to taste)
- 1 tablespoon allspice (can sub additional cinnamon and clove for the allspice if desired) (optional)
- 1/2 lemon, juice of
- 1 1/2 cups sugar
- pastry dough (Tammy's Fried Pie Pastry Tammy's Fried Pie Pastry or Traditional Fried Pie Pastry Traditional Fried Pie Pastry suggested)

Direction

- Wash and dice dried apricots, then place in a sauce pan and cover with water (about 1 inch above fruit).
- Cook slowly until tender.
- Do NOT pour off water.
- Add spices to taste and lemon juice.
- Thicken with a corn starch slurry.
- **Be careful of scorching after cornstarch is added.
- Roll out a ball of pastry about the size of a golf ball.

- Spoon 1 heaping tablespoon of fruit filling on 1/2 of pastry circle leaving about a half inch edge.
- Fold over and seal with a fork.
- ***Pies may be frozen at this point.
- Fry frozen or thawed pies in a skillet of hot oil (preferred Crisco at 375 degrees in cast iron skillet) until golden brown.
- Remove to a paper towel lined plate.
- Can be eaten as is (preferred) or sprinkle with powdered sugar, lightly.
- Enjoy! ;).

Nutrition Information

- Calories: 134.8
- Saturated Fat: 0
- Fiber: 1.4
- Total Fat: 0.1
- Sodium: 1.7
- Sugar: 33
- Total Carbohydrate: 35
- Cholesterol: 0
- Protein: 0.5

239. Parmesan Shortbread

Serving: 16 savory cookies | Prep: 5mins | Ready in:

Ingredients

- 1/2 cup unsalted butter, softened
- 1 tablespoon sugar
- 1/2 cup fresh grated parmesan cheese (no, not the sandy stuff that comes in a can)
- 1/4 teaspoon black pepper or 1/8 teaspoon cayenne pepper
- 1/2 teaspoon chopped fresh rosemary (or thyme) (optional)
- 1 1/4 cups flour

Direction

- Preheat oven to 325.
- Line an 8 inch square pan with buttered foil.
- Beat all ingredients except flour in a mixing bowl with an electric mixer until light and creamy, 3-4 minutes.
- Add flour and continue to mix at lowest speed until smooth dough forms.
- Scrape dough into pan and press evenly with the back of a spoon.
- Pierce dough randomly with a floured fork.
- Bake 35 minutes until firm.
- Let cool slightly then invert pan over your cutting board.
- Remove the foil and cut the shortbread into 2 inch squares.

Nutrition Information

- Calories: 103
- Total Fat: 6.7
- Sodium: 48.8
- Fiber: 0.3
- Protein: 2.3
- Cholesterol: 18
- Saturated Fat: 4.2
- Sugar: 0.8
- Total Carbohydrate: 8.4

240. Peanut Butter Cut Out Cookies

Serving: 3 dozen cookies, 36 serving(s) | Prep: 20mins | Ready in:

Ingredients

- FOR THE COOKIES
- 1/2 cup butter or 1/2 cup margarine
- 1 cup peanut butter chips
- 2/3 cup light brown sugar, packed
- 1 egg
- 3/4 teaspoon vanilla extract
- 1 1/3 cups all-purpose flour
- 3/4 teaspoon baking soda
- 1/2 cup pecans, finely chopped

- FOR THE CHOCOLATE CHIP GLAZE
- 1 cup hershey's special dark chocolate chips or 1 cup semi-sweet chocolate chips
- 1 tablespoon shortening
- FOR THE PEANUT BUTTER CHIP GLAZE
- 2/3 cup peanut butter chips
- 1 tablespoon shortening

Direction

- Combine butter and peanut butter chips in saucepan; cook over low heat, stirring constantly, until melted. Pour into large bowl; add brown sugar, egg and vanilla. Beat well. Stir in flour, baking soda and pecans; blend well. Refrigerate 15 to 20 minutes or until firm enough to roll.
- Heat oven to 350°F Roll out dough, a small portion at a time, on lightly floured board or between 2 pieces of wax paper, to 1/4-inch thickness. (Keep remaining dough in refrigerator.) With cookie cutters, cut into desired shapes; place on ungreased cookie sheet.
- Bake 7 to 8 minutes or until almost set (do not over bake). Cool 1 minute; remove from cookie sheet to wire rack. Cool completely.
- Drizzle CHOCOLATE CHIP GLAZE or PEANUT BUTTER CHIP GLAZE onto each cookie; garnish as desired.
- CHOCOLATE CHIP GLAZE: Place 1 cup HERSHEY'S SPECIAL DARK Chocolate Chips or HERSHEY'S Semi-Sweet Chocolate Chips and 1 tablespoon shortening (do not use butter, margarine, spread or oil) in small microwave-safe bowl. Microwave at MEDIUM (50%) 1 minute; stir. If necessary, microwave at MEDIUM an additional 15 seconds at a time, stirring after each heating, just until chips are melted and mixture is smooth.
- PEANUT BUTTER CHIP GLAZE: Place 2/3 cup REESE'S Peanut Butter Chips and 1 tablespoon shortening (do not use butter, margarine, spread or oil) in small microwave-safe bowl. Microwave at MEDIUM (50%) 30 seconds; stir. Microwave at MEDIUM an additional 10 seconds at a time, stirring after each heating, just until chips are melted and mixture is smooth. About 1/3 cup glaze.
- VARIATION: SLICE AND BAKE PEANUT BUTTER COOKIES: Prepare dough as directed above. Refrigerate 15 to 20 minutes or until firm enough to handle. Shape dough into two 6-inch rolls. Wrap rolls in wax paper or plastic wrap; freeze 1 to 2 hours or until firm enough to cut. Cut dough into 1/4-inch thick slices. Proceed as directed for baking and cooling.

Nutrition Information

- Calories: 137.4
- Total Fat: 8.3
- Sugar: 9.7
- Protein: 2.4
- Saturated Fat: 3.8
- Sodium: 68
- Fiber: 0.9
- Total Carbohydrate: 14.3
- Cholesterol: 12.7

241. Peanut Chubbies

Serving: 4 dozen cookies | Prep: 20mins | Ready in:

Ingredients

- 2 cups lightly packed brown sugar
- 1/2 cup evaporated milk
- 2 tablespoons butter or 2 tablespoons margarine
- 3/4 cup peanut butter
- 1/2 teaspoon vanilla
- 1 cup rolled oats
- 1/2 cup chopped pretzel
- 1/2 cup salted peanuts
- 1/2 cup chocolate chips

Direction

- In a saucepan, combine brown sugar, evaporated milk and butter; bring to a boil and

cook, stirring constantly, until thickened and smooth (about 5 minutes); remove from heat.
- Stir in peanut butter and vanilla, then blend in the remaining ingredients.
- Drop from a teaspoon onto wax paper and chill until set.

Nutrition Information

- Calories: 1245.7
- Saturated Fat: 16.1
- Sodium: 957.6
- Fiber: 9.2
- Sugar: 124.1
- Total Carbohydrate: 175.3
- Cholesterol: 24.4
- Total Fat: 54.9
- Protein: 28.1

242. Peanut Parfait Dessert

Serving: 16 serving(s) | Prep: 20mins | Ready in:

Ingredients

- Brownie base
- 4 ounces unsweetened chocolate (100 grams)
- 2/3 cup shortening
- 2 cups sugar
- 4 eggs
- 1 1/4 cups flour
- 1 teaspoon baking powder
- 1/2 teaspoon salt
- 1 (12 ounce) package chocolate chips
- Filling
- 1 1/2 cups powdered sugar
- 3/4 cup peanut butter
- 1 (8 ounce) package cream cheese, softened
- 2 1/2 cups milk
- 1 (8 ounce) container frozen whipped topping, thawed
- 1 package vanilla instant pudding mix (6-serving size)
- chopped peanuts, if desired (to garnish)
- grated milk chocolate, if desired (to garnish)

Direction

- To make the base:
- Melt chocolate and shortening.
- Stir in sugar with whisk until blended.
- (Mixture will be dry).
- Add eggs, beating well.
- Stir in dry ingredients.
- Finally, add the chocolate chips.
- Spread in greased 13x9" pan.
- Bake 25 minutes, or until set.
- Don't overbake.
- Cool completely.
- To make the filling and assemble:
- In small bowl, combine powdered sugar and peanut butter until crumbly and set aside.
- In a large bowl, beat cream cheese until smooth.
- Add milk, whipped topping and pudding mix; beat 2 minutes or until well blended.
- Pour half of cream cheese mixture over cooled brownie base and spread evenly.
- Sprinkle with half of peanut butter mixture.
- Repeat layers.
- Top with chopped peanuts and grated milk chocolate, if desired.
- Cover; refrigerate or freeze until serving time.

Nutrition Information

- Calories: 621.5
- Sugar: 58
- Cholesterol: 73.8
- Sodium: 326.1
- Fiber: 3.4
- Total Carbohydrate: 72.9
- Protein: 9.9
- Total Fat: 36.1
- Saturated Fat: 17

243. Pear Pudding Cake (Or Apple, Peach...) In Crock Pot

Serving: 6-8 serving(s) | Prep: 15mins | Ready in:

Ingredients

- 1 cup Bisquick
- 1/2 cup sugar
- 1/2 cup brown sugar
- 1 cup buttermilk
- 1 tablespoon melted butter
- 2 eggs
- 2 1/2 cups sliced pears (or fruit of your choice)
- 2 tablespoons vanilla
- 3/4 tablespoon cinnamon

Direction

- Lightly butter a 4-5 crock slow cooker.
- In a large bowl combine sugars and baking mix.
- In a separate bowl beat the eggs lightly and stir in milk, melted butter, vanilla cinnamon. Stir to combine then pour into dry ingredients.
- Add the pears last and gently stir.
- Pour batter into the slow cooker. Cover with a thick clean dish cloth (to absorb the moisture).
- Cook on low for 6 hrs. or high for 3 hours.
- Serve warm w/ice cream or whipped topping -- YUM!

Nutrition Information

- Calories: 331.6
- Fiber: 3
- Sugar: 46
- Protein: 5.4
- Total Fat: 7.1
- Saturated Fat: 2.8
- Total Carbohydrate: 61.1
- Cholesterol: 77.6
- Sodium: 343.5

244. Pears Poached In Red Wine

Serving: 4 serving(s) | Prep: 10mins | Ready in:

Ingredients

- 2 cups red wine
- 1/4 cup creme de cassis
- 1/2 cup raisins
- 1 cinnamon stick
- 1/2 cup honey
- 4 pears, cored and sliced
- whipped cream
- slivered almonds

Direction

- Simmer the wine, crème de cassis, raisins, cinnamon, and honey together for 5 to 10 minutes.
- Add the pears and cook gently for 10 to 15 minutes.
- Serve in bowls or sherbet glasses topped with freshly whipped cream and slivered almonds.
- This dish can be prepared hours in advance and is good hot, warm, or chilled.

Nutrition Information

- Calories: 379.2
- Saturated Fat: 0
- Sugar: 62.5
- Cholesterol: 0
- Protein: 1.4
- Total Fat: 0.3
- Sodium: 10.1
- Fiber: 5.9
- Total Carbohydrate: 78

245. Pecan Sandies Cake Mix Cookies

Serving: 24 cookies, 24 serving(s) | Prep: 5mins | Ready in:

Ingredients

- 1 (18 1/4 ounce) box butter pecan cake mix
- 1 egg
- vegetable oil
- water
- 1/2 cup chopped fresh pecans

Direction

- Pour cake mix into a large bowl. Whisk dry mix to remove lumps or sift it into the bowl.
- Add pecans to the dry cake mix and stir well.
- In a liquid measuring cup, add the egg. Add enough oil to the egg to bring the mixture to 1/2 cup. Add enough water to bring the mixture to 2/3 cup. Beat mixture together with a fork.
- Add egg mixture to cake mix in large bowl. Mix well.
- Using a teaspoon or small ice cream scoop, gather balls of dough, rolling them into perfect circles. Place 12 on a cookie sheet and bake 8-12 minutes at 350 degrees F. If they get golden brown, they are too done. Pulling them out around 10 minutes should be perfect.
- Let the cookies cool 5 minutes before transferring them to a plate or container.

Nutrition Information

- Calories: 18.8
- Fiber: 0.2
- Total Carbohydrate: 0.3
- Cholesterol: 8.8
- Total Fat: 1.8
- Saturated Fat: 0.2
- Sodium: 2.9
- Sugar: 0.1
- Protein: 0.5

246. Perfect Peanut Butter Cookies

Serving: 50 cookies | Prep: 15mins | Ready in:

Ingredients

- 1/2 cup butter, softened
- 1/2 cup packed brown sugar
- 1/2 cup white sugar
- 1 large egg
- 1 cup smooth peanut butter (not crunchy, I think crunchy ruins the texture)
- 1/2 teaspoon pure vanilla extract
- 1/2 teaspoon salt
- 1/2 teaspoon baking soda
- 1 3/4 cups all-purpose flour

Direction

- Preheat oven to 375°F; have ungreased shiny cookie sheets ready.
- In a large mixing bowl, with electric mixer, cream together the butter and sugars; next, beat in egg, peanut butter and vanilla.
- In a smaller bowl, sift together salt, baking soda and flour (I do this through a sieve, not with a sifter).
- With a wooden spoon, stir flour mixture into peanut butter mixture until a dough is formed.
- If desired, you could stir in about 1/2 cup (or more) of chocolate chips now; I usually don't (even though I'm a chocoholic) as I often just want a pure peanut butter cookie with nothing else in it, not even peanut bits.
- Stash dough in fridge while you clean up the dishes; this step isn't absolutely necessary but the fridge slightly firms up the dough, making it easier to work with.
- Drop by heaping teaspoons onto cookie sheets and press down, criss-cross style, with a fork-- the classic peanut butter cookie look.
- If fork sticks to cookies too much as you press down, lightly flour the fork.

- Bake in preheated oven for 7 to 9 minutes, or until edges are slightly darkened (I like to cook these at 7-1/2 minutes).
- Do not worry if they don't look done; cookies firm up as they cool and if you want chewier cookies it is very important not to over bake them.
- Add an extra minute if you like crispier cookies.
- Remove cookies from sheets after letting them rest on sheets for one minute, then let cooked cookies cool on racks.
- Store cookies in a tin or in cookie jar (airtight containers are best).
- I use a one-inch scoop to make the cookies; the approximate yield I get is 4-1/2 dozen cookies.

Nutrition Information

- Calories: 80.2
- Total Fat: 4.6
- Sugar: 4.6
- Cholesterol: 8.6
- Protein: 1.9
- Saturated Fat: 1.8
- Sodium: 77.9
- Fiber: 0.4
- Total Carbohydrate: 8.5

247. Pina Colada Cheesecake With Coco Nut Crust

Serving: 8-10 serving(s) | Prep: 20mins | Ready in:

Ingredients

- Coco Nut Crust
- 1 1/2-2 tablespoons butter, at room temperature
- 1 cup flaked coconut
- 1 cup ground toasted brazil nuts or 1 cup ground toasted filbert nut
- 1/4 cup sugar
- 1/4 cup butter, melted, cooled to room temperature
- Cheesecake
- 2 1/4 lbs cream cheese, at room temperature
- 3/4 cup unsweetened crushed canned pineapple, drained well, 1/2 cup juice reserved
- 1/3 cup coconut rum
- 1/4 cup sour cream
- 1 1/2 cups sugar
- 4 large eggs, at room temperature, slightly beaten
- 2 slices fresh pineapple, 1/2 cm thick (optional) or 2 slices canned pineapple (optional)

Direction

- Prepare coco nut crust.
- Place oven rack in center of oven, heat to 350 degrees.
- Coat bottom and sides of 9 inch springform pan evenly with unmelted butter, reserve.
- Stir coconut, Brazil nuts and sugar in medium bowl.
- Drizzle melted butter over nut mixture.
- Stir and toss mixture vigorously with fork until slightly darkened and uniform.
- Press nut mixture evenly on sides and bottom of reserved pan.
- Refrigerate 5 minutes.
- Bake crust 7 minutes.
- Cool on wire rack to room temperature before filling, about 30 minutes.
- Cheesecake-------------.
- Place oven rack in center of oven, heat to 350 degrees.
- Cut cream cheese into 1 inch cubes, place in large mixer bowl.
- Beat at medium speed, scraping down sides of bowl as needed, until completely smooth.
- Continue beating while gradually adding crushed pineapple.
- Gradually beat in reserved pineapple juice and the liqueur until blended, scraping down sides of bowl as needed.

- Add sour cream to cheese mixture, beat at medium speed until blended.
- Continue beating while very slowly adding sugar, scraping down sides of bowl as needed, beat until sugar is absorbed.
- Add eggs, about 1/4 cup at a time, beating well and scraping down sides of bowl after each addition.
- (Batter will be thin) Pour patter into baked cooled coconut crust.
- Gently rotate pan several quarter turns to settle batter.
- Bake until sides of cheesecake are set 2 1/2 inches in from edges and center is still pudding like, 60 to 65 minutes for a creamy center.
- For a firmer center, bake until center is just set, about 10 minutes longer (cake may crack at sides).
- Transfer pan to wire rack away from drafts.
- Let cool undisturbed until sides and bottom of pan are completely cooled to room temperature.
- Remove sides of pan.
- Refrigerate cake uncovered overnight or at least 8 hours.
- Cover cake loosely with plastic wrap, refrigerate until serving time.
- Make optional garnish just before serving.
- Pare and core pineapple slices, cut out eyes of pineapple making small notches in outer edge of slices (or use canned slices).
- Cut slices into quarters.
- Place 6 to 8 pineapple quarters in border around top of cheesecake.

Nutrition Information

- Calories: 924
- Fiber: 1.9
- Sugar: 50.3
- Total Fat: 71
- Saturated Fat: 40
- Sodium: 497.2
- Total Carbohydrate: 56.1
- Cholesterol: 270.2
- Protein: 16

248. Pine Bark (Homemade Toffee)

Serving: 8 serving(s) | Prep: 10mins | Ready in:

Ingredients

- 35 saltine crackers
- 1 cup butter
- 1 cup light brown sugar, packed
- 1/4 teaspoon almond extract
- 1/4 teaspoon vanilla extract
- 20 ounces milk chocolate candy bars, broken into pieces
- cooking spray

Direction

- Preheat oven to 400°F.
- Line a 15 x 10 x 1 inch jelly roll pan with tin foil. Lightly spray the foil with a non-stick cooking spray.
- Place the crackers salty side up in the prepared pan.
- In a saucepan, boil the butter and sugar 2 to 3 minutes, stirring constantly. Remove from heat and stir in almond extract.
- Pour the mixture evenly over the crackers so that all pieces are covered, and bake for 4 to 6 minutes.
- Remove from the oven, top with the candy bar pieces, and spread them evenly as they begin to melt.
- Cool slightly and transfer to wax paper. Allow to cool completely.

Nutrition Information

- Calories: 746.6
- Saturated Fat: 25
- Sodium: 371.4
- Sugar: 63.4

- Total Carbohydrate: 78.6
- Cholesterol: 77.5
- Total Fat: 45.7
- Fiber: 2.8
- Protein: 6.9

249. Pineapple Coconut Cream Dream Pie

Serving: 8 serving(s) | Prep: 20mins | Ready in:

Ingredients

- Crust
- 20 crisp oatmeal cookies (You can find sugar-free ones or make your own.)
- 1/4 cup reduced fat margarine, melted
- Filling
- 3/4 cup Splenda sugar substitute
- 1/3 cup cornstarch
- 1 (20 ounce) can crushed pineapple in juice, drained (reserve juice)
- 1 (14 ounce) can coconut milk (not cream!)
- 5 large egg yolks
- 2 tablespoons reduced fat margarine, cut small
- 1 cup unsweetened flaked coconut, chopped finer
- Topping
- 1 cup light whipped topping or 1 cup whipping cream, whipped
- 2 tablespoons Splenda sugar substitute

Direction

- Heat oven to 350 degrees. Generously coat a 9 inch pie plate with spray.
- Process the cookies in a food processor until fine crumbs. Add margarine and process until crumbs are moist. Press into the pie plate. Bake 12 minutes until toasted around the edges and cool on a wire rack.
- Mix Splenda and cornstarch in a 2-qt. saucepan. Add enough pineapple juice to the coconut milk to make 2 1/2 cups. Stir into the sugar mixture, then bring to a boil over medium heat, stirring occasionally, but not briskly. Boil one minute. Remove from heat.
- Whisk yolks to mix; gradually whisk in about half the hot mixture; return to saucepan. Stir over low heat for 2 minutes. Remove from heat, stir in margarine till melted. Stir in pineapple and coconut. Pour into crust. Cover surface with plastic wrap to prevent a skin from forming and refrigerate 3 hours.
- Before serving: beat the cream and sugar to stiff peaks if using cream. Spread over pie and garnish with pineapple chunks, shredded coconut, or mint sprigs.

Nutrition Information

- Calories: 527.2
- Sugar: 27.6
- Cholesterol: 131.3
- Protein: 7.2
- Saturated Fat: 19
- Sodium: 319.4
- Fiber: 4.8
- Total Carbohydrate: 56.4
- Total Fat: 32.5

250. Pink Fantasy Salad

Serving: 12 serving(s) | Prep: 5mins | Ready in:

Ingredients

- 1 can cherry pie filling
- 1 can crushed pineapple, drained well
- 1 can sweetened condensed milk
- 8 -12 ounces Cool Whip

Direction

- Mix all ingredients.
- Chill until serving.

Nutrition Information

- Calories: 260.2
- Saturated Fat: 6.6
- Sugar: 28.6
- Cholesterol: 15.2
- Total Carbohydrate: 42.5
- Protein: 3.9
- Total Fat: 8.7
- Sodium: 70.2
- Fiber: 0.3

251. Plum Streusel Kuchen

Serving: 9 serving(s) | Prep: 15mins | Ready in:

Ingredients

- 1 2/3 cups all-purpose flour, divided
- 1/2 cup sugar
- 1/2 teaspoon ground cinnamon
- 1 tablespoon vegetable oil
- 2 teaspoons light corn syrup
- 1/3 cup sugar
- 1 teaspoon baking powder
- 1/4 teaspoon salt
- 1/4 cup chilled stick margarine or 1/4 cup butter, cut into small pieces
- 1/2 cup plain fat-free yogurt
- 2 tablespoons water
- 1 1/2 teaspoons vanilla extract
- 3/4 teaspoon grated lemon rind
- 1 large egg
- cooking spray
- 2 cups sliced plums (about 3/4 pound)

Direction

- Preheat oven to 400°.
- Lightly spoon flour into dry measuring cups; level with a knife.
- Place 1/3 cup flour, 1/2 cup sugar, and ground cinnamon in a food processor, and pulse the mixture 2 to 3 times.
- With processor on, slowly add the oil and corn syrup through food chute, processing until the mixture resembles coarse meal.
- Remove the streusel mixture from the food processor, and set aside.
- Place 1 1/3 cups flour, 1/3 cup sugar, baking powder, and salt in a food processor, and pulse mixture 2 to 3 times.
- Add the margarine, and process until mixture resembles coarse meal. Place margarine mixture in a large bowl.
- Combine yogurt, water, vanilla, rind, and egg, and stir with a whisk.
- Stir yogurt mixture into margarine mixture in a large bowl until blended.
- Spoon batter into a 9-inch round cake pan coated with cooking spray.
- Sprinkle half of streusel mixture evenly over batter.
- Top with plums, arranging in a circular pattern.
- Sprinkle the remaining streusel mixture evenly over the plums.
- Bake kuchen at 400° for 45 minutes or until a wooden pick inserted in center comes out clean.
- Cool on a wire rack.

Nutrition Information

- Calories: 254.3
- Total Carbohydrate: 43.1
- Cholesterol: 23.8
- Total Fat: 7.5
- Sodium: 183.9
- Sugar: 23.8
- Saturated Fat: 1.3
- Fiber: 1.2
- Protein: 4.2

252. Poppy Seed Plum Cake

Serving: 1 10 inch cake | Prep: 25mins | Ready in:

Ingredients

- Poppy Seeds Filling Mix

- 62 g ground poppy seeds
- 30 ml hot milk
- 1/2 teaspoon vanilla extract
- 12 g butter, softened
- 25 g sugar
- Cake Batter
- 140 g butter, softened
- 80 g sugar
- 1/4 teaspoon vanilla extract
- 1 pinch salt
- 3 eggs
- 250 g flour
- 2 teaspoons baking powder
- Topping
- 400 g plums, quartered (about 6 medium ones)

Direction

- To make the poppy seed filling place ground poppy seeds in a bowl and add the hot milk and vanilla extract. Allow to steep for 15 minutes, then add the butter and sugar. Mix well and set aside.
- For the cake batter cream butter and sugar in a big bowl for 6 minutes. Add vanilla extract and salt.
- Beat in each egg separately for 30 seconds.
- Then fold in the poppy seed filling mix.
- In a second bowl combine flour and baking powder. Add this to the butter mixture and stir to combine using a wooden spoon.
- Spread batter in a paper-lined or greased springform pan (26 cm/10 in in diameter).
- Stick the plum quarters into the dough arranging them in circles on the batter.
- Bake in the preheated oven at 180°C/350°F for 65 minutes or until tester inserted in the centre comes out clean.
- Allow to cool in the pan for 10 minutes, then remove to a wire rack to cool completely or serve at room temperature.
- Enjoy!

Nutrition Information

- Calories: 3156.2
- Cholesterol: 886.9
- Protein: 60.9
- Total Fat: 167.2
- Saturated Fat: 86.2
- Sugar: 148.1
- Total Carbohydrate: 364
- Sodium: 2209.8
- Fiber: 24.5

253. Poppycock

Serving: 8-10 serving(s) | Prep: 30mins | Ready in:

Ingredients

- 1 (10 ounce) bag popcorn (4 to 6 qts. popped)
- 1 cup butter
- 2 cups brown sugar
- 1/2 cup white Karo
- 1 teaspoon salt
- 1 teaspoon butter flavoring
- 1/2 teaspoon baking soda
- almonds or peanuts or other nuts, of choice

Direction

- In a large pan melt the butter.
- Add brown sugar, white Karo and salt and cook for 5 minutes stirring occasionally.
- Remove from stove and add butter flavoring extract and soda.
- Stir in almonds, peanuts or other nuts of choice.
- In a very large pan or bowl pour caramel syrup over popcorn.
- Stir quickly to coat.
- Pour out on cookie sheets.
- Bake at 250 degrees for 1 hour turning mixture halfway through baking with a spatula.
- Cool slightly, break apart and store when cooled completely in air tight bags or jars.

Nutrition Information

- Calories: 959.6
- Saturated Fat: 15.3
- Sodium: 610.6
- Fiber: 18.2
- Sugar: 60.2
- Total Carbohydrate: 168.3
- Cholesterol: 61
- Total Fat: 28.8
- Protein: 16.6

254. Possum's Apple Crisp

Serving: 6 serving(s) | Prep: 15mins | Ready in:

Ingredients

- 4 cups sliced and peeled apples
- 3/4 cup brown sugar
- 1/2 cup flour
- 1/2 cup oats
- 1/3 cup soft margarine or 1/3 cup butter
- 3/4 teaspoon cinnamon
- 3/4 teaspoon nutmeg
- 1/2 teaspoon vanilla

Direction

- Peel and slice apples.
- Grease a deep baking pan.
- Lay the apples in the pan.
- In a separate bowl, combine the remaining ingredients.
- Stir thoroughly.
- Spread mixture over apples.
- Bake at 375° for 30 minutes.
- Enjoy!

Nutrition Information

- Calories: 328.8
- Total Carbohydrate: 55.4
- Cholesterol: 0
- Protein: 3.6
- Total Fat: 11.3

- Sugar: 35.3
- Saturated Fat: 2
- Sodium: 130.2
- Fiber: 3.9

255. Potato Salad With Sweet Onion Dressing

Serving: 8 serving(s) | Prep: 10mins | Ready in:

Ingredients

- 1 kg new potato
- Dressing
- 2 red onions, finely minced
- 2 garlic cloves, finely minced
- 3 tablespoons olive oil
- 1 tablespoon balsamic vinegar
- 1 tablespoon cider vinegar
- 1/2 teaspoon caster sugar

Direction

- Boil potatoes in salted water for 10-15 minutes until tender.
- While the potatoes are cooking, mix together the ingredients for the dressing.
- Drain the potatoes.
- While they are still hot, mix together with the dressing.
- Serve.
- NOTE: Makes a great take-along dish for a picnic or pot-luck.

Nutrition Information

- Calories: 0
- Fiber: 0
- Sugar: 0
- Protein: 0
- Total Fat: 0
- Sodium: 0
- Total Carbohydrate: 0
- Cholesterol: 0

- Saturated Fat: 0

256. Praline Brownies

Serving: 12 serving(s) | Prep: 10mins | Ready in:

Ingredients

- 1/2 cup butter
- 4 baking chocolate squares
- 4 eggs
- 2 cups sugar
- 1 1/2 cups flour
- 2 teaspoons vanilla extract
- 1 pinch salt
- Topping
- 3 tablespoons butter, melted
- 3/4 cup light brown sugar
- 3/4 cup pecans, chopped

Direction

- Melt the chocolate squares and butter together.
- Mix lightly beaten eggs with the sugar, flour, vanilla extract and a pinch of salt.
- Add the melted chocolate mixture.
- Spread in a 13 x 9 x 2 inch pan.
- Combine the 3 tablespoons of the melted butter, the brown sugar and pecans.
- Sprinkle evenly over the batter.
- Bake for 25 to 30 minutes in a 350 degree oven.
- Do not overcook.
- Brownies should be creamy in the center.

Nutrition Information

- Calories: 453
- Fiber: 2.7
- Sugar: 47.2
- Total Carbohydrate: 62.7
- Saturated Fat: 10.8
- Cholesterol: 98.5
- Protein: 5.7
- Total Fat: 22.3

- Sodium: 119.2

257. Praline Pumpkin Pie

Serving: 8 serving(s) | Prep: 30mins | Ready in:

Ingredients

- 1 cup all-purpose flour, divided
- 3 1/2 tablespoons ice water
- 1 teaspoon granulated sugar
- 1/4 teaspoon salt
- 3 tablespoons vegetable shortening
- cooking spray
- 1 (15 ounce) can pumpkin
- 1 cup 2% low-fat milk
- 1/2 cup packed brown sugar
- 1 tablespoon all-purpose flour
- 3 tablespoons maple syrup
- 2 tablespoons Bourbon
- 1 teaspoon ground cinnamon
- 1/2 teaspoon salt
- 1 1/2 teaspoons vanilla extract
- 1/4 teaspoon ground nutmeg
- 1/4 teaspoon ground allspice
- 2 large egg whites, lightly beaten
- 1 large egg, lightly beaten
- 1/3 cup chopped pecans
- 1/4 cup packed brown sugar
- 1 1/2 teaspoons maple syrup

Direction

- Preheat oven to 400 degrees.
- Combine 1/4 cup flour and ice water; stir with a whisk until well-blended.
- Set aside.
- Combine 3/4 cup flour, granulated sugar, and 1/4 teaspoon salt in a bowl; cut in shortening with a pastry blender or 2 knives until mixture resembles coarse meal.
- Add ice-water mixture; mix with a fork until flour mixture is moist.

- Gently press mixture into a 4-inch circle on heavy-duty plastic wrap; cover with additional plastic wrap.
- Roll dough, still covered, into an 11-inch circle; chill 10 minutes or until plastic wrap can be easily removed.
- Remove 1 sheet of plastic wrap.
- Fit dough into a 9-inch pie plate coated with cooking spray; remove top sheet of plastic wrap.
- Fold edges of dough under; flute.
- Pierce bottom and sides with a fork.
- Place a 10-inch square of foil over dough.
- Place pie weights evenly over foil.
- Bake at 400 degrees for 5 minutes; cool on a wire rack.
- Remove foil and pie weights.
- Combine pumpkin and next 12 ingredients; stir well with a whisk.
- Pour into crust.
- Bake at 400 degrees for 40 minutes; shield edges of crust with foil after 30 minutes.
- Combine nuts, 1/4 cup brown sugar, and 1 1/2 teaspoons syrup.
- Sprinkle over pie; bake an additional 15 minutes or until filling is set.
- Cool completely on a wire rack.

Nutrition Information

- Calories: 293
- Sodium: 263
- Total Carbohydrate: 45.1
- Protein: 5.4
- Total Fat: 9.6
- Saturated Fat: 2.3
- Fiber: 1.3
- Sugar: 28.3
- Cholesterol: 28.9

258. Pumpkin Cake Bars With Cream Cheese Frosting!

Serving: 12-24 serving(s) | Prep: 20mins | Ready in:

Ingredients

- 4 large eggs
- 1 2/3 cups white sugar
- 1 cup vegetable oil
- 1 (15 ounce) can pumpkin puree
- 2 cups all-purpose flour
- 2 teaspoons baking powder
- 1 teaspoon salt
- 1 teaspoon baking soda
- 2 teaspoons ground cinnamon
- 6 ounces cream cheese
- 6 tablespoons butter, softened
- 3 cups confectioners' sugar

Direction

- Preheat oven to 350°F.
- Grease and flour one glass 9 x 13 inch pan.
- In a mixing bowl, beat together the eggs, sugar, oil and pumpkin.
- Sift together the flour, baking powder, salt, baking soda, salt and cinnamon; add to wet ingredients and mix thoroughly.
- Spread into prepared pan.
- Bake at 350° for 25 to 30 minutes.
- Remove from oven and allow to cool.
- For the frosting: beat together the cream cheese, butter and confectioner's sugar.
- Evenly spread over bars after they have cooled.

Nutrition Information

- Calories: 594.7
- Sodium: 480.8
- Sugar: 58.1
- Total Carbohydrate: 77.2
- Cholesterol: 92.9
- Total Fat: 30.6
- Saturated Fat: 9.3

- Fiber: 1
- Protein: 5.5

259. Pumpkin Gooey Butter Cake (Paula Deen)

Serving: 10 serving(s) | Prep: 30mins | Ready in:

Ingredients

- Cake
- 1 (18 1/4 ounce) package yellow cake mix
- 1 egg
- 8 tablespoons butter, melted
- Filling
- 1 (8 ounce) package cream cheese, softened
- 1 (15 ounce) can pumpkin
- 3 eggs
- 1 teaspoon vanilla
- 8 tablespoons butter, melted
- 1 (16 ounce) box powdered sugar
- 1 teaspoon cinnamon
- 1 teaspoon nutmeg

Direction

- Preheat oven to 350.
- To make the cake: Combine all of the ingredients and mix well.
- Pat batter into a lightly greased 13x9-inch baking pan with hands into an even layer.
- Prepare filling.
- To make the filling: In a large bowl, beat the cream cheese and pumpkin until smooth.
- Add the eggs, vanilla, and butter, and beat together.
- Next, add the powdered sugar, cinnamon, nutmeg, and mix well.
- Spread pumpkin mixture over cake batter and bake for 40 to 50 minutes.
- Make sure not to over bake as the center should be a little gooey.
- Serve with fresh whipped cream or cinnamon-flavored ice cream.

Nutrition Information

- Calories: 683.7
- Total Fat: 34.2
- Sodium: 605.5
- Saturated Fat: 17.7
- Fiber: 1
- Sugar: 68.3
- Total Carbohydrate: 90
- Cholesterol: 149.3
- Protein: 6.8

260. Pumpkin Apple Cake(s)

Serving: 10-12 serving(s) | Prep: 20mins | Ready in:

Ingredients

- 1/2 cup butter
- 2 eggs
- 1 1/2 cups sugar
- 1 3/4 cups flour
- 1 teaspoon baking soda
- 1/2 teaspoon cinnamon
- 1/2 teaspoon nutmeg
- 1/4 teaspoon salt
- 1/4 teaspoon clove
- 1/4 teaspoon ginger
- 1 cup canned pumpkin
- 1/2 cup apple juice
- 1 1/2 cups powdered sugar
- 1 -2 tablespoon milk

Direction

- Bring butter and eggs to room temperature.
- Grease and flour ten 4 inch baby Bundt pans or one 8 1/2 inch large Bundt pan.
- In a large bowl beat the butter until creamy and fluffy.
- Gradually add the sugar, beating at medium speed about 6 minutes or until light and fluffy and sugar is dissolved.

- Add egg, one at a time, beating about 1 minute after each; scrape bowl frequently.
- Stir together flour, soda, salt and spices.
- Add to creamed mixture alternately with pumpkin and apple juice, beginning and ending with flour.
- Beat just until thoroughly blended.
- Turn batter into prepared pans, filling small pans about 2/3 full.
- Bake individual cakes for 25 minutes or 45 minutes for the large pan in 350* oven.
- Cool 10 to 15 minutes and turn onto wire rack to cool completely.
- Stir together powdered sugar and milk to make a glaze of drizzling consistency; spoon over cooled cakes.

Nutrition Information

- Calories: 378.2
- Saturated Fat: 6.3
- Sodium: 324.4
- Sugar: 49.9
- Total Fat: 10.6
- Fiber: 1.4
- Total Carbohydrate: 68.4
- Cholesterol: 66.9
- Protein: 4

261. Pumpkin Spice Bundt Cake

Serving: 1 Bundt Cake, 12 serving(s) | Prep: 20mins | Ready in:

Ingredients

- Cake
- 3 1/4 cups all-purpose flour
- 1 tablespoon baking powder
- 2 1/2 teaspoons ground cinnamon
- 1 teaspoon baking soda
- 1 teaspoon ground nutmeg
- 1/4 teaspoon salt
- 1 1/2 cups fresh pumpkin puree or 1 1/2 cups canned pumpkin puree
- 1/2 cup applesauce
- 1 1/2 cups granulated sugar
- 1/2 cup margarine, softened
- 3 large egg whites
- 2 teaspoons vanilla extract
- cooking spray
- Glaze
- 3 tablespoons dark brown sugar or 3 tablespoons light brown sugar
- 1 tablespoon dark rum
- 1 teaspoon skim milk
- 3 tablespoons powdered sugar

Direction

- Preheat oven to 350°.
- Combine first 6 ingredients; set flour mixture aside.
- Combine pumpkin and applesauce; set aside.
- Beat granulated sugar and margarine in a large bowl at medium speed of a mixer until well-blended (about 5 minutes).
- Add egg whites and vanilla, beating well.
- Add flour mixture to sugar mixture alternately with pumpkin mixture, beginning and ending with flour mixture.
- Pour batter into a 12-cup Bundt pan coated with cooking spray.
- Bake at 350° for 50 minutes or until a wooden pick inserted in center comes out clean.
- Cool in pan 10 minutes; remove from pan.
- Combine brown sugar, rum, and milk in a small saucepan, and cook over low heat until brown sugar dissolves.
- Remove sugar mixture from heat, and add powdered sugar, stirring with a whisk.
- Spoon glaze over warm cake.

Nutrition Information

- Calories: 332.1
- Fiber: 1.4
- Protein: 4.7
- Sodium: 352.1

- Sugar: 30.8
- Total Carbohydrate: 60.2
- Cholesterol: 0
- Total Fat: 8
- Saturated Fat: 1.4

262. Queen Elizabeth's Own Cake

Serving: 1 cake | Prep: 10mins | Ready in:

Ingredients

- 1 cup boiling water
- 1 cup dates, chopped
- 1 teaspoon baking soda
- 1 cup sugar
- 4 tablespoons butter, softened
- 1 egg, beaten
- 1 teaspoon vanilla extract
- 1 1/2 cups sifted all-purpose flour
- 1 teaspoon baking powder
- 1/2 teaspoon salt
- 1/2 cup coconut or 1/2 cup chopped pecans
- ICING
- 5 tablespoons light brown sugar
- 5 tablespoons cream
- 2 tablespoons butter
- 1/2 cup coconut or 1/2 cup chopped pecans

Direction

- Preheat the oven to 350°F; grease a 9-inch square cake pan.
- In a bowl, pour the boiling water over the dates; add the soda and let stand while the remaining ingredients are prepared.
- Cream together the sugar and butter in a large bowl; add the eggs and vanilla; stir in the coconut, flour, baking powder and salt.
- Pour in the date mixture and blend well.
- Pour the batter into the cake pan; bake for 35 minutes or until toothpick inserted in center comes out clean; cool before icing.
- Combine all the ingredients for the icing; bring to a boil and cook, stirring constantly, for 3 minutes. While the icing is still warm, pour over the cooled cake; sprinkle with coconut.

Nutrition Information

- Calories: 3697.8
- Saturated Fat: 108.8
- Fiber: 33.2
- Sugar: 386.8
- Cholesterol: 477.9
- Sodium: 3441.4
- Total Carbohydrate: 568.2
- Protein: 38.2
- Total Fat: 154.7

263. Quick Easy Fruit And Dip

Serving: 8-10 serving(s) | Prep: 15mins | Ready in:

Ingredients

- 1 (8 ounce) package cream cheese
- 1/2 cup marshmallow creme
- 1 cup pineapple juice
- apples or strawberries or bananas or peaches or nectarines or plum

Direction

- Blend cream cheese and marshmallow crème in mixer.
- Slowly add ¼ C of juice.
- Mix until well blended.
- Cover and chill.
- Cut fruit up into bite size pieces.
- Dip the bananas and apples into the remaining pineapple juice to prevent the fruit from browning.
- (Works as well as lemon but adds some sweetness to the fruit) To serve, arrange fruit on a platter around the dip.

Nutrition Information

- Calories: 161.2
- Total Fat: 10
- Saturated Fat: 6.2
- Fiber: 0.1
- Protein: 2.4
- Sodium: 95.9
- Sugar: 9.8
- Total Carbohydrate: 16
- Cholesterol: 31.2

264. Quick And Easy Chocolate Chip Cookie Dough Brownies

Serving: 48 brownies | Prep: 15mins | Ready in:

Ingredients

- 20 ounces brownie mix, Betty Crocker Original Supreme preferred (with chocolate syrup pouch)
- 1/3 cup vegetable oil
- 1/4 cup water
- 2 eggs
- 17 1/2 ounces chocolate chip cookie mix, Betty Crocker brand preferred
- 1/2 cup butter or 1/2 cup margarine, softened
- 1 egg
- 16 ounces chocolate frosting, Betty Crocker Rich Creamy preferred

Direction

- Heat oven to 350°F.
- Grease bottom only of 13x9-inch pan.
- Make brownie mix as directed on box, using oil, water and 2 eggs; Spread in pan.
- Make cookie mix as directed on pouch, using butter and 1 egg.
- Drop dough by rounded tablespoonfuls evenly onto brownie batter; press down lightly.
- Bake 35 to 40 minutes or until toothpick inserted 2 inches from side of pan comes out almost clean.
- Cool completely, about 1 hour then frost.
- **For brownies, cut into 8 rows by 6 rows.

Nutrition Information

- Calories: 178.2
- Saturated Fat: 3.2
- Sugar: 5.5
- Total Carbohydrate: 22.4
- Protein: 1.5
- Total Fat: 9.9
- Sodium: 106.7
- Fiber: 0.1
- Cholesterol: 16.7

265. Quick And Easy Eggless Banana Bread

Serving: 1 loaf, 4 serving(s) | Prep: 15mins | Ready in:

Ingredients

- 4 very ripe bananas, mashed
- 1 1/2 cups all-purpose flour
- 1/2 cup butter, melted
- 3/4 cup brown sugar
- 1/2 cup milk or 1/2 cup buttermilk
- 1 teaspoon baking soda
- 1 teaspoon vanilla essence
- 1 pinch salt

Direction

- 1. Preheat oven to 350°F/180°C.
- 2. In a mixing bowl, combine mashed bananas with butter.
- 3. Add in milk, vanilla, and mix.
- 4. Add in sugar, baking soda, salt, and mix.

- 5. Add flour last and mix until just combined.
- 6. Pour mixture into a greased and floured bread loaf pan.
- 7. Bake for 1 hour or until a wooden pick comes out clean.
- 8. Allow to cool before removing from pan.

Nutrition Information

- Calories: 658.4
- Total Carbohydrate: 104.8
- Protein: 7.4
- Total Fat: 25
- Fiber: 4.3
- Sugar: 54.7
- Saturated Fat: 15.5
- Sodium: 584.7
- Cholesterol: 65.3

266. Quick And Easy German Chocolate Cake

Serving: 1 Cake | Prep: 15mins | Ready in:

Ingredients

- 1 box German chocolate cake mix
- 1 container pecan coconut frosting
- 3 eggs
- 1 cup water
- 1/3 cup vegetable oil

Direction

- Preheat oven to 350 degrees.
- Grease and flour 12-cup Bundt pan.
- Set pan aside.
- Mix all ingredients in large mixing bowl.
- Mix 3 minutes with electric mixer, batter should be thick and well combined.
- Pour batter into Bundt pan and bake for 48-52 minutes.
- Cool cake on rack for 20 minutes before removing from pan.
- Cool cake completely.

Nutrition Information

- Calories: 2935.4
- Saturated Fat: 30.6
- Fiber: 18.1
- Cholesterol: 634.5
- Total Fat: 136.6
- Total Carbohydrate: 415.3
- Protein: 39.5
- Sodium: 3539.1
- Sugar: 257.3

267. Quick And Easy Ice Cream Pie

Serving: 1 pie | Prep: 5mins | Ready in:

Ingredients

- 1 9-inch Oreo cookie pie crust
- 1/2 gallon ice cream (I like cookies 'n cream the best)
- squeezable chocolate syrup
- squeezable caramel ice cream topping (smuckers makes good ones)
- crushed Heath candy bars (for topping) or crushed Skor candy bar (for topping)

Direction

- Let ice cream soften slightly.
- Spread evenly in pie crust.
- Squeeze chocolate syrup over pie in a crisscross motion.
- Do the same with the caramel syrup in opposite direction.
- Sprinkle top of pie with the crushed candy topping.
- Freeze until ready to serve.
- Any combination of ice cream and toppings works wonderfully, this just happens to be my favorite combination!

Nutrition Information

- Calories: 2185.9
- Total Fat: 116.2
- Saturated Fat: 71.7
- Sodium: 844.8
- Fiber: 7.4
- Sugar: 224.1
- Total Carbohydrate: 249.2
- Cholesterol: 464.6
- Protein: 37

268. Raspberry Rave

Serving: 12 serving(s) | Prep: 12mins | Ready in:

Ingredients

- 2 (10 ounce) packages frozen red raspberries, in syrup, thawed
- 1 (20 ounce) can crushed pineapple
- 2 (3 ounce) packages raspberry gelatin powder
- 1 cup boiling water
- 1 cup sour cream

Direction

- In sieve, drain berries and pineapple over a bowl.
- Press the fruit with spoon until you have 2 cups juice.
- In med bowl, dissolve the gelatin in the boiling water.
- Stir in the 2 cups of juice, the fruit, and the sour cream until blended well.
- Pour into serving bowl and chill until firm.

Nutrition Information

- Calories: 148.1
- Sodium: 77.5
- Sugar: 21.1
- Total Carbohydrate: 26.7
- Saturated Fat: 2.5
- Cholesterol: 8.4
- Protein: 2.5
- Total Fat: 4.4
- Fiber: 3.5

269. Raspberry Sunshine

Serving: 6 serving(s) | Prep: 5hours | Ready in:

Ingredients

- 3/4 cup boiling water
- 1 (3 ounce) package orange gelatin
- 1 cup cold orange juice
- 1/2 cup fresh raspberry
- 1 (11 ounce) can mandarin oranges, drained (substitute fresh orange segments if you're ambitious)

Direction

- Place orange jello into a large bowl and stir in boiling water; keep stirring for 2 minutes or until jello completely dissolves.
- Stir in cold orange juice.
- Refrigerate for 90 minutes or until thickened (if you drag a spoon through it, it will definitely leave an impression).
- Measure out 3/4 cup of the thickened gelatin into a medium bowl and set aside.
- Stir raspberries and oranges into remaining gelatin and then divide fruit mixture into 6 dessert dishes.
- Beat reserved gelatin with mixer (on high speed) until it is fluffy and has doubled in volume.
- Spoon this over the fruit mixture.
- Refrigerate for 3 hours or until firm.
- If you wish, you can do this in one serving bowl rather than in six individual dishes.

Nutrition Information

- Calories: 105.5
- Fiber: 1.7
- Sugar: 21.6
- Total Fat: 0.3
- Saturated Fat: 0
- Sodium: 68.2
- Total Carbohydrate: 25.3
- Cholesterol: 0
- Protein: 1.9

270. Raspberry Apple Crumble (Volumetric)

Serving: 6 one cup servings, 6 serving(s) | Prep: 15mins | Ready in:

Ingredients

- 6 medium tart apples (such as Granny Smith)
- 1/3 cup orange juice
- 1/3 cup water
- 3 tablespoons raspberry jam (I use light jam)
- 1/3 cup oatmeal
- 3 tablespoons flour
- 3 tablespoons brown sugar (I use Splenda brown sugar blend)
- 1 1/2 teaspoons cinnamon
- 1 pinch salt
- 1 1/2 tablespoons reduced-calorie margarine (Melted)

Direction

- Preheat oven to 350 degrees.
- Combine juice, water, and jam.
- Core apples and slice thinly. (I usually slice in quarters and then slice each quarter into 4 more slices for a total of 16 per apple).
- As you slice each apple, place in juice mixture and stir to cover apples so they won't turn brown.
- Pour mixture into an 8x8 pan.
- Combine remaining dry ingredients and stir to mix well, then add melted margarine. Stir again to mix. Mixture will be crumbly.
- Sprinkle oat mixture over apple mixture.
- Bake 1 hour or until apples are tender.
- Serve hot or room temperature, on its own or with low fat ice cream. Keeps very well in the fridge (if there is any leftover) and is delicious cold the next day.
- Tip: prepare in advance and place in oven at the start of your meal for a hot dessert.

Nutrition Information

- Calories: 177.2
- Fiber: 4.3
- Total Carbohydrate: 40.5
- Cholesterol: 0
- Total Fat: 2
- Saturated Fat: 0.3
- Sodium: 68.5
- Sugar: 27.1
- Protein: 1.7

271. Rawai (Parsee Sweet)

Serving: 4 serving(s) | Prep: 20mins | Ready in:

Ingredients

- 1 cup semolina
- 1/2 cup ghee
- 3/4 cup sugar
- 1 cup milk
- 1 cup water
- 1 tablespoon fried silvered almonds
- 1 tablespoon fried sultana
- nutmeg

Direction

- Melt the ghee and add the semolina.
- Fry until light brown in colour.
- Add water, milk and sugar.
- Cook over medium heat until it is of porridge consistency.
- Serve in a deep dish.

- Decorate with grated nutmeg, almonds and sultanas.

Nutrition Information

- Calories: 583.3
- Sodium: 40.3
- Sugar: 39
- Total Carbohydrate: 73.2
- Cholesterol: 75.4
- Protein: 7.9
- Total Fat: 29.7
- Fiber: 2
- Saturated Fat: 17.7

272. Red Raspberry Holiday Trifle

Serving: 15 serving(s) | Prep: 1hours | Ready in:

Ingredients

- 1 purchased angel food cake, sliced
- 2 (16 ounce) bags frozen sweetened raspberries
- 1 cup raspberry-cranberry frozen juice concentrate, thawed
- 6 tablespoons Cointreau liqueur or 6 tablespoons brandy (or six tablespoons orange juice mixed with 1 tablespoon sugar)
- 4 cups cranberry-raspberry juice
- 2 tablespoons cornstarch
- For mousse layer
- 6 large egg yolks
- 3/4 cup sugar
- 1/2 cup fresh orange juice
- 4 tablespoons unsalted butter
- 2 tablespoons finely grated orange zest
- 1 pinch salt
- 8 ounces mascarpone cheese
- 1 cup heavy cream, whipped to medium firm peaks
- Garnish
- 1/2 cup heavy cream, whipped to medium-firm peaks and placed in decorating bag with piping tip or in plastic resealable b
- 6 fresh red raspberries

Direction

- To make the berry filling: In a large saucepan bring the 4 cups of raspberry-cranberry juice to a boil over high heat.
- Cook until reduced to about 1 1/2 cups, about 10 minutes.
- In a small bowl, stir together 4 tablespoons Cointreau with the cornstarch.
- Whisk into the reduced raspberry-cranberry juice and cook on medium heat until juice has thickened and become clear.
- Remove from the heat and add the two 16-ounce bags of frozen raspberries.
- Set aside and let stand until the berries have thawed.
- To make the mousse layer: In a heavy nonreactive saucepan (stainless steel or enamel) combine the egg yolks, sugar, orange juice and butter.
- Cook over medium heat, stirring to dissolve the sugar, until the butter melts.
- Reduce the heat to medium-low and stir constantly with a wooden spoon until the mixture thickly coats the back of the spoon, about 5 to 10 minutes.
- Strain mousse through a fine-mesh strainer to remove lumps, into a large bowl.
- The orange mousse mixture will be very thick.
- Refrigerate, covered with plastic wrap on the surface to prevent a skin from forming, until completely chilled, about half an hour.
- When mixture is chilled, in a large bowl, mash mascarpone cheese with a rubber spatula, add 1/4 cup of the orange mousse and stir until smooth and creamy.
- Stir in the remaining orange mousse and then fold in the whipped cream.
- To make the soaking liquid: In a small bowl, mix the 1 cup of thawed raspberry-cranberry concentrate with 2 tablespoons of Cointreau.
- Stir until blended and set aside.

- To assemble the Trifle:
- In a 12-cup trifle bowl or a glass bowl with straight sides, layer half the slices of the angel-food cake on the bottom, making sure that only the white, cut edges of the cake are visible against the sides of the trifle bowl.
- Drizzle cake with half the soaking liquid.
- Evenly spread half the orange mousse mixture over the soaked cake slices.
- Spread three-quarters of the berry filling carefully over the mousse.
- Layer the remaining angel-food cake slices on top of berry filling, cut sides against the glass.
- Drizzle cake with remaining soaking liquid.
- Spread remaining orange mousse mixture over cake.
- Mound remaining quarter of the raspberry mixture on top of the mousse in the center of the bowl.
- Pipe whipped cream on top of trifle to decorate.
- Garnish with fresh raspberries.
- Refrigerate for 4 to 6 hours or overnight before serving.

Nutrition Information

- Calories: 450
- Cholesterol: 124.7
- Protein: 4.5
- Total Fat: 13.9
- Saturated Fat: 8.1
- Sodium: 228.2
- Fiber: 3
- Sugar: 58.7
- Total Carbohydrate: 79.5

273. Red Velvet Chocolate Cake Icing

Serving: 1 cake | Prep: 5mins | Ready in:

Ingredients

- 1/2 teaspoon salt
- 1/4 cup Crisco
- 1/4 cup margarine
- 1/2 cup sugar
- 2 1/2 tablespoons flour
- 1/2 cup milk

Direction

- Beat salt, Crisco, margarine and sugar together in a bowl.
- In a saucepan, cook flour and milk on low heat.
- Cool to lukewarm.
- Add flour/milk mixture to creamed mixture and beat until fluffy.
- Spread evenly over cake.

Nutrition Information

- Calories: 1394.7
- Cholesterol: 17.1
- Saturated Fat: 26.3
- Sodium: 1754.8
- Fiber: 0.5
- Sugar: 100
- Total Carbohydrate: 121.1
- Protein: 6.5
- Total Fat: 101.3

274. Red, White, And Blueberry Pudding (Raw Vegan)

Serving: 2-4 serving(s) | Prep: 10mins | Ready in:

Ingredients

- 4 medium bananas
- 1/2 cup raspberries
- 1/2 cup young coconut water
- 1/2 cup blueberries
- raw coconut (to garnish) or left over berries (to garnish)

Direction

- Blend 1 banana with the raspberries and layer that into your parfait glasses. Rinse blender/food processor.
- Blend 2 bananas with the coconut water and layer on top of the red layer. Rinse blender.
- Blend 1 banana with the blueberries and layer on top of the white layer. Garnish with raw coconut or berries, enjoy!

Nutrition Information

- Calories: 247.1
- Fiber: 9
- Total Carbohydrate: 62.9
- Cholesterol: 0
- Protein: 3.2
- Total Fat: 1.1
- Saturated Fat: 0.3
- Sodium: 3
- Sugar: 33.9

275. Rhubarb Cake

Serving: 1 8x12 pan | Prep: 15mins | Ready in:

Ingredients

- 1 1/4 cups sugar
- 1/2 cup shortening
- 2 eggs
- 1/2 cup milk
- 2 cups flour
- 1 teaspoon baking soda
- 1 teaspoon cinnamon
- 1/4 teaspoon clove
- 1/4 teaspoon salt
- 1/2 teaspoon allspice
- 2 cups rhubarb, cut up
- Topping
- 1/3 cup brown sugar
- 1/2 teaspoon cinnamon
- 1/2 cup nuts

Direction

- Cream sugar, shortening and eggs.
- Sift flour.
- Then add soda, spices and salt.
- Mix well.
- Then stir in rhubarb.
- Pour into an 8"x 12" pan.
- Then mix the brown sugar, cinnamon and nuts (topping).
- Sprinkle over the top of the batter and Bake 350* for 30 to 35 minutes.

Nutrition Information

- Calories: 3755.3
- Saturated Fat: 36.8
- Sodium: 2544.3
- Protein: 56.7
- Total Fat: 155.3
- Fiber: 19.6
- Sugar: 327.6
- Total Carbohydrate: 550.7
- Cholesterol: 440.1

276. Rhubarb Upside Down Cake

Serving: 8 serving(s) | Prep: 20mins | Ready in:

Ingredients

- 2 tablespoons butter
- 1 cup brown sugar
- 2 cups diced rhubarb
- 1/4 cup shortening
- 1 cup sugar
- 1 egg
- 2 cups flour
- 2 1/2 teaspoons baking powder
- 1/2 teaspoon salt
- 1 cup milk

Direction

- Melt butter in a skillet.
- Add brown sugar and diced rhubarb.
- To make the batter, cream shortening and sugar together.
- Add egg and beat.
- Sift flour; add baking powder and salt, sift again.
- Sift dry ingredients together and add alternately with milk.
- Pour batter over rhubarb and bake at 375 degrees for 40 to 45 minutes.
- Turn upside down on plate to serve.
- Serve with cream.

Nutrition Information

- Calories: 432
- Sodium: 315.5
- Protein: 5.3
- Sugar: 51.9
- Total Carbohydrate: 78.8
- Cholesterol: 38.3
- Total Fat: 11.4
- Saturated Fat: 4.4
- Fiber: 1.4

277. Rice Cakes With Sweet Potatoes Soy Ginger Glaze

Serving: 24 appetizers | Prep: 30mins | Ready in:

Ingredients

- Rice cakes
- 2 cups medium grain rice, cooked
- 2 large eggs, lightly beaten
- 1 1/2 tablespoons green onions, chopped
- 1 1/2 tablespoons walnuts, chopped
- 2 tablespoons Italian parsley, chopped
- 1/2 teaspoon paprika
- 1 teaspoon kosher salt
- 1 teaspoon black pepper
- 1 tablespoon garlic, minced
- 1/2 cup flour
- 1/4 cup canola oil
- Sweet Potatoes and Soy Ginger Glaze
- 1 sweet potato, cooked, peeled and diced into small pieces
- 1 cup soy sauce
- 2 oranges, juice and zest of
- 3 tablespoons brown sugar
- 1 tablespoon fresh ginger, minced
- 1/4 cup cornstarch, mixed with water
- chopped chives (optional)

Direction

- In a bowl, combine rice, egg, green onions, walnuts, parsley, and half of the spices; refrigerate for about 2 hours.
- In a bowl, combine the flour and the rest of the spices.
- When rice mixture is chilled, form into 1-inch cakes and toss in the flour mixture.
- Sauté in oil until brown; about 3 minutes per side; press down softly with spatula while frying to slightly flatten.
- Sweet Potato and Soy Ginger glaze; Drizzle sweet potato with oil and roast in 425 degree oven until tender: or bake in Microwave until tender.
- Mix remaining ingredients in a sauce pan; bring to a boil and cook 2 to 3 minutes; add cornstarch mixed with a little water; cook until thickened.
- Mix sweet potatoes with sauce and place on rice cakes with chopped chives.

Nutrition Information

- Calories: 130.2
- Total Fat: 3.2
- Sugar: 2.2
- Total Carbohydrate: 22
- Saturated Fat: 0.4
- Sodium: 753.5
- Fiber: 1.3
- Cholesterol: 17.6
- Protein: 3.5

278. Rice Pudding Mexican Style, Arroz Con Leche

Serving: 6 serving(s) | Prep: 5mins | Ready in:

Ingredients

- 1 cup long-grain white rice (155 g)
- 3 cups water
- 3 inches cinnamon sticks or 1 teaspoon ground cinnamon
- 1 tablespoon very fine julienne strips lime peel (optional)
- 1 pinch salt
- 4 cups milk (or for richer pudding substitute 1 can of evaporated milk and add enough regular milk to equal 4 cup)
- 1 egg
- 1 1/2 cups sugar, to taste (375g)
- 1/3 cup raisins (60 g)
- 1 teaspoon vanilla extract

Direction

- Place the rice in a large saucepan with the water, cinnamon, lime peel and salt.
- Bring to a boil; lower the heat and cook, covered, until most of the water has been absorbed.
- Beat an egg into the milk.
- Stir in the milk, egg mixture and sugar, stirring constantly, over low heat until the mixture thickens.
- Add the raisins and vanilla and cook for 2 minutes.
- Remove from the heat and let cool for 10 to 20 minutes.
- Transfer to a platter or individual bowls and refrigerate.
- Garnish with ground cinnamon if desired.

Nutrition Information

- Calories: 448.1
- Total Carbohydrate: 88.7
- Protein: 8.8
- Total Fat: 7
- Saturated Fat: 4
- Sodium: 123.9
- Fiber: 0.7
- Sugar: 54.8
- Cholesterol: 53.8

279. Rich, Fudgy Vegan Brownies

Serving: 12 serving(s) | Prep: 10mins | Ready in:

Ingredients

- 1 1/2 cups unbleached flour
- 1/2 cup cocoa
- 1 1/2 cups brown sugar
- 3/4 teaspoon baking powder
- 1 1/2 teaspoons baking soda
- 1 teaspoon salt
- 3/4 cup brewed coffee
- 3/4 cup soymilk
- 1/3 cup vegetable oil
- 1/2 cup walnuts, roasted and chopped (optional)
- 1/2 cup chocolate chips or 1/2 cup carob chips
- Glaze for extra decadance
- 7 ounces dark Belgian chocolate (optional)
- 5 ounces margarine (optional)

Direction

- Sift together the flour, sugar, cocoa, baking powder and soda, and salt.
- In a separate bowl, combine the coffee, soy milk, and oil.
- Add the liquid to the dry ingredients and mix; then stir in the nuts and chocolate chips.
- Pour batter (it will be quite liquidy) into a greased 9x9" pan and bake at 325° for 25

minutes, or until a toothpick inserted in the middle comes out clean.
- (Note- for a smaller pan, the baking time could be substantially longer- a 7x10 pan took about 40 minutes).
- For glaze- melt the chocolate and margarine and whisk, then drizzle over brownies.
- (Note- this is a lot of glaze- an ounce of chocolate and a tablespoon of margarine makes a nice amount).

Nutrition Information

- Calories: 270.3
- Protein: 3.1
- Sodium: 390.6
- Sugar: 31.1
- Total Carbohydrate: 46.4
- Total Fat: 8.9
- Saturated Fat: 2.1
- Fiber: 1.6
- Cholesterol: 0

280. Roasted Pumpkin And Sweet Potato Soup

Serving: 4 serving(s) | Prep: 20mins | Ready in:

Ingredients

- 1 sugar pumpkin, approximately 1-2 pounds
- 1 medium sweet potato
- 2 1/2 cups chicken stock
- 2 shallots, diced
- 1 teaspoon cayenne pepper
- 1 teaspoon curry powder
- 1 teaspoon turmeric
- 1 tablespoon pumpkin pie spice
- 1 teaspoon salt
- 1 teaspoon fresh ground pepper
- 1 tablespoon vegetable oil

Direction

- Preheat oven to 400 degrees.
- Slice pumpkin in half and remove the seeds and strings.
- Season with salt and freshly ground pepper to taste, and wrap in aluminum foil.
- Use a fork to create vent holes all around the sweet potato.
- Wrap the sweet potato in foil and place with the pumpkin on a foil-lined baking sheet.
- Roast for one hour and ten minutes, or until both the pumpkin and the sweet potato are tender enough to pierce easily with a fork.
- Remove the pumpkin and sweet potato from the oven and allow to cool.
- Remove the skin from the shallots and dice them finely.
- Heat the vegetable oil in a sauté pan over a medium flame.
- "Sweat" the shallots by covering with foil and then topping the pan with a close-fitting lid.
- After 1-2 minutes, remove the cover and foil, and add the curry powder.
- Sauté for an additional minute, then remove from heat.
- Scoop the flesh from both the pumpkin and the sweet potato and place in a food processor.
- Add the curried shallots, the remaining spices, and one cup of the chicken stock.
- Puree until smooth.
- Thin with the remaining chicken stock until the desired consistency is reached.
- Serve hot, garnished with chervil, if desired.

Nutrition Information

- Calories: 130.4
- Total Fat: 5.6
- Sodium: 816.4
- Protein: 4.8
- Saturated Fat: 1.1
- Fiber: 1.7
- Sugar: 3.9
- Total Carbohydrate: 15.8
- Cholesterol: 4.5

- Saturated Fat: 0.6

281. Rocky Road Brownies

Serving: 8 serving(s) | Prep: 10mins | Ready in:

Ingredients

- 2 egg whites, whipped
- 1 whole egg, beaten
- 1/2 cup white sugar
- 1 tablespoon vanilla extract
- 1/2 cup cocoa, sifted
- 1/2 teaspoon baking powder
- 1/4 teaspoon salt
- 1/2 cup all-purpose flour
- 1 cup marshmallow cream
- 1 1/2 tablespoons chopped walnuts (optional)

Direction

- Preheat oven to 325F degrees.
- Grease and flour an 8-inch square pan and set aside.
- In a mixing bowl, combine baking powder, cocoa, salt, and flour.
- In another mixing bowl, combine beaten egg, egg whites, sugar, vanilla, and marshmallow creme.
- Mix dry ingredients with wet ingredients.
- Do not overmix or brownies will be too tough.
- Pour into prepared pan.
- Sprinkle nuts on top, if using.
- Bake for 18-20 minutes.
- Ice with your favourite chocolate or vanilla icing if you wish.

Nutrition Information

- Calories: 197.6
- Total Carbohydrate: 44.1
- Total Fat: 1.5
- Sodium: 140.9
- Fiber: 2
- Sugar: 26.2
- Cholesterol: 23.3
- Protein: 3.7

282. Rolled Chocolate Sugar Cookies

Serving: 42 large cookies | Prep: 15mins | Ready in:

Ingredients

- 2 1/2 cups flour
- 7 teaspoons baking cocoa
- 2 teaspoons baking powder
- 1/4 teaspoon baking soda
- 1/4 teaspoon salt
- 1/2 cup unsalted butter, room temperature
- 1 cup sugar
- 2 eggs
- 1 teaspoon vanilla extract
- additional sugar, for rolling and topping

Direction

- Preheat oven to 375*.
- Lightly grease cookie sheets.
- Sift together flour, cocoa, baking powder, baking soda and salt and set aside.
- Cream butter with sugar on medium speed until light, about 2 minutes.
- Add eggs and vanilla, beating well.
- Gradually add flour mixture and blend well.
- Gather dough into a ball and cover with foil or wrap.
- Refrigerate 1 to 2 hours, until firm.
- Using half of dough at a time, roll out a 1/4 inch thick on sugar sprinkled counter or pastry cloth.
- Cut out cookies and then lift with spatula onto sheets, leaving about 1 1/2" between cookies.
- Sprinkle with sugar or sprinkles, if desired.
- Bake 8 to 9 minutes or until cookies are firm and edges are just starting to brown.
- Remove to wire rack to cool.

Nutrition Information

- Calories: 69.5
- Saturated Fat: 1.5
- Sodium: 42.5
- Sugar: 4.8
- Total Carbohydrate: 10.7
- Total Fat: 2.5
- Fiber: 0.3
- Cholesterol: 15.9
- Protein: 1.1

283. Rum Cream Apple Pie

Serving: 1 pie | Prep: 10mins | Ready in:

Ingredients

- 1 1/3 cups regular rolled oats
- 1/3 cup melted butter
- 1/2 cup brown sugar
- 2 cups water
- 1 1/4 cups sugar, divided
- 2 tablespoons lemon juice
- 2 cooking apples, peeled, cored, and sliced
- 3 tablespoons cornstarch
- 1 dash salt
- 1 cup half-and-half
- 2 tablespoons rum
- 1 cup raisins, soaked in warm water
- sweetened whipped cream

Direction

- Combine the oats, butter, and brown sugar.
- Press mixture onto the bottom and sides of a 9-inch pie plate and bake at 350 degree F oven for 10 minutes; let cool.
- In a saucepan combine the water, 1 cup sugar, and lemon juice, and bring to a boil.
- Add the sliced apples and poach gently until apples are tender.
- Drain, reserving 1 cup of the syrup.
- In a saucepan combine the cornstarch, remaining 1/4 cup sugar, and salt; gradually blend in the reserved syrup and half and half and cook over medium heat, stirring constantly, until thickened.
- Remove from heat, stir in the rum and raisins, and then let cool slightly.
- Pour half of the cream mixture into the pie shell.
- Arrange the apple slices over the cream mixture (reserving a few slices for garnish), then top the apples with the remaining cream mixture.
- Arrange reserved apple slices on top for garnish.
- Refrigerate until set and well-chilled.
- Serve with sweetened whipped cream or vanilla ice cream.

Nutrition Information

- Calories: 3392.4
- Saturated Fat: 57.5
- Sugar: 472.8
- Total Carbohydrate: 617.1
- Total Fat: 97.1
- Fiber: 22.9
- Cholesterol: 252.1
- Protein: 30.4
- Sodium: 767.8

284. Russian Teacakes

Serving: 48 teacakes | Prep: 0S | Ready in:

Ingredients

- 1 cup butter
- 1/2 cup sifted powdered sugar
- 1 teaspoon vanilla
- 2 1/2 cups flour
- 1/4 teaspoon salt
- 3/4 cup nuts, chopped (usually pecans or walnuts)

Direction

- Mix butter, sugar and vanilla together. Mix flour and salt together and stir into batter. Add nuts and mix them into the batter. Chill until cold. With the oven at 400F, roll into balls and put on an ungreased pan. Put them in the oven for about 10-12 minutes. When they come out, roll them in powdered sugar while they are still warm. Let cool and roll again.

Nutrition Information

- Calories: 75.4
- Total Fat: 5
- Sugar: 1.4
- Cholesterol: 10.2
- Protein: 1.1
- Saturated Fat: 2.6
- Sodium: 60.4
- Fiber: 0.4
- Total Carbohydrate: 6.8

285. S'mores Pizza

Serving: 6-8 serving(s) | Prep: 10mins | Ready in:

Ingredients

- 1 (16 1/2 ounce) packagepillsbury refrigerated chocolate chip cookie dough
- 2 cups chocolate chips
- 2 cups graham crackers, broken in 1 inch pieces
- 2 cups miniature marshmallows
- chocolate syrup, for garnish (optional)

Direction

- Spread the softened cookie dough into a lightly greased pizza pan, flattening it to the edges.
- Bake at 350 degrees for 8-10 minutes until it begins to brown SLIGHTLY.
- Remove the cookie from the oven and sprinkle the top with the chocolate chips, graham crackers and marshmallows.
- Return the cookie to the oven for 5-8 minutes until crust is brown and chips and marshmallows are melted.
- Allow to cool slightly before serving.
- Garnish with chocolate syrup, if desired.

Nutrition Information

- Calories: 785
- Cholesterol: 18.7
- Sugar: 48.8
- Total Carbohydrate: 118.3
- Protein: 8
- Total Fat: 35.6
- Saturated Fat: 15.6
- Sodium: 351.8
- Fiber: 5.3

286. SO EASY SO GOOD Fruit Dip

Serving: 10-12 serving(s) | Prep: 20mins | Ready in:

Ingredients

- 2 (8 ounce) packages fruit-flavored cream cheese
- 2 (7 ounce) jars marshmallow cream
- 1 container Cool Whip
- mixed fruit, cut into chunks (cantaloupe, honeydew melon, pineapple, apple, banana, grapes, strawberries, etc....)

Direction

- Add marshmallow cream.
- When well blended, add cool whip.
- Serve with fruit chunks.

Nutrition Information

- Calories: 166.6
- Fiber: 0.1
- Cholesterol: 5.2
- Total Fat: 1.7
- Saturated Fat: 0.9
- Protein: 4.6
- Sodium: 169.3
- Sugar: 19.5
- Total Carbohydrate: 33.2

287. Salad With Eight Fruits

Serving: 10 serving(s) | Prep: 25mins | Ready in:

Ingredients

- 1/3 cup lemon juice
- 1/3 cup water
- 1/2 cup sugar
- 2 fresh peaches, thinly sliced
- 2 small bananas, sliced
- 1 pint blueberries
- 1 pint strawberry, sliced
- 1 cup watermelon, small pieces
- 1 cup cantaloupe, small pieces
- 1 cup grapes
- 2 kiwi, peeled and sliced

Direction

- Mix lemon juice, water, and sugar.
- Stir until sugar is dissolved.
- Add peaches and banana.
- Stir to coat well.
- In large bowl, combine remaining fruits.
- Add peaches and bananas.
- Stir gently.
- Cover tightly and refrigerate for 1 hour.

Nutrition Information

- Calories: 127.3
- Saturated Fat: 0.1
- Sugar: 25.6

- Cholesterol: 0
- Protein: 1.5
- Total Fat: 0.5
- Sodium: 4.7
- Fiber: 3.2
- Total Carbohydrate: 32.3

288. Santa's Whiskers

Serving: 4 dozen, 24 serving(s) | Prep: 15mins | Ready in:

Ingredients

- 1 cup softened butter
- 1 cup sugar
- 2 teaspoons milk
- 1 teaspoon vanilla
- 2 1/2 cups flour
- 1/4 cup chopped candied cherry (red or green or combination of both)
- 1/2 cup chopped nuts
- 3/4 cup flaked coconut

Direction

- Beat butter and sugar.
- Add milk and vanilla.
- Gradually stir in flour, mixing well.
- Stir in nuts.
- Form into 2 logs, approx. 1 1/2 inches in diameter.
- Roll in coconut until each log is well coated.
- Wrap in plastic wrap or waxed paper.
- Chill an hour or longer.
- Cut 1/4-inch slices and bake at 375°F for 12 minutes.

Nutrition Information

- Calories: 176.2
- Fiber: 0.7
- Sugar: 9.5
- Total Fat: 10
- Saturated Fat: 5.7

- Sodium: 80
- Total Carbohydrate: 20.1
- Cholesterol: 20.4
- Protein: 2

289. Scottish Fruited Gingerbread

Serving: 16 squares | Prep: 72hours | Ready in:

Ingredients

- 1/2 lb plain flour
- 2 teaspoons ground ginger
- 1 teaspoon baking powder
- 1 teaspoon baking soda
- 3 1/2 ounces light brown sugar
- 3 ounces unsalted butter
- 4 fluid ounces golden syrup or 4 fluid ounces light corn syrup
- 5 fluid ounces milk
- 2 eggs, lightly beaten
- 2 oranges, zest only
- 2 ounces dried apricots, finely chopped

Direction

- Grease and line a deep 7-inch square cake tin.
- Sift the flour, ginger, baking powder and bicarbonate of soda together.
- Place sugar, butter, syrup and milk in a pan and warm gently until melted and blended.
- Do not boil.
- Add to the flour with the eggs and mix thoroughly.
- Stir in orange zest and apricots.
- Turn into the baking tin and bake at 325°F for 60-65 minutes or until firm to the touch.
- Turn out and cool.
- The flavour of this cake improves with age.
- Store in an airtight container for 2-3 days before serving.

Nutrition Information

- Calories: 177.2
- Saturated Fat: 3.2
- Sodium: 125.3
- Fiber: 1.1
- Protein: 2.9
- Total Fat: 5.5
- Sugar: 12.5
- Total Carbohydrate: 30.3
- Cholesterol: 39.2

290. Scottish Tablet II

Serving: 5 pounds, 40-60 serving(s) | Prep: 2mins | Ready in:

Ingredients

- 1 cup unsalted butter
- 2 cups water
- 5 lbs extra finely granulated sugar (For a fuller texture, use 2½ lbs. extra fine, 2½ lbs. granulated)
- 1 (1 lb) can sweetened condensed milk

Direction

- Melt butter on low heat in water in a deep saucepan.
- Add sugar and bring to boil, stirring slowly all the time.
- When boiling, add condensed milk and simmer, stirring constantly to prevent sticking.
- Stop stirring when all bubbles vanish (excess moisture has now gone).
- Take off the heat and add any flavouring of your choice.
- Beat well for at least 5 minutes.
- Pour into a greased rectangular cookie sheet or rectangular pan.
- When cold, knife out and cut into bite-size cubes.
- Wrap in waxed paper to store.

Nutrition Information

- Calories: 296.8
- Sodium: 15.3
- Sugar: 62.9
- Cholesterol: 16.1
- Total Fat: 5.6
- Total Carbohydrate: 62.9
- Protein: 0.9
- Saturated Fat: 3.5
- Fiber: 0

291. Scripture Cookies

Serving: 8 serving(s) | Prep: 5mins | Ready in:

Ingredients

- 3/4 cup butter
- 3 cups oats
- 1/3 cup milk
- 1 cup raisins
- 1 1/2 cups sugar
- 2 eggs
- 2 cups flour
- 1 teaspoon cinnamon
- 1 teaspoon salt
- 1/2 teaspoon baking powder

Direction

- Drop by teaspoonfuls onto greased cookie sheet.
- Bake at 350* for 15 minutes.

Nutrition Information

- Calories: 719
- Saturated Fat: 12.3
- Sugar: 48.4
- Cholesterol: 100
- Fiber: 7.9
- Total Carbohydrate: 115.3
- Protein: 15.8
- Total Fat: 23.3
- Sodium: 462.3

292. Sex In A Pan

Serving: 10-15 serving(s) | Prep: 20mins | Ready in:

Ingredients

- 1 cup chopped pecans
- 1/4 cup icing sugar
- 1/2 cup melted margarine
- 1 cup flour
- 8 ounces Philadelphia Cream Cheese
- 1 cup white sugar
- 1 cup Cool Whip (buy large container)
- 1 (6 ounce) package instant chocolate pudding mix
- 1 (6 ounce) package instant vanilla pudding (do NOT buy pie filling!!!)
- chocolate shavings (optional)
- 3 cups milk

Direction

- Mix together the icing sugar, margarine, flour, and chopped pecans and press into a 9X13" pan.
- Bake for about 15 minutes at 350 degrees F; Cool.
- Mix cream cheese, white sugar, and ONE cup of cool whip; Spread on cool base.
- Mix both packages of pudding and add 3 cups of milk.
- Beat and spread on filling layer (don't worry it will thicken as it cools).
- Spread remaining cool whip on top, add some shaved chocolate if you want and set in the fridge.

Nutrition Information

- Calories: 566.8
- Saturated Fat: 10.7
- Protein: 7
- Total Fat: 29.9

- Sodium: 691
- Fiber: 2
- Sugar: 49.3
- Total Carbohydrate: 70
- Cholesterol: 35.2

293. Sheet Cake Icing

Serving: 1 sheet cake, 24 serving(s) | Prep: 15mins | Ready in:

Ingredients

- 1/2-1 cup butter
- 4 tablespoons cocoa powder
- 6 tablespoons sweet milk
- 1 (1 lb) box powdered sugar
- 1 teaspoon vanilla
- 1 cup chopped pecans

Direction

- In saucepan melt butter and add cocoa and milk.
- Melt altogether and bring to boil.
- Remove from heat.
- Add powdered sugar, vanilla and pecans.
- Stir well.
- Spread on cake while still warm.

Nutrition Information

- Calories: 156.4
- Fiber: 0.7
- Total Carbohydrate: 21.1
- Protein: 1.4
- Sodium: 37.6
- Sugar: 20
- Cholesterol: 12.7
- Total Fat: 8.1
- Saturated Fat: 3.2

294. Simple Cathedral Windows

Serving: 3 1 1/2 inch x 10 inch rolls/logs, 30-60 serving(s) | Prep: 20mins | Ready in:

Ingredients

- 1 1/2 cups chocolate chips, this can be milk, dark, bakers, etc. depending on your taste
- 1 1/2 cups peppermint candies, this can be crushed peppermint, spearmint, chopped candy, chopped nuts, coconut, dried fruit any com
- 1 1/2 cups miniature marshmallows, this can be white, colored, shaped, etc. depending on desired look
- wax paper
- tape, and string to tie it with
- 1 1/2 tablespoons margarine, can be butter instead if you like, use to coat inside of wax paper

Direction

- Spread out wax paper in medium sheets, apx 3 sheets 1 1/2 ft. long.
- Use small amount of butter or margarine to coat inside of wax paper, just towards middle - leave edges clean.
- Melt chocolate.
- Stir till smooth.
- Stir in additive of choice - nuts, candy, etc.
- Mixture should be cooled off just enough so marshmallows won't melt.
- Stir in marshmallows, enough to coat well with chocolate.
- Spoon out apx 1/3 mixture in a line onto wax paper in buttered area.
- Fold paper over compress mixture lengthwise.
- Roll firmly enough to keep mixture compressed without coming out of the ends of paper.
- Secure paper at middle of seam.
- Compress ends slightly secure them.
- Refrigerate 2hrs or more - this can last days wrapped up.

- Not sure if it last more than 1 1/2 weeks, somebody always eats it before then!
- But I suspect it last several weeks if needed.
- Slice in thin slices as needed.

Nutrition Information

- Calories: 53.2
- Cholesterol: 0
- Protein: 0.4
- Saturated Fat: 1.6
- Sodium: 9.6
- Total Carbohydrate: 7.3
- Sugar: 6
- Total Fat: 3.1
- Fiber: 0.5

295. Simple Chocolate Cupcakes

Serving: 20-30 cupcakes, 20-30 serving(s) | Prep: 25mins | Ready in:

Ingredients

- 1 1/3 cups flour
- 1/4 teaspoon baking soda
- 2 teaspoons baking powder
- 3/4 cup unsweetened cocoa powder
- 1 dash salt
- 3 tablespoons softened butter
- 1 1/2 cups sugar
- 2 eggs, beaten
- 1 teaspoon vanilla
- 3/4 cup milk

Direction

- Heat oven to 350°F.
- Put cupcake liner in muffin tin OR grease very well muffin tin.
- Sift flour, baking powder, baking soda, cocoa and salt.
- The in another bowl beat together the butter and sugar and then add the eggs beating very well then mix in the vanilla.
- Add the flour mixture alternately with the milk to the sugar and be sure to beat well each time!
- Spoon batter into the muffin cups 2/3 full.
- Bake for 15 to 17 minutes oven, or until a toothpick inserted into the cake comes out clean.
- It really depends on how full you fill the muffin tin to decide on the yield. If you want really domed cupcakes fill them almost full.

Nutrition Information

- Calories: 124.8
- Cholesterol: 24.5
- Total Fat: 3.1
- Saturated Fat: 1.7
- Sodium: 87.6
- Fiber: 1.3
- Sugar: 15.1
- Total Carbohydrate: 23.8
- Protein: 2.4

296. Simple Jello Salad

Serving: 6 serving(s) | Prep: 15mins | Ready in:

Ingredients

- 1 (12 ounce) carton whipped topping
- 1 (3 ounce) package Jello gelatin, any flavor
- 1 (8 ounce) carton cottage cheese
- 1 (8 ounce) can crushed pineapple, drained

Direction

- Empty whipped topping into a medium sized bowl.
- Sprinkle Jell-O over the top and fold in so it is well blended.

- Add cottage cheese and pineapple and fold into Jell-O mixture.
- Chill for about 4 hours so that the jello softens and slightly sets up.
- Serve.

Nutrition Information

- Calories: 270.7
- Protein: 7.7
- Fiber: 0.3
- Sugar: 23.5
- Cholesterol: 52.5
- Total Fat: 15.1
- Saturated Fat: 9
- Sodium: 292.5
- Total Carbohydrate: 27.6

297. Simply Fresh Fruit Salad

Serving: 8-10 serving(s) | Prep: 30mins | Ready in:

Ingredients

- 1 medium fresh pineapple, trimmed and cubed
- 1 cup fresh grapes, washed
- 3 fresh kiwi fruits, peeled and sliced
- 1 pint fresh strawberries, washed, hulled and sliced
- 1 fresh lemon (optional) or 1 lime (optional)
- honey, for drizzling (optional)
- fresh mint sprig, for garnish

Direction

- In a large bowl, toss together the fruit to combine well.
- Squeeze with fresh lemon or lime juice and drizzle with honey, if desired.
- Chill until serving time, and garnish with a fresh mint sprig.

Nutrition Information

- Calories: 99.7
- Fiber: 3.4
- Protein: 1.3
- Total Carbohydrate: 25.5
- Cholesterol: 0
- Total Fat: 0.4
- Saturated Fat: 0
- Sodium: 2.7
- Sugar: 18.6

298. Six Spice Oatmeal Raisin Cookies

Serving: 50 cookies | Prep: 15mins | Ready in:

Ingredients

- 1 cup butter or 1 cup margarine, softened
- 1 cup brown sugar
- 1 cup white sugar
- 1 egg
- 1 teaspoon vanilla
- 1 1/2 cups flour
- 1 teaspoon cinnamon
- 1 teaspoon nutmeg
- 1 teaspoon ground ginger
- 1 teaspoon cumin
- 1 pinch ground cloves
- 1 pinch cayenne
- 1/2 teaspoon baking soda
- 1/2 teaspoon salt
- 3 cups oats
- 1 cup raisins

Direction

- Cream together butter/margarine and sugar, then beat in egg and vanilla.
- Sift together flour, spices, baking soda and salt, and mix in.
- Add oats and raisins and mix well.
- Drop by spoonful onto cookie sheet.
- Bake for 8-10 minutes at 375°F.

Nutrition Information

- Calories: 125.8
- Sugar: 10
- Saturated Fat: 2.5
- Sodium: 65.8
- Cholesterol: 14
- Protein: 2.2
- Total Fat: 4.5
- Fiber: 1.2
- Total Carbohydrate: 19.8

299. Sky High Strawberry Pie

Serving: 8 serving(s) | Prep: 40mins | Ready in:

Ingredients

- 3 quarts strawberries, divided
- 1 1/2 cups sugar
- 6 tablespoons cornstarch
- 2/3 cup water
- 10 inches deep dish pie shells, baked and cooled

Direction

- Bake pastry shell according to direction on package and cool.
- In large bowl mash enough berries to make 3 cups
- In a sauce pan combine sugar and cornstarch use less sugar if berries are very ripe.
- Stir in mashed berries and water and mix well.
- Bring mixture to a boil over medium heat stirring constantly.
- Keep cooking and stirring for 2 minute.
- Remove from heat and pour into a large bowl.
- Chill 20 minutes in the refrigerator stirring occasionally until mixture is slightly warm.
- Cut remaining berries to desired size.
- Fold berries into mixture.

- Pour into pie shell. Careful it will be piled high above the edge.
- Chill for 2-3 hours before serving.

Nutrition Information

- Calories: 330.9
- Sugar: 48.8
- Total Carbohydrate: 69.2
- Cholesterol: 0
- Fiber: 4.8
- Saturated Fat: 1.9
- Sodium: 116.4
- Protein: 2.3
- Total Fat: 6.4

300. Slow Cooker (Crock Pot) Pumpkin Apple Dessert

Serving: 12 serving(s) | Prep: 15mins | Ready in:

Ingredients

- 1 (21 ounce) can apple pie filling
- 2 cups all-purpose flour
- 1 1/4 cups packed brown sugar
- 1 cup canned pumpkin (not pumpkin pie mix)
- 3/4 cup egg substitute
- 1/3 cup vegetable oil
- 2 teaspoons baking powder
- 1 teaspoon ground cinnamon
- 1/2 teaspoon ground nutmeg
- 1/4 teaspoon baking soda
- ice cream, if desired

Direction

- Spray 3 1/2- to 6-quart slow cooker with cooking spray; Spoon pie filling into cooker; spread evenly.
- Beat remaining ingredients except ice cream with electric mixer on low speed 1 minute, scraping bowl constantly; Beat on medium speed 2 minutes, scraping bowl occasionally.

- Pour batter over pie filling.
- Cover and cook on High heat setting 1 hour 30 minutes to 2 hours or until toothpick inserted in center comes out clean.
- Serve with ice cream.
- Note from Betty Crocker: This recipe was tested in slow cookers with heating elements in the side and bottom of the cooker, not in cookers that stand only on a heated base. For slow cookers with just a heated base, follow the manufacturer's directions for layering ingredients and choosing a temperature.

Nutrition Information

- Calories: 287.7
- Total Fat: 6.9
- Fiber: 1.8
- Total Carbohydrate: 53.4
- Protein: 4.3
- Saturated Fat: 1
- Sodium: 195.1
- Sugar: 29.8
- Cholesterol: 0.2

301. Slow Peaches

Serving: 4-6 serving(s) | Prep: 5mins | Ready in:

Ingredients

- 4 cups sliced peaches (I have always used fresh but maybe canned could be substituted. Don't know about the juice though!)
- 1/3 cup Bisquick
- 2/3 cup oatmeal (not instant--I use whole rolled oats)
- 1/4 teaspoon cinnamon
- 1/2 cup brown sugar
- 1/2 cup sugar

Direction

- Spray crockpot with non-stick spray.
- Mix dry ingredients together.
- Stir in peaches and pour into crockpot.
- Cook on low 4 to 6 hours.

Nutrition Information

- Calories: 361.9
- Total Fat: 2.8
- Sodium: 138.8
- Fiber: 4.2
- Sugar: 67.1
- Total Carbohydrate: 83.5
- Cholesterol: 0.2
- Protein: 4.5
- Saturated Fat: 0.6

302. Smucker's Strawberry Angel Cookies

Serving: 36 cookies, 36 serving(s) | Prep: 5mins | Ready in:

Ingredients

- 1 (18 ounce) package angel food cake mix
- 3/4 cup sugar-free strawberry jam
- 3 tablespoons semisweet mini chocolate chips

Direction

- HEAT oven to 325°F Coat baking sheet with no-stick cooking spray.
- 2 BEAT together cake mix and preserves (do not add water) at low speed of electric mixer 1 minute or until evenly moistened. Continue to beat an additional 1 minute. Stir in chocolate chips. Drop by rounded tablespoonfuls onto prepared baking sheet.
- 3 BAKE 10 to 12 minutes or until tops are just lightly browned. Cool 1 minute on baking sheet. Place on cooling rack to cool completely. Cookies will be soft and chewy.

Nutrition Information

- Calories: 57.3
- Saturated Fat: 0.2
- Sodium: 69.4
- Sugar: 6.8
- Total Carbohydrate: 12.7
- Protein: 1.3
- Total Fat: 0.3
- Fiber: 0.1
- Cholesterol: 0

303. Snickers Caramel Apple Salad

Serving: 12 serving(s) | Prep: 15mins | Ready in:

Ingredients

- 6 (2 1/4 ounce) Snickers candy bars, chill and chop
- 6 apples, cored and chopped into bite sized pieces (Granny Smith and or or Red Delicious)
- 1 (12 ounce) container Cool Whip
- 1 (5 ounce) box instant vanilla pudding (NO milk, use dry mix, DO NOT prepare!) or 1 (5 ounce) box butterscotch pudding mix (NO milk, use dry mix, DO NOT prepare!)
- Garnish for extra flair
- 1/2 cup caramel ice cream topping (optional) or 1/2 cup caramel apple dip (optional)
- 1/2 cup chopped peanuts, can also sprinkled on top (optional)

Direction

- Mix cool whip and dry pudding mix together.
- Chop apples and chilled Snickers.
- Mix together.
- Heat caramel sauce a bit in the microwave-- just enough to drizzle, not enough to heat up salad.
- Drizzle caramel sauce over salad and sprinkle peanuts on top.
- Chill for at least an hour-- Voila!

Nutrition Information

- Calories: 339.4
- Total Fat: 15.1
- Fiber: 2.9
- Protein: 3
- Saturated Fat: 9.2
- Sodium: 254.6
- Sugar: 43.1
- Total Carbohydrate: 49.8
- Cholesterol: 4.2

304. Soft 'N Chewy CHOCOLATE SANDWICH COOKIES

Serving: 48 sandwich cookies | Prep: 20mins | Ready in:

Ingredients

- 2 packages devil's food cake mix
- 4 eggs
- 2/3 cup vegetable oil
- Fillng
- 1 (8 ounce) package cream cheese, softened
- 1/2 cup butter, softened
- 1 teaspoon vanilla
- 3 1/2-4 cups confectioners' sugar
- food coloring, optional

Direction

- Preheat oven to 350 degrees.
- In a large mixing bowl, beat cakes mixes, eggs and oil.
- Roll into 1 inch balls and place on ungreased baking sheets, flatten slightly with back of spoon or fork.
- Bake for about 10 minutes or until almost set.
- Cool on wire racks.
- Filling: In a large mixing bowl, beat together cream cheese, butter and vanilla until fluffy.

- Add sugar gradually, until smooth and spreadable.
- Color with a few drops of food colouring, if desired, for any occasion.
- Spread half of the cookies with filling and top with remaining cookies.
- Store in airtight container in the refrigerator.

Nutrition Information

- Calories: 194.2
- Total Carbohydrate: 24.8
- Protein: 2.2
- Sugar: 17
- Cholesterol: 27.9
- Total Fat: 10.4
- Saturated Fat: 3.5
- Sodium: 213.7
- Fiber: 0.5

305. Sour Cream Fresh Blueberry Peach Cobbler

Serving: 6-8 serving(s) | Prep: 10mins | Ready in:

Ingredients

- FILLING
- 2 1/2 cups blueberries
- 2 1/2 cups peaches, sliced peeled
- 1 tablespoon cornstarch
- 1/3 cup sugar
- 1/4 teaspoon ground cinnamon
- TOPPING
- 1 cup flour
- 1 teaspoon baking powder
- 1/3 cup granulated sugar
- 1 large egg
- 1/3 cup low-fat sour cream
- 2 tablespoons soft margarine
- 1 tablespoon water

Direction

- Preheat oven to 350°F.
- Spray an 8-inch square cake pan with vegetable spray.
- FILLING: In a bowl, stir together the blueberries, peaches, and cornstarch.
- In another bowl, stir together the sugar and cinnamon.
- Set aside 1 tablespoons.
- Stir the remaining cinnamon sugar into the berry mixture.
- Pour the mixture into a prepared pan.
- TOPPING: In a bowl, stir together the flour and baking powder.
- In another bowl, mix the sugar, egg, sour cream, margarine, and water.
- With a wooden spoon, add the dry ingredients to the wet until everything is combined.
- Drop by spoonfuls on top of the fruit mixture.
- Sprinkle with the reserved cinnamon sugar.
- Place the pan in the centre of the oven and bake for 35 to 40 minutes or until a tester inserted in the centre comes out dry.
- Serve warm.

Nutrition Information

- Calories: 293.1
- Protein: 4.7
- Saturated Fat: 2
- Fiber: 3.1
- Total Carbohydrate: 55.7
- Total Fat: 6.8
- Sodium: 128.9
- Sugar: 34.3
- Cholesterol: 40.5

306. Southern Pride Sweet Cornbread

Serving: 12 serving(s) | Prep: 20mins | Ready in:

Ingredients

- 1 1/4 cups sugar
- 1/4 cup honey
- 2 eggs
- 1/2 cup butter (softened)
- 1 cup milk
- 1 cup water
- 2 cups white cornmeal (for less gritty) or 2 cups yellow cornmeal (I use white)
- 2 cups flour
- 1 tablespoon baking powder
- 1 teaspoon salt

Direction

- Grease a 9x13 inch baking pan with shortening.
- Preheat oven to 375°F.
- Mix sugar, butter, eggs, milk, honey and water together in a large bowl.
- Mix dry ingredients together in a separate bowl: cornmeal, flour, baking powder, and salt.
- While stirring, add dry ingredients to sugar, egg, and milk mixture and mix thoroughly.
- Mixture will be slightly lumpy.
- Pour into greased rectangular pan.
- Bake for 25-30 minutes or until golden brown on top.
- Serve with butter.

Nutrition Information

- Calories: 344.9
- Sugar: 26.8
- Total Carbohydrate: 59.5
- Protein: 5.6
- Saturated Fat: 5.7
- Sodium: 382.5
- Fiber: 2.1
- Cholesterol: 54.2
- Total Fat: 10.1

307. Spiced Sweet Potato Casserole

Serving: 10-12 serving(s) | Prep: 15mins | Ready in:

Ingredients

- 3 sweet potatoes (about 1 1/2 lbs total)
- 1/2 cup cream
- 1/2 cup light brown sugar, packed
- 1/2 cup white sugar
- 2 teaspoons cinnamon
- 1/8 teaspoon ground cloves
- 1/4 teaspoon powdered ginger
- 1/4 teaspoon ground nutmeg
- 1 -2 teaspoon vanilla extract
- 1 -2 tablespoon flour
- 1/2 cup butter, melted
- 2 eggs, beaten
- 1/2 cup flour
- 1 cup chopped pecans
- 1 cup light brown sugar, packed
- 1/2 teaspoon cinnamon
- 5 tablespoons butter, melted

Direction

- Cook your potatoes.
- You can bake them in the oven, you can bake them in the microwave, you could even boil them (which is how my mother always cooked them).
- Once the potatoes are cooked, scoop out the insides into a large bowl.
- Mash the potatoes.
- Add the cream and mix thoroughly until creamy.
- Add the brown sugar and white sugar and mix well.
- Add in the spices, 1-2 Tbsp flour and 1/2 cup butter and mix well.
- Add the eggs and mix well again.
- Spoon the mixture evenly into 9x9 baking dish.
- In a medium bowl combine the 1/2 cup flour, 1 cup pecans, 1 cup brown sugar, 1/2 tsp cinnamon and 5 Tbsp butter until crumbly.

- Spoon the topping mixture even over the top of the potatoes.
- Bake at 350 for 30 minutes until topping is bubbling and brown.
- Let cool for approx. 10 minutes before serving.

Nutrition Information

- Calories: 483.4
- Protein: 4.1
- Sodium: 181.1
- Fiber: 2.8
- Sugar: 44.2
- Total Carbohydrate: 58.2
- Total Fat: 27.6
- Saturated Fat: 12.8
- Cholesterol: 90.1

308. Spicy Baked Sweet Potato "fries"

Serving: 4 serving(s) | Prep: 15mins | Ready in:

Ingredients

- 2 medium sweet potatoes, washed and cut lengthwise into strips 1/3 inch on each side
- 1 1/2 tablespoons olive oil
- 1 teaspoon ground cumin
- 1/2 teaspoon chili powder
- 1/4 teaspoon salt
- 1/2 teaspoon onion powder

Direction

- Preheat oven to 450°F With aluminum foil or parchment paper, line a cookie sheet.
- In a medium bowl, combine sweet potatoes with olive oil and seasonings. Mix well to evenly coat potatoes. Place potato strips on the foil or parchment lined cookie sheet and leave space between strips for even baking.
- Bake for approximately 15 minutes or until potatoes become crispy. Turn strips every 5 to 7 minutes as needed. Serve immediately.

Nutrition Information

- Calories: 104.6
- Total Fat: 5.3
- Sodium: 187.8
- Sugar: 2.8
- Saturated Fat: 0.7
- Fiber: 2.2
- Total Carbohydrate: 13.7
- Cholesterol: 0
- Protein: 1.2

309. St. Paddy's Day Pound Cake

Serving: 1 cake, 4-6 serving(s) | Prep: 10mins | Ready in:

Ingredients

- 1 lb cake, loaf
- 1 (15 ounce) can crushed pineapple, drained
- 1 cup milk
- 1 (3 1/2 ounce) package pistachio pudding mix
- 1 (8 ounce) carton whipped topping
- 2 drops green food coloring

Direction

- Cut pound cake into three layers.
- Beat together pineapple and pudding mix and milk.
- Add whipped topping and food coloring.
- Layer pudding between pound cake.

Nutrition Information

- Calories: 257
- Saturated Fat: 9.7
- Sodium: 109

- Sugar: 20.2
- Cholesterol: 54.1
- Total Fat: 15.7
- Fiber: 0.8
- Total Carbohydrate: 27
- Protein: 4.4

310. Strawberry Angel Fluff

Serving: 12 serving(s) | Prep: 0S | Ready in:

Ingredients

- 1 angel food cake
- 1 packet strawberry gelatin
- 1 packet frozen whipped topping
- 1 packet frozen strawberries

Direction

- Tear the cake into walnut-size pieces and scatter over bottom of 10" X 13" sheet cake pan.
- Dissolve Jello in 2 cups of boiling water and then 2 cups cold water.
- Allow to jell a little.
- Fold in the frozen strawberries and whipped topping which has thawed a little.
- Pour over cake and refrigerate until set.
- Decorate with whipped cream or additional whipped topping and fresh strawberries.

Nutrition Information

- Calories: 154.6
- Sugar: 21.2
- Total Carbohydrate: 35.6
- Total Fat: 0.1
- Saturated Fat: 0
- Fiber: 0.1
- Cholesterol: 0
- Protein: 3.6
- Sodium: 285.8

311. Strawberry Cucumber Veloute

Serving: 4 serving(s) | Prep: 20mins | Ready in:

Ingredients

- 2 cups strawberries, washed and hulled
- 1/2 cucumber, peeled
- 2 tablespoons of fresh mint, chopped
- 1/8 teaspoon cayenne pepper
- 1 cup skim milk
- 1 cup plain yogurt
- 1/8 teaspoon ground pepper

Direction

- Puree the strawberries and cucumber in a blender or food processor.
- Add the mint, peppers and yogurt.
- Blend until smooth and uniform in colour.
- Chill for at least 2 hours before serving.

Nutrition Information

- Calories: 92.9
- Saturated Fat: 1.4
- Sugar: 6.8
- Protein: 5.4
- Sodium: 66.8
- Fiber: 1.9
- Total Carbohydrate: 13.5
- Cholesterol: 9.2
- Total Fat: 2.4

312. Strawberry Peach Gelatin Dessert

Serving: 3-4 serving(s) | Prep: 15mins | Ready in:

Ingredients

- 1 (2 3/4 ounce) packageRoyal or Jell-O strawberry gelatin
- 1 cup boiling water
- 1/2 cup cold water
- 1 (10 1/2 ounce) can peach pie filling or 1 (21 ounce) can peach pie filling (depending on how peachy you want it)
- whipped topping (optional)

Direction

- Put gelatin in a medium sized bowl.
- Add the boiling water and stir until gelatin is dissolved.
- Add the cold water and stir.
- Add the pie filling.
- Stir until well mixed.
- Keep the gelatin mixture in the bowl or pour it into a 6 1/2 inch square Pyrex or Corningware dish.
- Refrigerate until set.
- Serve in individual soup or salad bowls.
- Top with whipped topping. (If desired)

Nutrition Information

- Calories: 98.9
- Total Fat: 0
- Saturated Fat: 0
- Sodium: 123.4
- Fiber: 0
- Cholesterol: 0
- Sugar: 22.3
- Total Carbohydrate: 23.5
- Protein: 2

313. Strawberry Pretzel Potluck Salad

Serving: 1 salad, 5 serving(s) | Prep: 5mins | Ready in:

Ingredients

- 2 cups crushed pretzel rods
- 3/4 cup melted margarine
- 1/2 cup sugar
- 8 ounces cream cheese
- 8 ounces Cool Whip
- 1 cup sugar
- 6 ounces strawberry gelatin
- 1 lb strawberry

Direction

- Mix margarine pretzels and sugar press on pan and bake on 350 for 8 minutes.
- Beat cream cheese, sugar and strawberries and spread over crust.
- Make jello with water and let it partially jell, then add over cream cheese layer.

Nutrition Information

- Calories: 812.4
- Sugar: 105.5
- Cholesterol: 50
- Protein: 6.7
- Total Fat: 41
- Saturated Fat: 21.5
- Sodium: 477
- Fiber: 1.8
- Total Carbohydrate: 110.2

314. Strawberry Streusel Squares

Serving: 12 serving(s) | Prep: 15mins | Ready in:

Ingredients

- 1 (18 ounce) box2 layer yellow cake mix
- 3 tablespoons uncooked old fashioned oats
- 1 tablespoon margarine
- 1 1/2 cups sliced strawberries
- 3/4 cup water, plus
- 2 tablespoons water, divided
- 3/4 cup diced strawberry
- 3 egg whites

- 1/3 cup unsweetened applesauce
- 1/2 teaspoon cinnamon
- 1/8 teaspoon ground nutmeg

Direction

- Preheat oven to 350.
- Grease and flour 13x9 inch baking pan.
- Combine 1/2 cup cake mix and oats in a small bowl.
- Cut in margarine until mixture resembles coarse crumbs.
- Set aside.
- Place 1 1/2 cups sliced strawberries and 2 TBS water in blender or food processor.
- Process until smooth.
- Transfer to small bowl and stir in 3/4 cup diced strawberries.
- Set aside.
- Place remaining cake mix in large bowl.
- Add 3/4 cup water, egg whites, applesauce, cinnamon and nutmeg.
- Blend 30 seconds at low until moistened.
- Beat at medium for 2 minutes.
- Pour into prepared pan.
- Spoon strawberry mixture evenly over batter spreading lightly.
- Sprinkle evenly with oat mixture.
- Bake 31-34 minutes until toothpick comes clean.
- Cool completely on wire rack.

Nutrition Information

- Calories: 213.1
- Total Fat: 6.1
- Sodium: 305
- Sugar: 19.8
- Total Carbohydrate: 37
- Cholesterol: 0.8
- Saturated Fat: 0.9
- Fiber: 1.3
- Protein: 3.2

315. Strawberry Trifle No Cream Cheese

Serving: 8 serving(s) | Prep: 30mins | Ready in:

Ingredients

- 1 (3 1/2 ounce) package vanilla flavored instant pudding mix
- 1 cup sour cream
- 1 cup milk
- 1 teaspoon orange peel, grated
- 2 cups whipped cream
- 1 angel food cake or 1 white cake, torn into bite-size pieces
- 1 liter fresh strawberries, hulled and sliced

Direction

- In a large mixing bowl beat, instant pudding mix, orange peel, sour cream, and milk.
- Beat at low speed until thick.
- Using a spatula fold in whipped cream and mix (do not beat).
- In trifle bowl layer 1/2 of cake pieces.
- Next layer 1/3 strawberries.
- Next layer 1/2 pudding mixture.
- Repeat layers.
- Arrange strawberries on top.
- Cover and refrigerate at least 2 hours.

Nutrition Information

- Calories: 382.1
- Sodium: 608.4
- Sugar: 39
- Total Carbohydrate: 65.6
- Cholesterol: 28.3
- Protein: 7.4
- Total Fat: 11
- Saturated Fat: 6.6
- Fiber: 1.7

316. Sue B's Blueberry Buckle

Serving: 12 serving(s) | Prep: 15mins | Ready in:

Ingredients

- FOR CAKE
- 3/4 cup sugar
- 1/4 cup butter or 1/4 cup margarine
- 1 large egg
- 1 cup milk
- 2 cups flour
- 2 teaspoons baking powder
- 1/4 teaspoon salt
- 2 cups blueberries
- FOR TOPPING
- 2/3 cup sugar
- 2/3 cup flour
- 2 teaspoons cinnamon
- 1/4 cup butter, melted

Direction

- Preheat oven to 375°.
- Grease and flour an 8-inch square pan.
- Mix together first 7 ingredients.
- Gently stir in blueberries.
- Place in prepared pan.
- To make topping, mix last 4 ingredients together and sprinkle over cake mixture.
- Bake in preheated oven for 45-50 minutes.
- Serve warm or cooled.

Nutrition Information

- Calories: 294.8
- Total Fat: 9.2
- Saturated Fat: 5.5
- Sugar: 26.1
- Protein: 4.3
- Sodium: 193.5
- Fiber: 1.6
- Total Carbohydrate: 49.9
- Cholesterol: 38.7

317. Sugar Dusted Banana Cake

Serving: 8-10 serving(s) | Prep: 10mins | Ready in:

Ingredients

- 1 teaspoon baking powder
- 1 teaspoon baking soda
- 1/2 teaspoon salt
- 1 1/2 cups granulated sugar
- 1/2 cup butter flavor shortening (I like Crisco)
- 2 eggs
- 1 tablespoon vanilla
- 3/4 cup milk
- 4 bananas, smashed (the riper the bananas, the better)
- 2 cups all-purpose flour
- confectioners' sugar, for dusting

Direction

- Grease and flour a 9-inch by 11-inch baking pan.
- Preheat the oven to 375 degrees F.
- All mixing must be done by hand with a wooden spoon.
- In a small bowl, mix all the dry ingredients except flour and granulated sugar.
- In a large mixing bowl, cream the granulated sugar and shortening.
- Add the dry ingredients (not the flour), the eggs, vanilla, and milk to the sugar and shortening mixture.
- Mix thoroughly.
- Add the smashed bananas and mix.
- Add the flour, continuing to mix.
- Pour in the batter and bake at 375°F for 25 minutes or until a knife through the centre of the cake comes out dry.
- Cover with confectioners' sugar.
- Let cool and cover again with confectioners' sugar.

Nutrition Information

- Calories: 462.6

- Protein: 6.2
- Saturated Fat: 4.2
- Fiber: 2.4
- Sugar: 45.1
- Total Carbohydrate: 76.3
- Cholesterol: 56.1
- Total Fat: 15.4
- Sodium: 378.1

318. Sugarless Apple Cookies

Serving: 18 cookies | Prep: 20mins | Ready in:

Ingredients

- 3/4 cup chopped dates
- 1/2 cup finely chopped peeled apple
- 1/2 cup raisins
- 1/2 cup water
- 1 cup all-purpose flour, plus
- 1 tablespoon all-purpose flour
- 1 teaspoon ground cinnamon
- 1 teaspoon baking soda
- 2 eggs
- 1 teaspoon liquid artificial sweetener

Direction

- In a large saucepan, combine dates, apple, raisins and water.
- Bring to a boil; reduce heat and simmer for 3 minutes.
- Remove from heat and cool.
- Combine flour, cinnamon and baking soda.
- Stir into apple mixture and mix well.
- Combine eggs and sweetener; add to batter and mix well.
- Drop by tablespoonfuls onto a nonstick baking sheet.
- Bake at 350 degrees for 10 minutes.

Nutrition Information

- Calories: 66.2

- Total Fat: 0.7
- Cholesterol: 20.7
- Protein: 1.8
- Sugar: 6.7
- Total Carbohydrate: 14
- Saturated Fat: 0.2
- Sodium: 78.8
- Fiber: 1

319. Sunflower Centerpiece

Serving: 25 serving(s) | Prep: 20mins | Ready in:

Ingredients

- 1 (8 inch) one layer chocolate cake
- 1 (16 ounce) can chocolate frosting
- 1/2 cup chocolate chips
- 15 individual Little Debbie Boston cream rolls

Direction

- Make a chocolate layer cake from your favourite mix or recipe. Use 8" round pans.
- Place one layer of cooled chocolate cake in centre of 16" pizza pan or platter. You can freeze the other layer for a future use.
- Frost with 1 can of chocolate icing.
- Arrange chocolate chips on top only of cake to resemble sunflower seeds.
- Unwrap Boston Crème cakes and arrange around chocolate cake.
- Note: Preparation time does not include making and baking a layer cake.

Nutrition Information

- Calories: 256.9
- Sugar: 12.3
- Cholesterol: 26.4
- Total Fat: 11.1
- Saturated Fat: 4.1
- Sodium: 176.8
- Fiber: 1.1

- Total Carbohydrate: 37.9
- Protein: 2.8

320. Super Easy Peanut Butter Fudge

Serving: 48 1 inch squares, 20 serving(s) | Prep: 20mins | Ready in:

Ingredients

- 4 cups granulated sugar
- 1 cup milk
- 2 cups peanut butter
- 1 tablespoon butter
- 1 tablespoon vanilla extract

Direction

- Prepare a 9x11 glass dish by buttering the bottom.
- In heavy bottom sauce pan combine sugar and milk.
- Measure and set aside remaining ingredients.
- Cook over MEDIUM HEAT (temperature too high will cause it to reach temperature sooner and lead to overcooking) stirring occasionally till it comes to a boil then stir constantly.
- Let boil for 4 minutes EXACTLY, over cooking leads to crumbly fudge as it has moved past softball stage and into soft-crack (measure from the first sight of littlest bubbles or use a thermometer - softball stage) I use a stop watch. Remove from heat.
- Stir in remaining ingredients till all melted and smooth.
- Pour into prepared dish and refrigerate until firm.

Nutrition Information

- Calories: 321.3
- Total Carbohydrate: 45.7
- Total Fat: 14
- Sodium: 129.9
- Fiber: 1.6
- Sugar: 42.4
- Cholesterol: 3.2
- Protein: 6.9
- Saturated Fat: 3.4

321. Super Easy Peach Cobbler

Serving: 8 serving(s) | Prep: 15mins | Ready in:

Ingredients

- 0.5 (18 ounce) box white cake mix
- 1 lb canned peaches in heavy syrup
- 1/2 cup margarine, thinly sliced

Direction

- In a square baking dish, pour canned peaches (or whatever other canned fruit you choose) into the bottom, using only about 1/2 the syrup that's in the can.
- Cover the peaches with 1/2 a box of white cake mix.
- Thinly slice a stick of margarine (or butter) and arrange the slices so they (basically) cover the surface of the white cake mix.
- Bake at about 350F for about an hour, or until the peach juice seems to have been well-absorbed, and the butter has melted on top, creating a nice, lightly-browned, crumbly topping.
- Serve topped with vanilla ice cream, if desired.

Nutrition Information

- Calories: 229.7
- Total Fat: 9.2
- Cholesterol: 0
- Protein: 1.8
- Saturated Fat: 1.7
- Sodium: 283.4

- Fiber: 1
- Sugar: 28.1
- Total Carbohydrate: 36.5

322. Super Rich No Bake Chocolate Peanut Butter Pie

Serving: 8 serving(s) | Prep: 15mins | Ready in:

Ingredients

- 1 (14 ounce) caneagle brand sweetened condensed milk (NOT evaporated milk)
- 1 cup crunchy peanut butter
- 1 (1 ounce) packagejell-o sugar-free instant chocolate fudge pudding mix (4 serving size)
- 1 (8 ounce) container Cool Whip Topping, thawed
- 1 (9 inch) Oreo cookie pie crusts
- peanuts (to garnish)
- chocolate shavings (to garnish)

Direction

- Combine sweetened condensed milk, peanut butter and pudding mix until smooth.
- Fold in whipped topping.
- Pour into pie crust.
- Garnish with peanuts and chocolate shavings.
- Refrigerate for at least two hours. (Cook time is refrigeration time).
- Note: If you use pudding mix with sugar, the pie will turn out grainy-the sugar doesn't dissolve.
- TIP: Use the top of the pie crust container as a cover for your pie. Just remove the paper, give it a good wash and replace it UPSIDE-DOWN over the pie. Re-crimp the edges to hold the lid on. It's the perfect size and your lovely pie won't get squished!

Nutrition Information

- Calories: 588.8
- Saturated Fat: 13.8
- Sodium: 417.9
- Fiber: 3
- Total Carbohydrate: 49.9
- Cholesterol: 56.3
- Total Fat: 39.7
- Protein: 13.7
- Sugar: 35.9

323. Swedish Rice Dessert

Serving: 8 serving(s) | Prep: 10mins | Ready in:

Ingredients

- 2 cups mini marshmallows
- 2 cups cooked and chilled rice
- 1 (8 1/4 ounce) can crushed pineapple (well drained)
- 1/2 cup maraschino cherry, halves
- 1/2 cup slivered almonds (toasted)
- 1 cup heavy cream
- 1/4 cup sugar
- 1 teaspoon vanilla

Direction

- Combine all ingredients but the heavy cream, sugar and vanilla.
- Whip the cream.
- Gradually add the sugar and vanilla.
- Combine the rice mixture with the whipped cream mixture.
- Refrigerate to chill.
- Makes 8 servings.

Nutrition Information

- Calories: 400.1
- Sugar: 18.1
- Cholesterol: 40.8
- Total Fat: 14.8
- Sodium: 22.2
- Fiber: 1.7

- Saturated Fat: 7.2
- Total Carbohydrate: 61.9
- Protein: 5.6

324. Sweet Fry Bread Enough For An Army!

Serving: 48 taco breads, 48 serving(s) | Prep: 1hours | Ready in:

Ingredients

- Sponge
- 4 1/2 teaspoons yeast
- 1/4 cup sugar
- 1/2 teaspoon salt
- 1 cup warm water
- The Rest of the Story
- 1 1/2 teaspoons salt
- 1/2 cup sugar
- 1 cup butter, softened
- 2 cups warm water
- 8 1/2 cups flour (set aside 1 cup)

Direction

- Mix the sponge items in a large bowl; then let "sponge" for 15 minutes or so until foamy.
- Mix remaining dry ingredients in another bowl, and alternate adding dry stuff and water to the first mixture, allowing mixer to work ingredients before adding more.
- WARNING: You may need the extra cup of flour--the dough should NOT be sticky when finished.
- Knead the dough, working in the remaining flour as you knead.
- Grease a large glass or plastic bowl; shape dough into a large ball, place in bowl--turning to grease all sides; cover loosely with plastic and place in a warm place; let rise until doubled.
- Heat about a half-inch of oil in a large frying pan (375 - 400 degrees).
- While the oil heats, remove dough from bowl and divide into 4 balls. Each ball will make one dozen (12) balls (so a total of 48 balls).
- Flatten each small ball into a thin disk (about 4 inches), make a little hole in the center of each. Keep a uniform shape, but these don't have to look "perfect."
- Carefully drop into hot oil; fry until bottom is golden brown, flip with a spatula in one hand and a fork in the other to prevent oil from splashing out.
- SERVING IDEA #1: Lay bread on plate, cover with my Recipe #219826, grated cheese, topped with sour cream, lettuce, and olives for an "Indian Taco" (this is straight from the school lunch menu on an Indian Reservation!).
- SERVING IDEA #2: Sprinkle with powdered sugar, slather on some jam or marmalade.
- OAMC PLANNED OVERS: Use fresh for supper tonight, freeze ALL the leftovers in meal-size portions in plastic zipper bags.

Nutrition Information

- Calories: 127.7
- Sodium: 125.1
- Fiber: 0.7
- Total Fat: 4.1
- Saturated Fat: 2.5
- Sugar: 3.2
- Total Carbohydrate: 20.2
- Cholesterol: 10.2
- Protein: 2.5

325. Sweet Iced Cinnamon Tea

Serving: 3 quarts | Prep: 5mins | Ready in:

Ingredients

- 10 tea bags (regular or decaff)
- 1 cup red-hot candies
- 1/4 cup sugar (optional)

- 1/2 cup water (if adding sugar) (optional)
- water, for iced tea pot
- ice

Direction

- Put the cinnamon candies in the bottom of the container/well the tea bags go in Put tea bags on top of them.
- Fill the water well of the Iced Tea Pot with water.
- If you don't want to have ice in the pitcher while tea is brewing, you can fill water well a second time.
- Turn the Iced Tea Pot on.
- As tea is brewing, make sure candies are melting.
- You might have to help them along with a fork or spoon.
- If a sweeter tea is desired, put the sugar in the 1/2 cup water and mix well to dissolve sugar.
- Pour into pitcher of tea and stir.
- Pour tea over ice in tall glasses.
- Can also be poured into a cup and heated in a microwave oven for hot tea.

Nutrition Information

- Calories: 0
- Sodium: 0
- Total Carbohydrate: 0
- Cholesterol: 0
- Total Fat: 0
- Saturated Fat: 0
- Fiber: 0
- Sugar: 0
- Protein: 0

326. Sweet Pineapple Cranberry Sauce

Serving: 3 cups, 9-12 serving(s) | Prep: 15mins | Ready in:

Ingredients

- 1 (12 ounce) bag fresh cranberries
- 1 cup sugar
- 1 (20 ounce) can crushed pineapple, in juice
- 1 large orange
- pumpkin pie spice
- ground cinnamon

Direction

- Put the sugar into your saucepan.
- Zest the orange over the sugar.
- Cut the orange in half and squeeze the juice into a measuring cup. You want approximately 1/2 cup of orange juice. Discard the rinds/pulp.
- Place a mesh strainer over your measuring cup and dump in the crushed pineapple. Use the back of a spoon to press the pineapple until you have gotten 1/2 cup of pineapple juice (making 1 full cup including the orange juice).
- Set aside half of the strained pineapple, and discard or save the rest.
- Dump the cup of juice into the saucepan with the sugar and orange zest. Stir well.
- Rinse your cranberries in a pot of water. Discard any sinkers and overripe (mushy) berries.
- Put your rinsed berries into your saucepan with the sugar, juice, and orange zest.
- Bring everything to a boil over medium heat, stirring frequently. Continue to boil (and frequently stir) for about 20 minutes. This is much longer than it takes for all the berries to pop, but it thickens the sauce.
- Remove the sauce from heat and stir in the pineapple that you set aside.
- Season with a couple small shakes (1/8 teaspoon?) of pumpkin pie spice and some generous shakes (1/4 teaspoon?) of ground cinnamon.
- Refrigerate overnight. The warm sauce might taste bitter, but the cold sauce shouldn't.

Nutrition Information

- Calories: 153
- Saturated Fat: 0
- Sodium: 1.7
- Protein: 0.6
- Total Fat: 0.1
- Fiber: 3
- Sugar: 34.9
- Total Carbohydrate: 39.7
- Cholesterol: 0

327. Sweet Potato Boats

Serving: 6 serving(s) | Prep: 15mins | Ready in:

Ingredients

- 3 sweet potatoes
- 1 cup cranberries
- 1/4 cup raisins
- 1/2 cup walnuts
- 2 tablespoons honey
- 1 teaspoon cinnamon

Direction

- Bake the sweet potatoes in their skins.
- Allow them to cool.
- When the potatoes are cool, slice them in half lengthwise and gently scoop out the flesh, leaving behind enough to hold the shell together.
- In a food processor, grind the cranberries.
- Then add the raisins, walnuts, honey, cinnamon and the reserved sweet potato and process until well mixed.
- Mound the filling back into the sweet potato shells and bake in a 350°F oven for 20 minutes.
- If the potatoes are large, slice each boat in half before serving.

Nutrition Information

- Calories: 167.3
- Total Fat: 6.5

- Sodium: 37.3
- Cholesterol: 0
- Saturated Fat: 0.6
- Fiber: 3.8
- Sugar: 12.9
- Total Carbohydrate: 27.2
- Protein: 2.8

328. Sweet Potato With Brandy And Raisins

Serving: 4-6 serving(s) | Prep: 20mins | Ready in:

Ingredients

- 1/2 cup seedless raisin
- 1/4 cup brandy
- 4 medium sweet potatoes, boiled until just tender then peeled and sliced into 1/4 inch slices
- 2/3 cup packed brown sugar
- 1/4 cup margarine
- 2 tablespoons water
- 1/4 teaspoon ground cinnamon

Direction

- Mix raisins and brandy in small bowl, let stand 20 minutes.
- Drain raisins.
- Layer sweet potatoes in 9 x9 x2 inch baking pan, top with raisins.
- Mix brown sugar, margarine, water and cinnamon in small saucepan, heat to boil.
- Pour over sweet potatoes.
- Bake in preheated oven at 350 degrees for 40 minutes, basting with pan juices occasionally.

Nutrition Information

- Calories: 447.1
- Total Fat: 11.5
- Sodium: 221.1
- Fiber: 4.7

- Total Carbohydrate: 76.5
- Saturated Fat: 2
- Sugar: 51.5
- Cholesterol: 0
- Protein: 2.7

329. Sweet Potatoes (Yams) With Apricots

Serving: 6-8 serving(s) | Prep: 5mins | Ready in:

Ingredients

- 1 (16 ounce) can yams, drained
- 1 (16 ounce) can apricots, pitted, drain reserving 1/2 cup juice
- 1/4 cup pecan halves
- 1 1/4 cups brown sugar
- 1 1/2 tablespoons cornstarch
- 1/4 teaspoon salt
- 1/8 cup butter
- 1/8 teaspoon cinnamon
- 1 teaspoon orange peel, grated

Direction

- Layer sweet potatoes and apricots in casserole dish.
- Sprinkle with pecan halves.
- In a saucepan, combine remaining ingredients, including the apricot juice, bring to a boil, and continue to cook for 2 minutes, stirring constantly.
- Pour sauce over casserole and bake at 375 degrees F. for 25 minutes.

Nutrition Information

- Calories: 369.1
- Total Fat: 7.2
- Saturated Fat: 2.7
- Total Carbohydrate: 76.7
- Protein: 2.6
- Cholesterol: 10.2

- Sodium: 149.8
- Fiber: 5.1
- Sugar: 51.7

330. Sweet Potatoes With Rum

Serving: 8 serving(s) | Prep: 20mins | Ready in:

Ingredients

- 6 medium sweet potatoes
- 4 tablespoons margarine or 4 tablespoons butter, cut into small pieces
- 1/3 cup packed brown sugar
- 1/4 cup dark rum (substitute freshly-squeezed orange juice if you wish; it will taste different though)
- 1/2 cup golden raisin

Direction

- Boil the whole, unpeeled, sweet potatoes until tender but not too soft-- it will take anywhere from 20 to 40 minutes depending on the thickness of your potatoes.
- Drain and, when cool enough to handle, peel and slice into 1/4-inch slices.
- Preheat oven to 350F degrees.
- Arrange the slices in an attractive overlapping pattern in a buttered shallow baking dish.
- Dot with butter pieces, then sprinkle with brown sugar and raisins, if using.
- Drizzle the rum over all.
- Bake in preheated oven, uncovered, until bubbly and glazed, about 30 minutes.

Nutrition Information

- Calories: 212.5
- Total Fat: 5.8
- Sodium: 124.8
- Fiber: 3.3
- Sugar: 18.2
- Total Carbohydrate: 35.8

- Saturated Fat: 1
- Cholesterol: 0
- Protein: 1.9

331. Sweet Tea Chicken

Serving: 8 serving(s) | Prep: 1hours | Ready in:

Ingredients

- 8 chicken leg quarters, cut into thighs and drumsticks
- 1 quart brewed tea, double strength
- 1 lemon, quartered
- 1 cup sugar
- 1/2 cup kosher salt
- 1 quart ice water
- 2 cups all-purpose flour
- 2 cups cornflour (or fish fry)
- 2 tablespoons Old Bay Seasoning
- 1 tablespoon chili powder
- salt and pepper
- 1 cup all-purpose flour
- 1 cup buttermilk
- 8 eggs
- peanut oil

Direction

- Combine tea, lemon, sugar and salt and simmer for 5 minutes or until salt and sugar are completely dissolved.
- Pour in ice water and cool brine completely. Submerge thighs and drumsticks in brine for 48 hours. Remove to a wire rack and allow chicken to drain.
- Combine the 2 cups flour, corn flour, Old Bay, chili powder, salt, and pepper in a large bowl. In a medium bowl have the 1 cup flour, and in a third bowl beat the 8 eggs with the buttermilk.
- Line up containers of flour, egg-buttermilk mixture, and flour-corn flour mix in that order. Bread the chicken in the flour, then the egg, and then the flour-corn flour mix, applying pressure to ensure even adherence. Let the chicken sit in the refrigerator for 1/2 hour before frying.
- Pour oil into a heavy pot to a depth of at least 3 inches. Heat oil to 300°F
- Fry chicken, submerged in oil, for 15 minutes or until an instant-read thermometer registers 170°F for dark meat, 160°F for white meat. Drain on a rack.
- Cool to room temperature, and then place in refrigerator for at least 4 hours and no more than 24. Serve cool from a picnic basket or cold, straight from the fridge.

Nutrition Information

- Calories: 775.1
- Cholesterol: 325.8
- Total Fat: 27
- Fiber: 4
- Sugar: 27.2
- Total Carbohydrate: 86.6
- Protein: 44.7
- Saturated Fat: 7.7
- Sodium: 7334.8

332. Tate's Bake Shop Chocolate Chip Cookies

Serving: 8-10 serving(s) | Prep: 15mins | Ready in:

Ingredients

- 2 cups all-purpose flour
- 1 teaspoon baking soda
- 1 teaspoon salt
- 1 cup salted butter, 2 sticks
- 3/4 cup sugar
- 3/4 cup dark brown sugar, firmly packed
- 1 teaspoon water
- 1 teaspoon vanilla
- 2 large eggs
- 2 cups semi-sweet chocolate chips

Direction

- Preheat oven to 350°F.
- Grease or line 2-3 cookie sheets with parchment paper.
- In a large bowl, stir together flour, baking soda and salt.
- In another large bowl, cream the butter and sugars, then add the water and vanilla. Mix until just combined.
- Add eggs to the butter mixture and mix them lightly.
- Stir in the flour mixture. When flour is mixed in, fold in the chocolate chips.
- Drop 2 tablespoonfuls of the cookie dough 2-inches apart onto prepared cookie sheets. Make sure the cookie sheets are well greased. I like to use parchment paper.
- Bake for 12-17 minutes or until the edges and centers of the cookies are golden brown.
- Remove from oven and allow to cool on wire racks.

Nutrition Information

- Calories: 689.1
- Sugar: 61.8
- Total Carbohydrate: 89.8
- Saturated Fat: 22.5
- Sodium: 679.6
- Fiber: 3.3
- Cholesterol: 107.5
- Protein: 6.8
- Total Fat: 37.1

333. That Yummy Pink Salad

Serving: 8 serving(s) | Prep: 5mins | Ready in:

Ingredients

- 1 (8 ounce) container Cool Whip
- 3 ounces strawberry Jell-O gelatin dessert
- 8 ounces cottage cheese
- 8 ounces strawberry yogurt

Direction

- Mix cool whip and dry jello well.
- Stir in cottage cheese and yogurt.
- Chill well.

Nutrition Information

- Calories: 191.8
- Total Fat: 8.9
- Saturated Fat: 7.3
- Sugar: 15.8
- Total Carbohydrate: 22.2
- Protein: 6.4
- Sodium: 198.6
- Fiber: 0
- Cholesterol: 6.3

334. The Bestest Butter Cookies (Rolled)

Serving: 2 dozen cookies | Prep: 15mins | Ready in:

Ingredients

- 2/3 cup butter, softened
- 1/2 cup sugar
- 1 egg, beaten well
- 1/2 teaspoon vanilla
- 1 3/4 cups all-purpose flour
- 1/2 teaspoon baking powder
- decorator icing, in various colors or confectioner's sugar icing, colored with food coloring (optional)

Direction

- Cream butter and sugar well.
- Add egg and vanilla and beat well.
- Combine baking powder and flour.
- Add gradually to creamed mixture.
- Chill until firm.

- Preheat oven to 400 degrees.
- Roll out dough to about 1/4" thickness and cut into desired shapes.
- Bake for 6 to 8 minutes.
- When cool, decorate with frosting or icing if desired.

Nutrition Information

- Calories: 1176.2
- Total Fat: 65.1
- Fiber: 3
- Total Carbohydrate: 134.1
- Protein: 15.1
- Saturated Fat: 40
- Sodium: 672
- Sugar: 50.5
- Cholesterol: 256.5

335. The Only Chocolate Cake Recipe You'll Ever Need! (Devil's Food)

Serving: 16 serving(s) | Prep: 30mins | Ready in:

Ingredients

- Cake
- 2 cups all-purpose flour
- 1 teaspoon salt
- 1 teaspoon baking powder
- 2 teaspoons baking soda
- 3/4 cup unsweetened cocoa powder
- 2 cups sugar
- 1 cup vegetable oil
- 1 cup hot coffee
- 1 cup milk
- 2 large eggs
- 1 teaspoon vanilla
- Frosting
- 1 cup milk
- 5 tablespoons all-purpose flour
- 1/2 cup butter, softened
- 1/2 cup shortening
- 1 cup sugar
- 1 teaspoon vanilla

Direction

- Preheat oven to 325°F.
- In a large mixing bowl, sift together dry ingredients. Add oil, coffee and milk and mix at medium speed for 2 minutes. Add eggs and vanilla and beat 2 more minutes. Expect batter to be thin.
- Pour into a 9" x 13" greased and floured pan or 2- 9" round pans. Bake 9 x 13 pan for about 45 minutes or 9" pans for about 30 minutes. Cool in pans for about 15 minutes and then cool completely on racks.
- While cake is cooling make the icing: Combine the milk and flour in a saucepan and cook over low heat until thick, whisking constantly. Cover and refrigerate until chilled.
- In a medium bowl, beat butter, shortening, sugar and vanilla until creamy. Add chilled milk and flour mixture and beat for 10 minutes. Frost cooled cake and enjoy! The frosting sounds intimidating, but it is worth it! By the way, for some reason, we prefer this cake chilled, right out of the refrigerator. The rich chocolate and cool frosting just seem to taste best this way.

Nutrition Information

- Calories: 477.9
- Total Carbohydrate: 55.1
- Protein: 4.5
- Total Fat: 28.2
- Saturated Fat: 8.2
- Sodium: 401.8
- Sugar: 37.6
- Fiber: 1.8
- Cholesterol: 42.8

336. The Ultimate Strawberry Shortcake

Serving: 12 serving(s) | Prep: 20mins | Ready in:

Ingredients

- 1 quart fresh strawberries (or more if you like)
- 1/2 cup sugar
- 8 ounces cream cheese, softened
- 1 cup powdered sugar
- 1 (8 ounce) container frozen whipped topping
- 1 (14 ounce) angel food cake, cut into cubes (I buy the cake already made)

Direction

- Wash, stem, and cut strawberries in half.
- Add sugar; toss to mix well.
- Chill.
- Beat cream cheese and powdered sugar well.
- Fold in whipped topping and cake cubes.
- Spread cake into an ungreased 13x9 dish.
- Cover and chill for at least 2 hours.
- Cut cake into squares; top with strawberries.

Nutrition Information

- Calories: 296.8
- Saturated Fat: 7.8
- Sodium: 235.3
- Total Carbohydrate: 46.6
- Protein: 3.7
- Cholesterol: 20.8
- Total Fat: 11.6
- Fiber: 1
- Sugar: 35.5

337. Theepless (Almost Funnel Cake)

Serving: 12 serving(s) | Prep: 5mins | Ready in:

Ingredients

- 4 cups self-rising flour
- 4 tablespoons sugar
- 1 cup sugar
- 4 eggs
- 1 lemon, rind of
- 2 tablespoons oil
- oil (for cooking)
- 2 cups honey
- cinnamon
- coarsely chopped walnuts

Direction

- Place the flour in a big, deep bowl.
- Mound the flour and make an opening in the middle.
- Meanwhile, beat eggs with the sugar, lemon rind and oil.
- Place the egg mixture in the opening and knead the dough until firm.
- Divide the dough equally many times and roll each division into thin pieces.
- Cut the pieces in triangle sections.
- Heat the oil well, and stick the dough strips in the hot oil one by one.
- Quickly, using two large forks roll each strip of dough in a cylindrical shape and cook the pieces until golden brown.
- Take them out, and place somewhere to cool.
- Heat the honey with one cup of sugar until boiling.
- Spoon out the froth that forms, and lather the ready the less with the honey syrup, and sprinkle cinnamon and walnuts as a garnish.

Nutrition Information

- Calories: 444.6
- Saturated Fat: 0.9
- Sodium: 554.8
- Fiber: 1.2
- Sugar: 67.5
- Total Carbohydrate: 98.5
- Total Fat: 4.3
- Cholesterol: 70.5
- Protein: 6.4

338. Tikvenik Bulgarian Sweet Pumpkin Pie

Serving: 8-12 serving(s) | Prep: 30mins | Ready in:

Ingredients

- 1 1/2 lbs pumpkin (peeled and seeded) or 1 1/2 lbs any suitable squash (peeled and seeded)
- 1 cup sugar
- 2 ounces walnuts (chopped)
- 1 teaspoon ground cinnamon
- 1/2 lb butter, melted (optional)
- 1 (1 lb) package phyllo pastry
- 2 -3 tablespoons caster sugar (for sprinkling)

Direction

- Cut the pumpkin or squash into large pieces and boil. You could do that in a sauce pan with water to cover, or even better steam boil it.
- When soft enough drain, place in a bowl, and puree with a fork.
- VARIANT: Some people, instead of boiling the pumpkin, prefer to grate it and sauté it with some butter or vegetable oil. Others prefer to grate it and put it in raw. Downsides are that in the first case it ends up quite greasy, and in the second quite crunchy.
- Add the sugar, walnuts, and cinnamon; mix in with the pumpkin.
- If you decide to use the butter, melt it.
- Take two sheets of phyllo pastry and drizzle some melted butter on the top one. You could also use a single sheet, butter both sheets, or do as I do and skip the butter altogether.
- Spoon some of the pumpkin mixture over the pastry and roll loosely. Repeat with the rest of the pastry.
- Take a non-stick baking sheet or tin (or else oil it). If it is rectangular place the rolls parallel to each other. If it is round, start lining the rim with the rolls, slowly spiraling them towards the center (you can see what I mean in one of the photos I've submitted).
- VARIANT: You could decide to do one whole pie instead of individual rolls. For that choose a baking tin slightly smaller than the size of the phyllo sheets (it could be round). Layer the sheets one by one slightly folding them to fit into the tin and to allow air between them. If you are using butter, drizzle some over each sheet you lay. When you have laid two sheets, spoon some pumpkin mixture on top.
- Continue layering the pastry and the pumpkin mix and finish off with a single sheet of dough.
- Place the baking tin in the oven.
- Bake at medium heat for about 20 to 30 minutes. After 10 minutes baking you could take the pie out and spread some butter on it, but I do not do that.
- Let the pie cool down and serve sprinkled with some caster sugar.

Nutrition Information

- Calories: 348.1
- Sodium: 275.6
- Protein: 6
- Saturated Fat: 1.3
- Fiber: 2.1
- Sugar: 29.6
- Total Carbohydrate: 64.8
- Cholesterol: 0
- Total Fat: 8.1

339. Toffee Almond Bars

Serving: 15 bars | Prep: 10mins | Ready in:

Ingredients

- 1 cup butter (no substitutions)
- 1/2 cup sugar
- 2 cups flour

- 1 3/4 cups crushed chocolate-covered toffee bits (Heath or Skor)
- 3/4 cup light corn syrup
- 1 cup sliced almonds
- 3/4 cup sweetened flaked coconut

Direction

- Preheat oven to 350 degrees F.
- Grease a 13x9x2-inch baking pan and set aside.
- In a large bowl, cream butter and sugar until light and fluffy.
- Add flour in small amounts, and mix until blended.
- Press the dough evenly into the baking pan.
- Bake in the preheated oven for 15-20 minutes or until edges lightly brown.
- In a saucepan, stir toffee bits and corn syrup over med-low heat, stirring constantly until toffee melts.
- Stir in half of the almonds and 1/2 cup of the coconut.
- Spread this mixture over the crust, leaving a 1/4-inch margin all around.
- Sprinkle the rest of the almonds and coconut over the top.
- Bake in oven another 15 minutes or until top becomes bubbly.
- Set the pan on a wire rack to cool completely (allow to cool before cutting).

Nutrition Information

- Calories: 302
- Sodium: 110.3
- Protein: 3.3
- Total Fat: 17.2
- Saturated Fat: 9.5
- Fiber: 1.4
- Sugar: 13.6
- Total Carbohydrate: 35.9
- Cholesterol: 32.5

340. Toffee Cornflake Cookies

Serving: 15 cookies | Prep: 0S | Ready in:

Ingredients

- 3 macintosh toffee bars
- 3 tablespoons margarine or 3 tablespoons butter
- 3 tablespoons condensed milk
- 3 cups corn flakes

Direction

- In large pot melt first three ingredients on low heat.
- When many bubbles appear, pour in cornflakes.
- Immediately drop spoonfuls onto cookie sheet coated with waxed paper.
- Eat!

Nutrition Information

- Calories: 52.5
- Sugar: 2.6
- Total Carbohydrate: 6.9
- Total Fat: 2.6
- Sodium: 71.8
- Fiber: 0.1
- Protein: 0.7
- Saturated Fat: 0.6
- Cholesterol: 1.3

341. Torrones A Christmas Time Nougat Candy

Serving: 12-16 serving(s) | Prep: 15mins | Ready in:

Ingredients

- 2 2/3 cups superfine sugar
- 2/3 cup light corn syrup
- 1/2 cup water

- 2 egg whites, at room temperature
- 2 teaspoons vanilla extract
- 1 teaspoon almond extract
- 1 teaspoon orange extract (optional)
- 1/2 cup candied fruit (optional)
- candied fruit, garnish (optional)
- 1 cup sliced almonds

Direction

- Combine sugar, corn syrup and water in saucepan.
- Cook over medium heat until candy thermometer registers at 260°F.
- In an electric mixer, beat egg whites to form stiff peaks.
- When sugar reaches 260°F pour slowly in a thin stream into egg whites, while mixer is running.
- Add extracts and beat on medium speed for 13 minutes; then fold in candied fruit, if using, and mix for another 2 minutes.
- Now fold in 1/2 cup sliced almonds.
- Pour mixture in buttered and lightly dusted floured 9" pan.
- Top with remaining almonds.
- Let sit overnight and then cut into pieces.
- Serve on a "festive" decorated plate.

Nutrition Information

- Calories: 275.6
- Saturated Fat: 0.3
- Fiber: 0.9
- Sugar: 49.9
- Total Carbohydrate: 60.8
- Cholesterol: 0
- Protein: 2.2
- Sodium: 21.8
- Total Fat: 3.8

342. Tres Leches (Three Milk Cake)

Serving: 12 serving(s) | Prep: 15mins | Ready in:

Ingredients

- 8 large eggs
- 1 1/2 cups sugar
- 2 cups all-purpose flour
- 1 tablespoon baking powder
- 1 (14 ounce) can sweetened condensed milk
- 1 (12 ounce) can evaporated milk
- 1 cup milk
- 1/4 cup Kahlua (or strong coffee)
- 1 teaspoon vanilla
- lightly sweetened softly whipped cream
- sliced strawberry

Direction

- In a large bowl, with a mixer on high speed (use whip attachment if available), beat eggs and sugar until thick and pale yellow, 5 to 6 minutes.
- In a small bowl, mix flour and baking powder.
- With mixer on medium speed, gradually add flour mixture in small increments and beat until smooth.
- Scrape batter into a buttered 9 by 13 inch baking pan.
- Bake in a 325 degree oven until a toothpick inserted in the center comes out clean, 30 to 40 minutes.
- Meanwhile, in a blender, whirl condensed milk, evaporated milk, regular milk, Kahlua, and vanilla until well blended.
- Pour evenly over hot cake; let cool about 15 minutes, then cover and chill until cake has absorbed all the milk mixture, at least 3 hours, or up to 1 day.
- Cut cake into squares or rectangles, lift out with a wide spatula, and set on plates.
- Top each piece of cake with a spoonful of whipped cream and garnish with strawberries.

Nutrition Information

- Calories: 397.9
- Total Carbohydrate: 66
- Saturated Fat: 4.7
- Sodium: 221.3
- Fiber: 0.6
- Sugar: 45.9
- Total Fat: 9.2
- Cholesterol: 146.3
- Protein: 11.6

343. Triple Dark Chocolate Mousse Pie

Serving: 8 serving(s) | Prep: 30mins | Ready in:

Ingredients

- Crust
- 8 sheets cinnamon graham crackers, finely crushed
- 1/4 cup unsweetened cocoa powder
- 1/4 cup butter, melted
- Mousse
- 1 (19 ounce) package reduced-fat soft tofu, well drained
- 1 (8 ounce) package bittersweet chocolate, melted
- 1/4 cup chocolate syrup
- 3 tablespoons powdered sugar
- 2 teaspoons vanilla
- 4 egg whites or 4 liquid egg substitute, to equal 4 whites
- Garnish
- whipped topping (optional)
- chocolate curls (optional)
- raspberries (optional)

Direction

- Crust; in a 9-inch pie plate, combine the graham cracker crumbs, cocoa, and butter until well blended.
- Press the mixture into the bottom and up the side of pie plate, set aside.
- Mousse; in a food processor or blender process the tofu until smooth.
- Add the melted chocolate, chocolate syrup, sugar and vanilla.
- Combine until mixture is smooth.
- With a mixer at high speed, beat egg whites until stiff peaks form.
- Fold the chocolate mixture into the egg white mixture until smooth.
- Spoon mixture into the prepared pie crust.
- Refrigerate for at least 3 hours, or until the pie is set.
- Garnish with whipped topping and chocolate curls or raspberries.
- Enjoy.

Nutrition Information

- Calories: 172.8
- Cholesterol: 15.4
- Protein: 3.8
- Sodium: 186.5
- Fiber: 1.6
- Sugar: 10.8
- Total Carbohydrate: 21.4
- Total Fat: 8.4
- Saturated Fat: 4.5

344. Tropical Breakfast Ambrosia

Serving: 8 serving(s) | Prep: 25mins | Ready in:

Ingredients

- 4 1/2 cups fresh pineapple, "medium, peeled, cored, and cut into bite size pieces
- 11 ounces mandarin oranges, canned and drained
- 1 medium mango, peeled, seeded, and cut into 1/2 inch pieces

- 1 cup frozen dark sweet cherries, thawed, pitted, unsweetened
- 2 tablespoons Amaretto (optional)
- 2 medium bananas, cut into 1/2 inch slices
- 1 cup flaked coconut
- 1/2 cup macadamia nuts or 1/2 cup sliced almonds, chopped

Direction

- In a large bowl combine pineapple, oranges, mango, cherries, and amaretto.
- Transfer mixture to an ungreased 3-quart casserole.
- Bake in a 350 degree oven, uncovered for 15 minutes.
- Stir in bananas, sprinkle with coconut and macadamia nuts or sliced almonds. Bake for approximately 15 minutes or until fruit is heated through and coconut/nuts are golden brown.
- Serve warm, spooning liquid in bottom of casserole over fruit.

Nutrition Information

- Calories: 238.4
- Sugar: 30.6
- Total Carbohydrate: 40.1
- Cholesterol: 0
- Protein: 2.6
- Total Fat: 9.8
- Saturated Fat: 3.7
- Sodium: 26.9
- Fiber: 5

345. Tropical Paradise

Serving: 2 serving(s) | Prep: 10mins | Ready in:

Ingredients

- 1 cup peeled and diced ripe mango
- 1/2 cup orange juice
- 2 tablespoons lime juice
- 4 scoops vanilla ice cream

Direction

- In a blender container, place all ingredients, cover.
- Blend until combined.

Nutrition Information

- Calories: 230.1
- Protein: 3.4
- Sugar: 33
- Total Carbohydrate: 38.8
- Saturated Fat: 5
- Sodium: 60.2
- Fiber: 2.2
- Cholesterol: 31.7
- Total Fat: 8.3

346. Ultimate Mars Bar Slice

Serving: 1 Slice, 12 serving(s) | Prep: 5mins | Ready in:

Ingredients

- 8 ounces Mars bars (chopped) or 8 ounces Milky Way bars (chopped)
- 1/2 cup unsalted butter
- 3 cups rice bubbles or 3 cups Rice Krispies
- 8 ounces milk chocolate chips
- 1/8 cup unsalted butter (extra)

Direction

- Grease a 9 x 9 pan with butter.
- On low heat in a medium saucepan, combine Mars Bars (or Milky Ways) and 1/2 cup Butter.
- Stir constantly until the mixture is smooth and melted.
- Remove from heat and fold in Rice Bubbles / Rice Krispies
- Press into the 9 x 9 pan.

- In a small saucepan, melt together the Chocolate Morsels and 1/8 cup Butter
- Once melted, spread over the top of the Rice Bubbles / Rice Krispies mixture in pan.
- Refrigerate until chocolate is set.
- Slice, serve and enjoy!

Nutrition Information

- Calories: 300.4
- Cholesterol: 33
- Protein: 3.5
- Total Fat: 19.6
- Sodium: 85.6
- Total Carbohydrate: 28.8
- Saturated Fat: 11
- Fiber: 1.1
- Sugar: 20.3

347. Unemployment Cake (Poudding Chomeur)

Serving: 6-8 serving(s) | Prep: 10mins | Ready in:

Ingredients

- Sauce
- 2 cups water
- 1 cup brown sugar
- 3 -4 tablespoons flour (see note)
- 1 1/2 teaspoons vanilla or 1 1/2 teaspoons maple flavoring
- 3 tablespoons butter
- Cake
- 3/4 cup sugar
- 3 tablespoons butter
- 3/4 cup milk
- 1 pinch salt
- 1 1/2 cups flour
- 2 teaspoons baking powder

Direction

- For sauce melt butter and stir in water, brown sugar and flavoring. Stir in flour and pour into deep baking dish. For the cake cream together butter and sugar. Mix dry ingredients together and add to butter and sugar. Mix in milk. Drop dough into sauce.
- Cook at 350 degrees for 30-40 minutes. Check to see if it is cooked by inserting a toothpick into cake. If it comes out clean, your cake is cooked.
- Serve warm with vanilla ice cream.
- **4 tbsp. of flour will give you more of a custard, where 2-3 tbsp. will be more of a sauce. It depends on your preference and how you like it*.

Nutrition Information

- Calories: 489.2
- Total Fat: 13
- Sugar: 60.8
- Protein: 4.8
- Fiber: 0.9
- Total Carbohydrate: 89.7
- Cholesterol: 34.8
- Saturated Fat: 8
- Sodium: 276.9

348. Vanilla Cinnamon Fruit Salad

Serving: 8-10 serving(s) | Prep: 20mins | Ready in:

Ingredients

- 1 cup green seedless grape
- 1 cup red seedless grapes
- 1 cup purple seedless grapes
- 1 large apple, chopped with skin on
- 1 cup strawberry, sliced
- 3 kiwi, peeled and sliced
- 1 (11 ounce) can pineapple chunks in juice, drained, reserve 3 t juice
- 1 (11 ounce) can mandarin oranges, drained

- 1 (3 1/4 ounce) package fat free sugar-free instant vanilla pudding mix or 1 (3 1/4 ounce) package vegetarian fat free sugar-free instant vanilla pudding mix
- 1 tablespoon cinnamon

Direction

- Combine all fruit in large bowl.
- In small bowl, combine pudding mix and cinnamon.
- Sprinkle over fruit and stir lightly.
- Sprinkle juice over fruit 1 T at a time, stirring lightly until slightly pasty.
- (Fruit will add wetness over time.).

Nutrition Information

- Calories: 121.6
- Total Fat: 0.5
- Fiber: 3.9
- Cholesterol: 0
- Saturated Fat: 0.1
- Sodium: 3.6
- Sugar: 24.6
- Total Carbohydrate: 31.4
- Protein: 1.4

349. Vanilla Fruit Salad For Sixty Plus

Serving: 64 serving(s) | Prep: 10mins | Ready in:

Ingredients

- 5 (20 ounce) cans pineapple chunks (reserve juice!)
- 1 (8 ounce) can pineapple chunks (reserve juice)
- 4 (5 1/8 ounce) boxes vanilla instant pudding mix
- 8 (15 ounce) cans mandarin oranges, drained
- 10 red apples, chopped

Direction

- Drain pineapple, reserving juice.
- Place pudding mix in large bowl.
- Measure pineapple juice, and add as much water as needed to make 6 cups.
- Stir pineapple juice into pudding mix until thickened, about 4 or 5 minutes.
- Fold fruit into pudding.
- Divide fruit salad into four 13 x 9 inch pans that have been lightly sprayed with non-stick cooking spray (like Pam)--each pan should hold about 8 cups of fruit salad.
- Refrigerate until chilled.

Nutrition Information

- Calories: 102.3
- Saturated Fat: 0.1
- Sodium: 132.4
- Fiber: 1.9
- Total Carbohydrate: 26
- Cholesterol: 0
- Total Fat: 0.3
- Sugar: 23.2
- Protein: 0.7

350. Vegan Cranberry Cashew Biscotti

Serving: 36 biscottis | Prep: 20mins | Ready in:

Ingredients

- 1/3 cup margarine, softened (Earth Balance)
- 2/3 cup organic sugar
- 2 Ener-G Egg Substitute
- 1 teaspoon vanilla extract (I like vanilla paste)
- 1/4 teaspoon almond extract
- 1 1/2 cups unbleached all-purpose flour
- 1/2 cup whole wheat pastry flour
- 1 teaspoon baking powder
- 1/2 cup dried cranberries, roughly chopped
- 1/4 cup raw unsalted cashews, chopped

Direction

- Preheat oven to 350°F.
- Cream margarine and sugar together until light and fluffy. Blend in the "eggs" and extracts. Mix in the flour and baking soda. Stir in the cranberries and cashews. Chill for 10 minutes.
- Divide the chilled dough in half and shape into a 1 inch-thick rectangular slabs on a lined, oiled baking sheet. Flatten the slabs slightly by evenly patting them down. Bake until they are golden brown and a toothpick inserted in the center comes out clean, about 25 minutes. Remove from the oven and reduce the oven temperature to 275°F.
- Let slabs cool for 10 minutes, then cut each slab into 1/2 inch-wide slices. Place sliced biscottis on their sides on an ungreased baking sheet (just simply remove the lining from the one you just used) and bake for another 8-10 minutes until they are crisp and dry. Let cool completely before storing in an airtight container. They will keep for a few days, but I suggest freezing half. They taste great frozen!

Nutrition Information

- Calories: 60.2
- Total Fat: 2.2
- Saturated Fat: 0.4
- Sodium: 30.1
- Total Carbohydrate: 9.4
- Cholesterol: 0
- Protein: 0.9
- Fiber: 0.4
- Sugar: 3.8

351. Vegetarian Sweet Potato Pie

Serving: 8 pieces of pie, 8 serving(s) | Prep: 10mins | Ready in:

Ingredients

- 1 1/2 cups soymilk
- 1/3 cup egg substitute (equal to 2 eggs)
- 1 tablespoon cornstarch
- 1 teaspoon vanilla
- 2 cups cooked sweet potatoes, mashed (or pumpkin or winter squash)
- 1/2 cup flour
- 2 teaspoons baking powder
- 1/2 cup sugar
- 1 teaspoon pumpkin pie spice
- 1 teaspoon cinnamon
- 1/2 teaspoon salt

Direction

- Preheat oven to 350 degrees.
- Spray a 9-inch deep dish pie pan with cooking spray. A deep dish is recommended because this pie will rise a lot during cooking but will shrink back as it cools.
- Put the first 4 ingredients in the blender and blend well. Add the sweet potatoes and puree. Add the remaining ingredients and blend on high, stopping to scrape the sides a few times to make sure everything is thoroughly blended.
- Pour into the pie pan and bake for about 60 minutes. A standard toothpick or knife test does not work on this pie. Look for the center to be moist, but cooked. Remove from the oven and allow to cool.

Nutrition Information

- Calories: 179.2
- Total Fat: 1.5
- Saturated Fat: 0.2
- Sodium: 302.5
- Fiber: 3.1
- Total Carbohydrate: 37
- Cholesterol: 0.1
- Sugar: 17.6
- Protein: 5.3

352. Walnut Squares

Serving: 1 8x8 square pan | Prep: 25mins | Ready in:

Ingredients

- 1 cup flour
- 2 tablespoons brown sugar
- 1/2 cup butter
- 1/2 cup chopped walnuts
- 2 eggs, well beaten
- 1 1/4 cups brown sugar
- 1 teaspoon baking powder
- 1/2 cup coconut
- 2 tablespoons flour
- 1/2-1 teaspoon almond extract

Direction

- Set oven to 350 degrees.
- Grease an 8-in square pan.
- Mix together 1 cup flour and 2 tbsp. brown sugar.
- Cut butter into mixture.
- Press into pan.
- Bake for 10 mins; leave to cool.
- In a bowl, mix together chopped walnuts, beaten eggs, remaining 1-1/4 cup brown sugar, baking powder, grated coconut, 2 tbsp. flour and almond extract.
- Evenly spread over cooled baked crust.
- Bake for approx. 10 mins, or until mixture thickens.

Nutrition Information

- Calories: 3285.1
- Total Fat: 169
- Saturated Fat: 89.5
- Sodium: 1294.8
- Sugar: 297.3
- Cholesterol: 667
- Fiber: 14.7
- Total Carbohydrate: 422.1
- Protein: 39.9

353. Whipped Minted Yoghurt

Serving: 4 serving(s) | Prep: 5mins | Ready in:

Ingredients

- 1/4 cup sugar
- 1/2 cup shredded fresh mint leaves
- 1/2 cup water
- 1 cup yoghurt, well chilled
- 1 cup cream, well chilled

Direction

- Place sugar, mint and water in a saucepan over low heat, stirring till the sugar has dissolved.
- Allow it to simmer for another 4 minutes, then let it stand for 5 minutes.
- Strain and cool the mixture.
- Place the yoghurt, cream and mint syrup in the bowl of a mixer, and beat till light and creamy.
- Serve the minted yoghurt with fresh fruit for breakfast or dessert.
- Garnish with a couple of extra mint leaves.

Nutrition Information

- Calories: 262.4
- Saturated Fat: 12.8
- Sodium: 50.1
- Fiber: 0.3
- Cholesterol: 74.3
- Total Fat: 20.5
- Sugar: 15.4
- Total Carbohydrate: 17.6
- Protein: 3.5

354. White Chocolate Chunk Macadamia Cookies

Serving: 72 cookies | Prep: 15mins | Ready in:

Ingredients

- 1 cup butter or 1 cup margarine, softened
- 1 cup light brown sugar, firmly packed
- 1/2 cup sugar
- 2 large eggs
- 1 teaspoon vanilla
- 2 1/4 cups all-purpose flour
- 1 teaspoon baking soda
- 1 teaspoon salt
- 1 cup macadamia nuts, coarsely chopped
- 2 cups white chocolate, broken into bite size chunks

Direction

- Preheat oven to 350°F.
- Cream butter and sugars together until light and fluffy; beat in the eggs and vanilla.
- Mix together the flour, baking soda, and salt; add gradually to the butter mixture.
- Fold in the macadamias and chocolate.
- Drop by heaping tablespoonfuls onto greased baking sheets.
- Bake at 350° for 10-12 minutes or until undersides are lightly golden.
- Cool slightly before removing from cookie sheets.

Nutrition Information

- Calories: 94.8
- Protein: 1
- Total Fat: 5.7
- Saturated Fat: 2.8
- Fiber: 0.3
- Sugar: 7.2
- Total Carbohydrate: 10.4
- Sodium: 79.6
- Cholesterol: 12.9

355. White Chocolate No Bake Cheesecake Pie

Serving: 8 serving(s) | Prep: 10mins | Ready in:

Ingredients

- 1 cup white chocolate chips
- 2 (8 ounce) packages cream cheese, cut up in small pieces
- 1 (8 ounce) container frozen whipped topping, thawed
- 1 9-inch graham cracker crust
- 1/3 cup toffee pieces (or other topping of your choice)

Direction

- Melt the chocolate chips slowly in microwave, stirring often until smooth.
- Stir in cream cheese until smooth.
- Fold in whipped topping.
- Pour into crust.
- Cover and chill until set (about 4-5 hours).
- Sprinkle with topping.

Nutrition Information

- Calories: 547.2
- Cholesterol: 66.9
- Protein: 6.2
- Saturated Fat: 22.9
- Sodium: 379.2
- Total Carbohydrate: 41
- Total Fat: 40.9
- Fiber: 0.5
- Sugar: 32.4

356. White Dessert

Serving: 1 dessert, 5 serving(s) | Prep: 5mins | Ready in:

Ingredients

- 4 cups whipped cream
- 1 cup cream cheese
- 6 tablespoons vanilla frosting (use a whole tube or 1/2 container)
- 1 tablespoon vanilla ice cream
- 1/4 cup coconut (shredded)
- 1 tablespoon skim milk
- 1 tablespoon white sauce (optional)

Direction

- Stir very well.
- Chill 15 minutes before serving at least.

Nutrition Information

- Calories: 318.1
- Total Fat: 29.8
- Sugar: 4.6
- Total Carbohydrate: 8.8
- Saturated Fat: 19.4
- Sodium: 204.5
- Fiber: 0.7
- Cholesterol: 88.4
- Protein: 5.5

---

357. Whole Wheat Chocolate Chip Cookies

Serving: 24-36 serving(s) | Prep: 5mins | Ready in:

Ingredients

- 3/4 cup granulated sugar (or equivalent Splenda substitute)
- 3/4 cup light brown sugar
- 1/2 cup unsalted butter
- 1/2 cup unsweetened applesauce
- 1 teaspoon vanilla
- 1/4 cup Egg Beaters egg substitute (or other egg substitute)
- 2 cups whole wheat flour
- 1 teaspoon baking soda
- 1/2 teaspoon salt
- 1 1/2 cups semi-sweet chocolate chips
- 1 cup chopped walnuts (optional)

Direction

- Preheat oven to 375 degrees
- Mix sugars, butter, applesauce until well blended.
- Add in vanilla and eggbeaters
- Stir in flour, baking soda and salt (dough may be stiff)
- If necessary, add approximately 1/3 cup more flour, depending on consistency of batter.
- Stir in chocolate chips and walnuts.
- Drop dough by rounded tablespoonfuls about 2 inches apart onto ungreased cookie sheet.
- Bake 8 to 11 minutes or until light brown (centers will be soft).
- Cool slightly; remove from cookie sheet. Cool on wire rack.

Nutrition Information

- Calories: 170.9
- Total Fat: 7.2
- Saturated Fat: 4.3
- Sugar: 18.6
- Protein: 1.9
- Sodium: 105.9
- Fiber: 1.9
- Total Carbohydrate: 27.4
- Cholesterol: 10.2

---

358. Whoopie Pies (Lightened Up)

Serving: 16 cookies, 16 serving(s) | Prep: 30mins | Ready in:

Ingredients

- 3/4 cup granulated sugar

- 1/2 cup smart balance 50/50 butter (butter blend spread)
- 1 egg white
- 2 teaspoons vanilla extract, divided
- 2 cups all-purpose flour
- 1/2 cup cocoa
- 1 1/2 teaspoons baking soda
- 1/2 teaspoon baking powder
- 1/2 teaspoon salt
- 1 cup nonfat milk
- 7 1/2 ounces marshmallow cream
- 1 cup confectioners' sugar

Direction

- Heat oven to 350. Grease 2 large baking sheets (or use parchment).
- Cream granulated sugar and spread with electric mixer in large bowl. Beat in egg white and 1 teaspoon of the vanilla extract.
- Mix flour, cocoa, baking soda, baking powder, and salt in bowl. Beat dry ingredients gradually into wet ingredients, alternating with milk. Drop by rounded tablespoonfuls onto pans to make 32 cookies. Press each cookie with a spoon dipped in water to flatten slightly.
- Bake until cookie springs back when touched lightly, 10-12 minutes. Cool completely.
- Beat marshmallow cream with electric mixer, gradually adding confectioners' sugar. Add remaining 1 teaspoon vanilla extract and beat well until smooth, about 3 minutes. Drop about 1 tablespoon of filling onto a cookie and top with another cookie, pressing so filling spreads.

Nutrition Information

- Calories: 230.2
- Total Fat: 6.3
- Sodium: 265.9
- Fiber: 1.3
- Cholesterol: 15.6
- Saturated Fat: 3.9
- Sugar: 23.9
- Total Carbohydrate: 41.6
- Protein: 3

359. Willamette Apple And Cheddar Tart

Serving: 6-8 serving(s) | Prep: 30mins | Ready in:

Ingredients

- 1 1/2 cups flour
- 3 tablespoons sugar
- 1/2 teaspoon cinnamon
- 1/2 cup cold butter
- 2 egg yolks
- 2 teaspoons ice water
- 1 cup strained apricot preserves
- 1 cup grated tillamook medium cheddar
- 1/3 cup chopped almonds, toasted
- 1 1/2 lbs tart apples, pared and thinly sliced
- 1/2 teaspoon grated lemon, rind of

Direction

- Put flour, sugar, and cinnamon in bowl.
- Cut butter into flour mixture until it resembles fine bread crumbs.
- Add egg yolks and ice water and mix until it almost forms a ball.
- Press over bottom and up sides of a 10-inch tart pan; chill for 30 minutes.
- Warm the preserves in saucepan or microwave.
- Spread a half cup of the preserves over the bottom of the chilled pastry.
- Sprinkle with cheese and nuts.
- Arrange apple slices over the mixture.
- Combine remaining warm preserves with lemon peel and brush over the apple slices.
- Bake in preheated oven at 400 degrees F for 15 minutes, then reduce the heat to 350 degrees F for 20 to 25 minutes.
- Makes 6 to 8 servings.

- Serve warm with slices of Tillamook cheese and vanilla ice cream.

Nutrition Information

- Calories: 600.6
- Total Carbohydrate: 82.3
- Cholesterol: 123.4
- Protein: 11.3
- Sodium: 277.5
- Sugar: 38.4
- Total Fat: 27.6
- Saturated Fat: 14.6
- Fiber: 4.8

360. Wonderful Lemon Fruit Salad

Serving: 8 serving(s) | Prep: 5mins | Ready in:

Ingredients

- 4 1/3 ounces lemon cook serve pudding, please DO NOT use instant I have tried it before and it tastes totally different
- 3 egg yolks
- 3/4 cup sugar
- 3 cups water
- 2 (15 ounce) cans fruit cocktail, well drained
- 1 -2 apple, use red skinned to give color and sweet taste, I like gala and red delicious
- 2 -3 bananas, sliced
- 8 ounces Cool Whip
- pecans, chopped (optional)

Direction

- Cooling time not included.
- In a medium saucepan stir pudding mix, sugar, 1/2 c water and egg yolks until combined; stir in remaining water.
- Stirring constantly, bring to a full boil (boils even while being stirred) remove from heat and pour into your serving bowl, let cool, stir about every 20 minutes. If I am in a hurry I will speed up the cooling process and put in the fridge.
- When cool add drained fruit cocktail, apples and bananas, stir to combine.
- Serve right away or store in fridge until ready, top with cool whip and if desired chopped pecans.
- Enjoy!

Nutrition Information

- Calories: 297.3
- Protein: 2.4
- Total Fat: 9.4
- Saturated Fat: 7
- Sodium: 39.1
- Fiber: 2.2
- Sugar: 48.7
- Total Carbohydrate: 54
- Cholesterol: 71.9

361. World's Most Amazing Simple Cobbler!! (Peach And Strawberry)

Serving: 6-8 serving(s) | Prep: 15mins | Ready in:

Ingredients

- For Topping
- 1/3 cup light brown sugar, packed
- 2 tablespoons granulated sugar
- 1 cup walnuts or 1 cup pecans, chopped
- 1 1/2 teaspoons ground cinnamon
- 1 cup all-purpose flour
- 8 tablespoons unsalted butter, softened
- 1 1/2 teaspoons vanilla extract
- 1/8 teaspoon salt
- For Fruit
- 3 fresh peaches, in eighths
- 8 -10 fresh strawberries, sliced
- 1/2 cup sugar

- 1 lemon, juice of
- 1/4 teaspoon cinnamon
- 1 tablespoon cornstarch

Direction

- Preset oven to 350°F.
- Put all fruit, sugar, lemon juice, cinnamon, and cornstarch in one bowl and mix with hands until fruit is covered. Pour this mixture into a small glass baking dish, making sure to include all the extra sugary juices from the bowl.
- Separately, mix all topping ingredients. This will make a crumbly mixture (not a dough). Pour this topping evenly over fruit in baking dish.
- Bake at 350°F for about 15 minutes.
- Serve warm, possibly with ice cream.

Nutrition Information

- Calories: 501.9
- Fiber: 3.3
- Total Carbohydrate: 59.8
- Cholesterol: 40.7
- Saturated Fat: 11
- Sodium: 56.7
- Total Fat: 28.5
- Sugar: 38.4
- Protein: 5.9

362. YUM YUMS (Chocolate Nut Cookies)

Serving: 48 cookies | Prep: 15mins | Ready in:

Ingredients

- 1/2 cup butter
- 2 ounces unsweetened chocolate
- 3/4 cup granulated sugar
- 1 egg
- 1 teaspoon vanilla
- 1/4 teaspoon salt
- 1 3/4 cups flour
- 1/2 cup chopped walnuts
- 1 cup confectioners' sugar

Direction

- Preheat oven to 375 degrees.
- Melt butter and chocolate together and set aside to cool for about 5 minutes.
- Stir chocolate mixture, granulated sugar, egg, vanilla and salt together until blended.
- Stir in flour and nuts.
- Shape into 1 inch balls and place 2 inches apart on ungreased cookie sheets.
- Bake for 8 to 10 minutes or until set.
- While still warm, roll in confectioner's sugar.
- Cool on wire racks and then roll in sugar again.

Nutrition Information

- Calories: 71
- Fiber: 0.4
- Cholesterol: 9.5
- Protein: 1
- Sodium: 27.6
- Sugar: 5.7
- Total Carbohydrate: 9.6
- Total Fat: 3.5
- Saturated Fat: 1.7

363. Yum Yum Yo Yo Biscuits

Serving: 20-24 Yum Yum Yo Yo Biscuits | Prep: 15mins | Ready in:

Ingredients

- 150 g butter, preferably unsalted
- 4 tablespoons icing sugar
- 1 cup self-raising flour, sifted
- 1/2 cup custard powder, sifted
- 1/8 cup slivered almonds (optional)

- Butter Cream
- 60 g butter, softened, preferably unsalted
- 1 1/2 cups icing sugar
- pink food coloring (optional)

Direction

- Cream the butter and icing sugar until light and fluffy; add the sifted self-rising flour and custard powder and mix to a firm dough; fold in the slivered almonds (if using).
- Taking a teaspoonful of the mixture, roll into balls and place onto a baking paper lined oven tray; press lightly with the back of a fork (see TIP below) and bake in a preheated oven at 180°C/350°-375°F/4-5 gas mark for 10-12 minutes.
- Make the butter cream by beating the butter and icing sugar together until the mixture is light and fluffy; add 1-2 drops of food coloring (if using) to make the cream pale pink; join the biscuits together with butter cream.
- TIP: When making the pattern with the fork, dip the fork in plain flour to prevent it sticking to the biscuit mixture.

Nutrition Information

- Calories: 150.6
- Sodium: 139.6
- Protein: 0.7
- Total Carbohydrate: 18.4
- Cholesterol: 22.4
- Total Fat: 8.5
- Saturated Fat: 5.4
- Fiber: 0.2
- Sugar: 13.5

364. Yummy Caramel Frosting

Serving: 12 serving(s) | Prep: 5mins | Ready in:

Ingredients

- 2 cups brown sugar
- 1/2 cup butter
- 1/2 cup milk
- 4 cups powdered sugar
- 1/4 teaspoon maple flavoring

Direction

- In med saucepan, mix brown sugar, butter, and milk.
- Cook and stir on med-hi until boiling.
- Boil for 3 minutes.
- Remove from heat and cool.
- Add powdered sugar and maple flavoring.
- Beat until creamy.

Nutrition Information

- Calories: 369.5
- Total Fat: 8
- Saturated Fat: 5.1
- Sugar: 74.7
- Total Carbohydrate: 76.3
- Cholesterol: 21.8
- Sodium: 83.6
- Fiber: 0
- Protein: 0.5

365. Yummy Gelatin Salad

Serving: 8 serving(s) | Prep: 15mins | Ready in:

Ingredients

- 1 cup unsweetened applesauce
- 1 (1/2 ounce) package sugar-free cherry gelatin
- 1 (12 ounce) can ginger ale
- 1 (8 ounce) can unsweetened crushed canned pineapple, undrained

Direction

- In a saucepan, bring the applesauce to a boil; remove from the heat.

- Stir in gelatin until dissolved.
- Slowly add ginger ale and pineapple.
- Pour into a 2-qt. bowl.
- Chill until set.
- Garnish with apple slices.

Nutrition Information

- Calories: 41
- Saturated Fat: 0
- Sodium: 19.4
- Fiber: 0.6
- Sugar: 9
- Total Fat: 0.1
- Total Carbohydrate: 11.2
- Cholesterol: 0
- Protein: 0.5

Index

A

Almond 3,4,5,7,45,47,49,57,61,122,123,199

Apple 3,4,5,6,7,12,13,14,29,33,83,101,102,104,108,129,134,135,146,153,156,162,170,178,180,188,210

Apricot 3,4,7,15,77,194

B

Baking 30,101,119

Banana 3,4,5,6,17,18,19,20,21,53,72,95,102,103,136,159,187

Berry 3,23

Biscotti 7,205

Biscuits 7,212

Blackberry 4,81

Blueberry 3,6,23,27,28,102,164,181,187

Bran 3,4,7,11,29,74,193

Brazil nut 148

Bread 3,4,5,6,27,63,98,100,109,131,136,159,191,195

Buns 3,5,10,111,113

Butter 3,4,5,6,7,17,18,31,41,42,53,56,69,76,82,106,112,119,123,128,143,144,147,156,189,190,196,203,204,213

C

Cake 3,4,5,6,7,8,11,12,16,17,20,21,24,26,31,32,35,36,38,39,44,45,47,55,60,66,69,72,74,78,82,84,85,88,101,104,108,111,112,114,121,123,129,130,132,137,139,141,146,147,151,152,155,156,157,158,160,164,165,166,175,183,187,197,198,201,204

Caramel 3,5,6,7,33,34,112,120,180,213

Carob 3,35

Carrot 3,35,36

Cashew 3,7,36,205

Cheddar 7,210

Cheese 3,4,5,6,7,9,19,37,38,46,61,69,94,115,117,121,127,148,155,174,186,208

Cherry 3,4,5,38,39,40,47,56,71,110

Chicken 3,7,8,195

Chips 30,144

Chocolate 3,4,5,6,7,11,25,26,34,40,44,45,46,47,48,49,50,51,52,53,54,56,61,66,74,76,77,88,89,100,102,118,127,135,137,141,144,159,160,164,169,176,190,195,197,202,204,208,209,212

Cinnamon 3,4,7,12,91,191,204

Coconut 4,6,57,61,150

Coffee 3,4,12,24,31,39,58

Cola 6,148

Cranberry 4,7,60,61,192,205

Cream 3,4,5,6,18,19,34,35,48,57,60,61,62,66,69,76,95,107,109,110,111,118,121,126,130,134,136,137,141,150,155,158,159,160,165,169,170,174,177,181,186,196,206,208,210,213

Crumble 4,5,6,67,71,85,108,162

Cucumber 6,184

Curry 5,127

Custard 4,59,64,65,86,93

D

Dab 37

Date 4,67

E

Egg 3,4,6,20,75,121,159,205,209

F

Fat

3,4,5,8,9,10,11,12,13,14,15,16,17,18,19,20,21,22,23,24,25,26,27,28,29,30,31,32,33,34,35,36,37,38,39,40,41,43,44,45,46,47,48,49,50,51,52,53,54,55,56,57,58,59,60,61,62,63,64,65,66,67,68,69,70,71,72,73,74,75,76,77,78,79,80,81,82,83,84,85,86,87,88,89,90,91,92,93,94,95,96,97,98,99,100,101,102,103,104,105,106,107,108,109,110,111,112,113,114,115,116,117,118,119,120,121,122,123,124,125,126,127,128,129,130,131,132,133,134,135,136,137,138,139,140,141,142,143,144,145,146,147,148,149,150,151,152,153,154,155,156,157,158,159,160,161,162,163,164,165,166,167,168,169,170,171,172,173,174,175,176,177,178,179,180,181,182,183,184,185,186,187,188,189,190,191,192,193,194,195,196,197,198,199,200,201,202,203,204,205,206,207,208,209,210,211,212,213,214

French bread 98,109

Fruit 3,4,5,6,7,22,25,38,60,86,87,105,110,121,133,138,158,171,172,173,177,204,205,211

Fudge 3,4,6,35,45,83,88,189

G

Gin 3,4,5,6,44,55,79,84,89,90,96,125,136,166,173

H

Ham 4,98

Hazelnut 3,5,50,100

Honey 5,104,105,139

I

Icing 3,4,6,49,66,69,118,164,175

J

Jelly 4,75

Jus 18,72,190

L

Lemon 4,5,7,77,80,89,112,113,114,115,126,211

Lime 5,105,113

M

Macadamia 7,208

Macaroon 3,4,40,88

Mandarin 74

Mango 3,14,102

Marsala wine 70

Marshmallow 3,4,32,58

Mascarpone 3,4,51,58

Meringue 3,5,25,114

Milk 3,7,11,13,97,201,203

Mince 5,129

Mint 7,207

N

Nougat 7,200

Nut 3,4,5,6,7,8,9,10,11,12,13,14,15,16,17,18,19,20,21,22,23,24,25,26,27,28,29,30,31,32,33,34,35,36,37,38,39,40,41,42,43,44,45,46,47,48,49,50,51,52,53,54,55,56,57,58,59,60,61,62,63,64,65,66,67,68,69,70,71,72,73,74,75,76,77,78,79,80,81,82,83,84,85,86,87,88,89,90,91,92,93,94,95,96,97,98,99,100,101,102,103,104,105,106,107,108,109,110,111,112,113,114,115,116,117,118,119,120,121,122,123,124,125,126,127,128,129,130,131,132,133,134,135,136,137,138,139,140,141,142,143,144,145,146,147,148,149,150,151,152,153,154,155,156,157,158,159,160,161,162,163,164,165,166,167,168,169,170,171,172,173,174,175,176,177,178,179,180,181,182,183,184,185,186,187,188,189,190,191,192,193,194,195,196,197,198,199,200,201,202,203,204,205,206,207,208,209,210,211,212,213,214

O

Oatmeal 3,4,5,6,12,42,76,80,91,102,130,133,134,135,177

Oil 16,39

Olive 1,2

Onion 6,153

Orange 4,5,74,97,138,139,140,141

P

Parfait 4,5,75,145

Parmesan 5,143

Pastry 4,5,96,115,142

Peach 3,4,5,6,7,36,62,63,85,99,116,146,179,181,184,189,211

Pear 3,5,14,16,92,101,102,131,146

Pecan 5,6,101,124,147

Peel 12,17,18,32,101,111,153

Pie 3,4,5,6,7,18,20,24,79,93,95,99,106,110,126,127,129,142,143,150,154,155,160,170,178,190,199,202,206,208,209

Pineapple 4,5,6,7,62,80,82,102,117,150,192

Pizza 3,4,5,6,50,86,121,171

Plum 6,151

Popcorn 3,34

Potato 3,5,6,7,15,28,36,105,111,131,153,166,168,182,183,193,194,206

Praline 5,6,120,154

Pumpkin 5,6,7,106,117,121,127,154,155,156,157,168,178,199

R

Raisins 3,7,48,193

Raspberry 4,5,6,93,102,115,161,162,163

Rhubarb 4,6,78,93,165

Rice 4,6,43,53,64,68,114,136,166,167,190,203,204

Rum 3,6,7,16,31,170,194

S

Salad 3,4,5,6,7,9,73,87,94,95,97,105,110,125,131,133,150,153,172,176,177,180,185,196,204,205,211,213

Seasoning 195

Seeds 151

Shortbread 4,5,89,116,143

Sorbet 5,102,103

Soup 6,168

Spaghetti 4,94

Strawberry 3,5,6,7,8,24,51,102,107,178,179,184,185,186,198,211

Sugar 6,8,9,10,11,12,13,14,15,16,17,18,19,20,21,22,23,24,25,26,27,28,29,30,31,32,33,34,35,36,37,38,39,40,41,43,44,45,46,47,48,49,50,51,52,53,54,55,56,57,58,59,60,61,62,63,64,65,66,67,68,69,70,71,72,73,74,75,76,77,78,79,80,81,82,83,84,85,86,87,88,89,90,91,93,94,95,96,97,98,99,100,101,102,103,104,105,106,107,108,109,110,111,112,113,114,115,116,117,118,119,120,121,122,123,124,125,126,127,128,129,130,131,132,133,134,135,136,137,138,139,140,141,142,143,144,145,146,147,148,149,150,151,152,153,154,155,156,157,158,159,160,161,162,163,164,165,166,167,168,169,170,171,172,173,174,175,176,177,178,179,180,181,182,183,184,185,186,187,188,189,190,191,192,193,194,195,196,197,198,199,200,201,202,203,204,205,206,207,208,209,210,211,212,213,214

Syrup 10,137

T

Taco 191

Tea 6,7,132,170,184,191,192,195

Toffee 4,5,6,7,52,134,149,199,200

Tomato 4,69

Truffle 4,67

V

Vanilla extract 38

Vegan 6,7,164,167,205

Vegetarian 7,206

W

Walnut 5,7,141,207

Wine 5,146

Y

Yam 7, 194

Yoghurt 7, 207

Z

Zest 192

L

lasagna 100

Conclusion

Thank you again for downloading this book!

I hope you enjoyed reading about my book!

If you enjoyed this book, please take the time to share your thoughts and post a review on Amazon. It'd be greatly appreciated!

Write me an honest review about the book – I truly value your opinion and thoughts and I will incorporate them into my next book, which is already underway.

Thank you!

If you have any questions, **feel free to contact at:** author@voilacookbook.com

Olive Chen

voilacookbook.com

Made in the USA
Middletown, DE
04 January 2023